Spatial Dynamics of International Capital

A Study of Multinational Corporations in India

Spatial Dynamics of International Capital

A Study of Multinational Corporations in India

Swapna Banerjee-Guha

Orient Longman

ORIENT LONGMAN LIMITED

Registered Office
3-6-272 Himayatnagar, Hyderabad 500 029 (A.P.), India

Other Offices
Bangalore, Bhubaneshwar, Calcutta, Chennai,
Ernakulam, Guwahati, Hyderabad, Jaipur,
Lucknow, Mumbai, New Delhi, Patna

First Published 1997

ISBN 81 250 1289 3

Printed in India by
Swapna Printing Works Pvt. Ltd.
Calcutta 700 009

Published by
Orient Longman Limited
17 Chittaranjan Avenue
Calcutta 700 072

For my parents

"Capitalism has found itself able to attenuate its internal contradiction and succeeded in achieving growth by occupying and producing space"

— Henri Lefebvre, 1973

Contents

Preface

This is a book about the spatial relations of international capital. More precisely, about the operations and organisations of multinational corporations—one of the most important organisational forms of international capital—with special reference to India as a host country during late eighties and early nineties. Given the status of geography in India as an analytical social science and the felt need of many geographers in the country to develop a geographical viewpoint for studying the local and the global on a continuous scale—that has assumed a critical urgency in the contemporary time—this endeavour has been especially significant for me, both at academic-social and personal level.

Formation of a transnational economic space by international capital within the boundaries of nation-states essentially brings the issue of absolute and relative space to the fore in a typical manner. Striking an integral accord with the regional attributes of different space economies, the spatial organisation of multinational corporations of late has brought the economy and society of various nation-states within the network of a universal interdependence that involves not only space-specific production processes but incorporate also the dynamics of political economy and social relations of all the constituent regions and countries. The so-called globalisation process has not eliminated absolute space altogether, but only created and recreated innumerable divisions in space by producing certain absolute spaces of its own as part of the larger production of relative space (Smith, 1986) by building, fragmenting and carving our newer spatial configurations with specific human practice and circumstances (Harvey, 1982).

The above conceptualisation of space by international capital characterising a fusion of horizontal and vertical differentiation and simultaneously featuring an integration of spatial form and structure is the major theme of the book. Significant behavioural arrangements are involved in this space-bound schema with a *pari passu* division of market, technology and labour. The resultant spatial division of production and other economic activities, a contemporary strategy of globalisation, is resting on a rigid concentration in decision making, production planning and control while allowing various stages and phases of production to be distributed over a wider geographical surface in a non-hierarchical manner to facilitate exploitation of region-specific characteristics at a global scale. Absolute and relative space get intertwined in this arrangement and the associated spatial division of labour becomes more an attribute of international pricing system, wage differentials and the relative immobility of labour rather than of mere division of work or levels of skill. The equalisation of profit rates also does not necessarily lead to equalisation of material condition of workers, rather unrestrained mobility of capital finally acts as a check on unrestrained mobility of labour. The latter has become a hallmark in the contemporary international spatial order.

This new international division of production that the multinational corporations have been fostering since eighties, tangibly represents the inherently contradictory and crisis-ridden tendencies of capitalism with which a diverse use of space is integrally connected. For example, while responding to the crisis of falling profit—an inherent feature of capitalism—international capital in recent times has been seeking to explore the possibility of reorganising and restructuring production and related economic activities over a still wider surface and opt for a more profitable spatial order. Its contemporaneous spread over a more variegated geographical environment having great diversity in production relations and labour power leads to a much more divergent use of space, and the related spatial attributes give rise to opposed tendencies of concentration and dispersal. The recent combination strategy of Fordist-Non Fordist (Ettlinger, 1990) production that the multinational corporations have adopted since eighties symbolises similar contradictions and crises. Although projected as a symbol of globalisation and internationalisation of the world economy, the strategy actually rests on a place and space-specific devaluation forming a part of an internationally operative process of accumulation and underdevelopment. The most significant fall-out of this strategy has been a discreet, planful, selective relocation of high-skill jobs to less developed host countries creating islands of capital intensive, automated production or *supra* office complexes and an associated labour aristocracy, on the one hand, and an acute informalisation of the economy with a simultaneous reduction of organised employment, on the other. Innumerable sweat shops engaging the cheapest possible labour, abound in the cities and countryside of the host countries manned by the same corporations that create the aforementioned labour aristocracy. Thus while promoting integration of space for the movement of goods and commodities, technology and information, international capital, as part of the same strategy, entails space differentiation exploiting various levels of income, wage and development disparities among countries and regions. Differentials in the value of labour power and material conditions of work happpen to be a premise of the arrangement that enables the corporations to organise production on geographically divided lines creating and recreating myriad divided spaces generating further differentiations in social relations, institutional arrangements and so on. Besides economic aspects, it also affects the social, political and environmental situations. The above divergence in the use of space and its attributes is the key dynamic of the book.

Locational decisions and regional concentration pattern of MNC offices and plants in the host country soil do not, therefore, reflect a search for only cheap labour but a complex set of factors such as, market, resource, institutions, etc. While locating, shifting or relocating units in the host countries, international capital has been systematically found to follow the trajectory, often inequable, of the regional growth and decline of the latter and establish an integral link with their internal space relations reflecting a set of complex factors. The distinct spatial scales that are thence created differentiate and divide regions within these countries tailored to the needs of an exogenous design. Aggravation of regional disparity, globalisation of selected third world cities, acute primacy in their urban systems, increasing rural-urban or town-country divide thus become coherent products of the diverse and intersecting operations of international capital. Sections on empirical analysis of multinational corporations operating the manufacturing sector in India deal with such issues.

The book is divided into six chapters. The introductory chapter discusses the significance of multinational corporations in the world economy by emphasising the spatial scale of their expansion, especially in the post War II era. The second chapter while presenting the key theme of the spatial organisation of multinational corporations focuses on the new international division of production and labour. The chapter also discusses the trends in geographical researches on international capital. Chapter 3 offers a brief outline of Indian policy towards foreign capital followed by identification, classification and selection of multinational corporations operating in India during late eighties. Numerous tables in the chapter serve to summarise details of policy and typology of the corporations. Chapter 4 deals with the spatial organisation of these corporations with a discussion on its impact on the regional settlement systems in India. Chapter 5 discusses the expansion of foreign capital in the consumer goods sector in India with a focus on two giant corporations, Procter and Gamble and Unilever. Socio-cultural effects of consumer goods MNCs have been touched upon in this chapter. The concluding chapter is a synthesis of my argument on the spatial dynamics of MNC operation in India. Using 1990 regional development indicators as a basis, the chapter seeks to demonstrate a plausible, functional link between the spatial organisation of MNCs and unevenness in the Indian space economy.

A clarification of one or two points. First, the data base for the typology of MNCs and their parent country origin included in the analysis of Chapter 4 onwards is of late eighties when Germany was a divided country. Similarly, till 1992 Coca-Cola was yet to stage a come-back to India and hence excluded from the analysis of the consumer goods MNCs in the Chapter 5. However, had I done the work later and included Coca-Cola, I am sure, my overall argument would have remained the same. For the same reason I have not changed Bombay and Madras to Mumbai and Chennai.

Since long I have been contemplating to work on such a theme. *Ab initio*, it was David Harvey from whom I got a solid encouragement to undertake such a work while I was a Visiting Fellow at the Johns Hopkins University in mid-eighties. I recall his active intervention on a work of mine relating to neocolonialism and regional disparity. Peppered with challenging criticism it was at the same time unsparing in encouragement.

The long informal discussions often I had with him, almost always spiced with enchanting dinners, made a durable mark on my later arguments. His friendship, no less than his works, has always been a source of inspiration for me. Way back in Presidency College, Calcutta, it was Satyesh Chakraborti who made me see the potential of the subject for the first time. I value his friendship till today.

During the finalisation of the book I received the most active support from Amiya Bagchi. For days together he gave me a patient hearing while I read out the draft, raised questions, offered suggestions and shared views on spatial questions. I found his interest in the spatial perspective in political economic analysis something rare among non-geographer social scientists around. I have been greatly rewarded by his response.

To a large extent this book is a product of a long research project funded by the Indian Council of Social Science Research run in the Department of Geography, University of Bombay. I acknowledege the infrastructural and organisational support received from the Department of Geography and the Department of Accounts as well.

Ideas and works of many have enriched my vision. To name a few: Erica Schoenberger and Beatrice Nofal's project proposal on automobile multinational corporations that Erica had offered me to read for a totally different purpose and which I used years later while writing on the geographical perspectives on international capital in Chapter 2. An IDPAD report on Indian policy towards foreign capital has considerably helped me to formulate the section on Indian policy in Chapter 3; S. Aggrawal's piece on the history of Hindustan Lever that I have drawn on heavily to track the growth of the firm in India.

Data collection was a major part of the study. At the initial stage Anjali Masarguppi did a solid basework later followed up by V.A. Mathew, Krishnalina Basu, P.M.Deshpande and Baishakhi Datta. Manisha Divekar and Anagha Gore took up the challenge to tabulate date on MNC unit locations under a terrible time constraint. Smita Gandhi considerably involved herself in tabulation work and took the full responsibility to ensure that the computer work was done in time. S.R.Jog solved many a computer crisis when things went almost beyond control. K.V. S. Rao provided timely cartographical advice, and Prasad Gogote cartographical assistance. Jean Edge typed the manuscript at various stages. Theba Yumlembam assisted in a special way in the preparation of the index.

I had the good fortune to receive co-operation from a number of activists in the trade union front who supplied valuable data to help me substantiate my argument on consumer goods MNCs in Chapter 5. They were quite a few and I apologise for not mentioning everybody individually. But I would like to mention Sujata Gothoskar from Workers' Solidarity Centre, Bombay; Ashok Jagtap from the former Procter and Gamble (India) Workers' Union and Bennett D'costa from Hindustan Lever Workers' Union. Few others helped with their views and information; Sudip Chowdhury from Institute of Management, Calcutta; Chalapati Rao from Institute for Studies in Industrial Development, New Delhi; Girish Srinivasan from Research Unit for Political Economy, Bombay deserve mention. I also acknowledge the staff of Stock Exchange Library, Centre for Monitoring Indian Economy, Centre for Education and Documentation, Bombay; Institute for Studies in Industrial Development, Indian Institute for Public Administration, India Investment Centre and I.L.O. Area office, in New Delhi; Centre for Studies in Social Sciences, National Library and Indian Institute of Management, Calcutta and of course Jawaharlal Nehru Library of Bombay University. Pradip Banerjee did a wonderful job by sending me some special numbers of *Fortune* Magazine when I needed them most. Renate Kotzam offered her stimulating friendship especially during the final phase of the work.

And then there was Sambuddha, who showed almost uncanny consideration in tolerating my crazy schedule. I only hope he realises the significance of this topic when he grows up. Finally, I would like to share the finalé of the work with Sumit Guhathakurta (whose initial editing of the manuscript was of great help) from whom, as always, there was no dearth of comradeship. With him, goes my support towards struggles launched anywhere, in any form against international capital.

1
Multinational Corporations : Rise and Spread

1.1. The Significance of Multinational Corporaitons

The last two decades can be viewed as a period when fundamental changes took place in the world economy reshaping the process of economic development of countries and regions. This was also a period of transition to a new phase of internationalisation of capital including internationalisation of production. The resultant restructuration of the world industrial space and its fall-outs have posed major challenges to researchers in various branches of social sciences to reorient the perspective in understanding world economic development and underdevelopment. In the above major changes multinational corporations (MNCs) have been identified as an instrumental factor. In fact, few economic institutions have given rise to such varied responses and debates as the multinational corporations (MNCs) have. Besides becoming dominant organisational forms of capitalism and acting as vehicles through which changes in the capitalist systems are achieved (Magdoff, 1972) they have been exercising tremendous influence and power over the economic, social, political and cultural lives of many nations and people (Cohen *et al.*, 1979). They have a long history but their magnitude and efficiency of international operation assumed an omnipresent character especially in relation to the Third World in the post seventy era.

By the neo-classical school of thought these corporations have been portrayed as engines of growth capable of eliminating international economic inequality while the radical and marxian social scientists have portrayed them as major obstacles to independent development of the Third World, responsible for massive drain of surplus to advanced capitalist countries. On the other hand, they have also been portrayed as major causes of industrial decline and reduction of industrial employment in their parent countries, from which they often move out for exploring newer, greener pastures for production at cheaper cost. Irrespective of the lines of opinion, their overall significance in the international space economy cannot but be regarded as something astounding. Especially their role towards reorganising the world economic space.

Multinational corporations have been instrumental in distributing their production operation since early this century. But since the seventies they have got more closely associated with the reorganisation of the international industrial space economy of the Third World countries.

This spatial reorganisation is associated with a complex division and subdivision of production processes perpetuating an unequal competition between the industrial workforce of the developed countries and that of the Third World countries (Frobel, 1980)—unequal in terms of skill and wage. The competition even takes place within the host countries between the organised labour force and the unorganised labour force. The latter is hired by the multinational corporations frequently on contractual basis in their effort to bring down the production cost and raise the profit margin. At the same time there also exists substantial difference in earning within the developed countries expressing their respective control over the world market. Thus in the global village that the world has turned to be, economic space of any country or for that matter any region no longer represents isolatedness. Procurement of resource, mobilisation of labour, production, distribution, marketing, pricing, profiting all aspects of economic operations are now conceived at a global level, due to the vertical and horizontal integration of these corporations. The result is an interlacing of multi-locational, multi-product and multi-divisional organisations functioning at a global scale. With classical studies of Hymer (1960) followed by Baran and Sweezy (1966), Hymer (1972), Holland (1976), Palloix (1977), Wallerstein (1979), Bagchi (1972; 1982), Lall and Streeten (1977), Swamy (1980), Roychowdhury (1981) and others, a considerable volume of work has also been produced in geography to focus the impact of the structure, operations and locational decisions of these corporations on economic and social spaces of countries, parent or host. Analysis exists at all levels of regional, national and international scales (Massey and Meegan, 1979; Watts, 1980; Taylor and Thrift, 1982; Clarke, 1985).

Any serious attempt to understand the operation and effects of multinational corporations would, therefore, necessarily mean a journey into economics, sociology, geography and other social sciences including regional science. As the MNCs create patterns in space and society on a cross-country level, a proper analysis of their organisation and functioning certainly warrants crossing of the frontiers of various social science disciplines.

1.1.1. Defining the multinational corporations

Before we trace the history of these corporations, there is a need to conceptualise and define them. At the outset, it should be mentioned that these corporations are called international because of their international operation and not because of their parent country affiliation as most of them have a single country source e.g. Nestlé, IBM, Singer, Philips etc. and a few with cross-country parentage e.g. Unilever, Britannia, etc. In the seventies 65 per cent subsidiaries of the top US based MNCs were wholly owned by their parents and 72.5 per cent subsidiaries of the top 135 Europe and UK based enterprises were also wholly owned. Among the fifteen largest international companies listed in *Fortune* magazine in 1980, as many as 11 were US based, two UK based, one based in Holland and only one was part British and part Dutch. In 1989, out of the 500 largest industrial corporations listed in the same magazine only three were having cross-frontier identity e.g. Royal Dutch/Shell group and Unilever with parentage in Britain and Netherlands as principal countries and Pirelli having Italy and Switzerland as parent countries. In 1991 again out of the 500 largest industrial corporations, listed in the *Fortune* magazine, only two were having cross-country parentage e.g. Royal Dutch/Shell Group and Unilever with the same countries of 1989 as the principal ones. On this ground these corporations should be termed as transnational rather than multinational corporations. On the other hand, in matters like movement of funds, allocation of export markets to subsidiaries, locational decisions about new plants are always the privilege of the principal office and never given in the hands of the subsidiaries or collaborative firms. This control of the principal firm on the subsidiaries essentially reflects the domination of the parent country on all the units of the corporations located in different countries and a centralised control with diversified operations.

There is no universally accepted definition of such corporations (Deo, 1986). The broadest definition put forward by the UN Economic and Social Council refers to 'all enterprises which control assets—factories, mines, sales office and the like—in two or more countries (UNCTC, 1978). Usually the term denotes firms that control production in at least one foreign country. This means that the firms should have a minimum specified level of overseas activities, either in terms of the number of countries in which they operate or in their proportion of production or employment in foreign countries. The *Wall Street Journal* (1972) defined the multinational corporations as the children of the globe-girdling business concerns as old as the British Empire's East India Company. Multinational corporations, according to this journal, is a much post-World War II phenomenon attaining a spectacular growth in the past decade. These are the corporations that have production facilities in many countries, having access to world-wide capital and a 'global outlook' among the management. They can enter into collaboration with any private firm, individual of any other country or with any state or regional or local government of any country. To streamline their growth they evolve a well-integrated organisational system through intercorporate and intercountry stock holding, as well as acceleration or concentration of industry and banking. They also provide financial support to various political parties in foreign and parent countries and thereby exercise influence on the government machinery. Their system affects the world society in several ways, especially the economic divisions. These divisions determine the use of world's resources and distribution of world's production and hence control world's economic power.

Their selection of economic activities is also extremely noteworthy. Accelerating concentration of industry and banking with multinationalisation of operation has been the hallmark of their success (Swamy, 1980) and growth. In order to avoid inefficiency and streamline growth, they evolve a well integrated, organisational system through intercorporate and intercountry networking and penetrated all the major sectors of economy, starting from agriculture, agricultural marketing, manufacturing of agricultural inputs and machinery, heavy industrial machinery and sophisticated spare parts or finished items including consumer durables and products for international trade of all types of items and financing and banking at all levels. To do this, they use every possible economy of scale including both external and internal economies. Thus besides accounting for an important share of world production they also control a major part of direct foreign investment and trade. In 1983, 500 MNCs were responsible for 80 per cent of all foreign direct investment all over the world. Similarly in the early eighties 500 MNCs excluding their subsidiaries accounted for about 28 per cent of the total exports of the advanced capitalist countries. In this book the term 'multinational corporations' has been consistently used to represent these large corporations.

Significance of the MNCs in the world economy can be understood both in quantitative and qualitative terms. The quantitative approach considers primarily the size of the corporations, their volume of investment, production, employment, technology generation and trade. The qualitative approach looks at their growth as a part of the growth process of the world capitalism. These two need to complement each other.

MNCs have an overriding significance in constituting the most advanced form of capitalist system at its zenith. They manifest the process of internationalisation of capital by integrating the world economy in one single operative network. They also are the leaders in concentrating and centralising capital, especially industrial capital. During sixties and seventies the output of world's largest firms has outstripped the growth rate of world production (Trajtenberg, 1985). Simultaneously during the seventies the share of foreign subsidiaries in the total sales of MNCs rose from 30 per cent to 40 per cent (Jenkins, 1987).

Historically, many of the major exports of the Third World countries especially in the primary sector such as oil, copper, bauxite, banana or tea have been produced by the multinational corporations and they continue to dominate the marketing of such products. In many Third World countries, the expanding manufacturing sector, particularly dynamic industries like chemicals, rubber, machinery and transport equipment have a substantial multinational presence. In Brazil 44 per cent of the sales of manufactured items, were controlled by MNCs in 1977. In Ecuador MNCs controlled 66 per cent assets of the public corporations in 1973 and in 1974 MNCs controlled 43 per cent of the total industrial production in Colombia. In Nigeria foreign corporations controlled 70 per cent of the assets in 1968 while in Singapore they controlled 83 per cent of the total industrial output in 1978. However, this does not necessarily mean that these corporations are the major sources of investment or innovations. It is usually the small firms that are the real innovators. Only about $^{1}/_{5}$th of the post-war innovations have been originally introduced by the MNCs while (Vernon, 1977), although having played a major role in commercialising new technologies.

In terms of size, the largest MNCs have sales that exceed the total gross doemstic product of many Third World countries (Table 1.1).

Table 1.1. *World wide sale of leading MNCs compared to the GDP of select Third World countries*

Corporations	Parent Country	Industry	Sales ($ billion)	GDP ($ billion)	Country
Exxon	USA	Oil	73.6	83.2	South Korea
Royal Dutch/ Shell	Holland/ UK	Oil	72.6	80.6	Indonesia
General Motors	USA	Motor Vehicles	64.4	76.2	Argentina
Ford	USA	Motor vehicles	40.2	47.5	Venezuela
I B M	USA	Office equipment	35.2	42.0	Thailand
du Pont	USA	Chemicals and Energy	27.6	34.4	Colombia
General Electric	USA	Electrical	21.4	32.8	Philippines
Toyota	Japan	Motor vehicles	18.2	29.3	Malaysia
Unilever	UK/ Holland	Food	16.2	19.8	Chile
Hitachi	Japan	Electrical	13.4	13.3	Morocco.

Source : Times 1000 Leading Companies, World Bank, 1986.

In major industries like oil refining, aluminium, tobacco, transport, electricals or food, a considerable proportion of the capitalist world's production is accounted for by the MNCs that sometimes exceeds even the GNP of medium sized countries. In 1984 American Telephone and Telegraph produced more than the entire economic production of Greece, Israel, Norway and Venezuela put together.

General Motors produces more than the GNP of New Zealand or Pakistan. Royal Dutch Shell's sales are more than the GNP of Iran, Venezuela and Turkey put together. Chrysler alone sells more than the GNP value of Ethiopia. These corporations have more than $200 billion in physical assets under their control (Barnet and Muller, 1975). The enormous power that the MNCs wield emanates from the control of the means of creating wealth on a world wide scale. Simultaneously they also control the political machinery of many parent states in addition to some not so strong host countries (Deo, 1986).

Substantial control of MNCs in world market and trade is made possible for two specific reasons. First is the nullification of actual act of competition. Instead of increasing competition, multinational corporations are found to increase monopolisation in markets by using the advantages of their size and international expansion. In the mid eighties foreign controlled companies in India controlled 85 per cent of the markets of cosmetics, and 65 per cent of the storage batteries (Sachdeva, 1984). These companies like any other MNCs raise product differentiation barriers by introducing heavily advertised branded goods or capital requirements often *pari passu* with capital intensive technology (Lall, 1980). With these they adhere to the practice of predatory pricing, eliminate local competitors and thereby increase concentration. With a substantial domination over the market, they no longer remain 'price takers' but become 'price makers' and thereby abolish the law of single price. A large number of studies have indicated correlation between presence of MNCs and the level of concentration in any given manufacturing activity with relatively less constraint of competition (Jo, 1976, Longdon, 1978; Dunning, 1981; Jenkins, 1984; New Farmer, 1985). Interlocking directorships of more than one MNC also lead to pragmatic adjustments between competitors and reduce actual competition. In such situations to reduce the possibility of getting ousted and remain in the market local firms of host countries, expecially of the Third World, are found to adhere defensive mergers with the MNCs which the latter welcome as a measure to raise the average rate of profit (Jenkins 1987). Examples of mergers of Hindustan Lever and Tomco, Coca-Cola and Parle or Pepsi and Dukes in India in 1993 are appropriate examples. Besides mergers with the buying of indigenous firms of host countries, multinational corporations restructure and consolidate their position in similar or related industries of internatinoal level or take them over to consolidate and boost market share and benefit from economies of scale. Geographical diversification is thus becoming critical in attaining the goal of dominating the market. A consequent global strategy employed by large MNCs is to pursue acquisition of brands which give them a leading share in the market. In 1987 US firms took over 41 British owned and 11 German owned (FRG) firms. Between 1980 and 88, 75 US companies were taken over by companies of various countries with a transaction value of $ 500 million in each case (UNCTC, 1989). Thus instead of a sequence from monopoly through oligopoly to workable competition as suggested by Vernon (1977) what transpires in reality is oligopolistic control leading to corporate coalescence and formation of gigantic corporate structures with ultra-modern vertical and horizontal network. Newfarmer (1984) argues that in some industries of Latin America like cigarette, electronics or food, even if entry of MNCs created a short period of deconcentration through mergers and takeovers, it was followed by a new consolidation of an MNC-led oligopoly. As a general rule, he states, market structure does not undergo a transition from monopoly to workable competition. Rather it gives rise to a larger concentration and domination of market. Innumerable subsidiaries and collaborative firms having differential locations operating at different hierarchical levels sustains this concentration pattern. Through transactions between them and the principal units a huge proportion of the total market can be cornered. This brings us to the second reason behind MNCs' significance in trade and market which is replacement of market and transactions by non-market relationships due to the above transactions. In the seventies intra-firm trade accounted for 30 per cent of the world trade while 30 per cent to 60 per cent of the total exports of many countries was done on intra-firm basis. Since sale of goods from one affiliate to another is not subject to the discipline of the market, the concerned firms are free to set prices at the most advantageous levels to maximise their profits, subject to constraints imposed by governments (Newfarmer, 1983). Later the practice became more sophisticated and lucrative. Between 1986 and 1990 the most rapid growth of export in Colombia was in those industries, e.g. apparel, footwear and leather products in which a large number of local firms worked as subcontractors of MNCs. Export of sophisticated products from developing countries obviously depends on intra-firm transactions; for example export of semi-conductor products from several local firms in the Philippines and the Republic of Korea to their parent firms or export of aircraft components from Chinese firms to their principal firms like Boeing or McDonnell Douglas under subcontracting arrangements or even export of computer parts of Thailand firms to IBM, their parent oragnisation in the USA, (UNCTC, 1992). All these are popularly known as non-equity links with MNCs and their subcontracting firms. Through such transactions and manipulation of transfer prices by overpricing import to host countries and underpricing exports, a huge proportion of the total operation of the international market can be cornered. Several studies have indicated MNCs' inclination to use transfer prices against developing countries because of their high taxes, low import duties on intermediate goods, less stable currencies and stringent control on profit remittance (Lall, 1973; Robbins and Stobaugh (1973)).

In a thoroughly interdependent world, as it is since the seventies, MNCs have also been able to underscore the sovereignty of many states. Pervading power of the coalesce, it has been argued (Bennett and Sharpe, 1984), can supersede state powers if need arises. MNCs may view nation states as obstacles in the flow of their cross-country profit and, therefore, to their planetary development. 'The political boundaries of nation-states', declared William I Spencer (1972), President of the First National City Corporation having business with 90 countries, 'are too narrow and constricted to define the scope and sweep of modern business'. IBM chief (1969) felt 'the world's political structures are completely obsolete, woefully out of tune with technological progress'.

MNCs are major agents in the process of standardisation of production techniques, signifying another aspect of the internationalisation. The use of technology in this process becomes increasingly international, reflected through the increasing number of patents issued to firms of advanced capitalist countries. This also gets reflected through the payments for technology and personnel and royalty payments. Between 1970 and 81 such payments from the Third World countries to the advanced countries increased at an annual rate of 6 per cent in real terms (Vickery, 1984). According to Britton and Gilmour (1978), technology transfer by MNCs leads to truncated industrial system and high royalty license fees. Questions are also raised about their lack of interest in developing research and development in host countries. Chossoudovsky (1978) found that Ford in Canada conducted no research and development and employed not a single local scientist while Gordon and Fowler (1984) showed an association between foreign control and low level of R and D in Canada. In case of regional development also MNCs in general do not help establish backward and forward linkages among indigenous firms or suppliers in any region

(Bater and Walker, 1974; Britton 1976). Rather their centralised purchasing system favours purchases from other MNCs operating in raw material or processing sector rather than from local producers.

MNCs are major players in distorting the wage and market equations for industrial labour all over the world. On the one hand, they have created an elitist labour class at home and also in poor host countries thereby benefiting from a division in labour as a class and then aggravated it; On the other, they have given rise to peculiar competition between the labour of the parent countries and those of the host countries. Labour had never been used so deftly to control the international pricing system and to maintain profits. It has gone to the extent of even creating competition between organised and unorganised labour both hired simultaneously by these corporations.

Significance of the Multinational Corporations is, last but not the least, seen in the process of internationalisation of the consumption pattern leading to demonstration effect (Hirschman, 1958) and distorted consumerism in poor Third World countries. On this aspect the corporations truly sell a particular politico-economic system by selling their products. They have actually become much sophisticated players of a game that was already existing. They use their power of technology and market manipulation to shape the taste, goals and values of workers, suppliers and customers and thereby sell and resell themselves (Barnet and Muller, 1974). The products further assure the stability of the system in which they can sell at a more gigantic scale. The attractive power of international consumption (Enzenberger, 1975) is based not on the dictate of false needs alone but also the falsification of the real and legitimate ones. This gets expressed through the process of erosion of the regional cultures and surfacing of a false international one that is generated again not due to any social need at the customers' end at a mass level but at the producer's end in the form of a false desire especially tailor-made for the Third World countries. Handful of elite in these countries actually provide primary markets for such products but the desire to consume is created in the minds of the masses through media and communication that ensures future sale of their products. An indicator of this process has been the rapid growth of international advertising agencies (UNCTC, 1979) as well as use of public sector media network by the international corporations. These activities of the MNCs should be seen in the context of the development of a world capitalist system having institutional support. Large corporations should be essentially considered as modern institutional form of the capitalist mode of production encompassing the society in economic, cultural and political spheres (Peet, 1981). Internationalisation of the economic operation of the world capitalist system, accompanied by political and cultural domination has thus been made easier due to the global network created by the MNCs. It has led not just to an internationalisation of capital but an internationalisation of capitalist consciousness and culture.

1.2 Internationalisation of Production Space : Origin of MNCs

In order to trace the origin of the MNCs it is necessary to understand the situation that brought them to this level of growth and spatial domination especially in the context of the Third World. There is also a need to indicate some major features of the history of capital accumulation and underdevelopment of the Third World dating back to the days of colonial exploitation. Exploitation and exodus of raw material from these countries in exchange of manufactured goods from the coloniers dragged them into an international trade on unequal terms and gave rise to a clear-cut divide of core and peripheral status with a dominance dependency relationship. Internal development of these countries became truncated and distorted as bulk of the infrastructural development was meant for facilitating colonial exploitation and procurement of resources for transhipment to the manufacturing countries. In the process these countries were reduced to the position of mere satellites of the central countries and were not allowed to have any capital accumulation. Although investment was done in various infrastructure and economic activities e.g. mining or railways, it did not lead to any diversification of productive operations. The disjunction between and among the various sectors of the economy that it led to, perpetuated a process of underdevelopment associated with a lack of access to their own surplus and lack of power to decide their internal economic structure. Slow process of reinvestmnt of surplus value led to greater centralisation of the means of production including labour. Centralisation refers to a much faster change in the distribution of the concentrated capital brought about by competition through economies of scale (Marx, 1967). The entire process clearly reflected that economic development and underdevelopment are not just relative and quantitative but relational and qualitative in being structurally different from each other but caused by its relation to each other (Frank, 1967). Hence the same process of development in capitalist countries apart from imposing deadweight loss on the colonial peoples, was essentially a zero-sum game, so that some countries had to stay underdeveloped if metropolitan countries had to go along the capitalist path (Bagchi, 1972). Contradiction, existed between and among the capitalist powers, but the major relationship between them and the underdeveloped countries was one of dominance-dependence. Industrial revolution further established an exchange pattern of trade featuring a flow of manufactured and mineral products among the developed countries and manufacured products and raw materials between developed countries and colonies (Amin, 1976) while expropriation of surplus from colonies helped the centres in their primitive accumulation process.During the nineteenth century, finance became mobile and foreign investment flowed but to different directions expecially towards the colonies of new settlement and to other European countries. Britain was the primary capital exporter followed by France, Holland and Germany. Most of this capital flow, however, was in the form of foreign direct investment mainly of portfolio type, made in Government and Municipal bonds, railways, other transport and public utilities. During 1865-1914, 45 per cent of British portfolio investment flowed to North America and Australia, 13 per cent to Europe and 17 per cent to South America, mostly to those with substantial European populations (Bagchi, 1972). In other words, about 68 per cent of the total went to the temperate regions of recent settlements (Simon, 1967). Simultaneously during different periods of nineteenth century huge surplus of balance of payments was accumulated by Britain from India to meet deficit with Europe or North America. From the point of view of capitalist growth this method was extremely important as it enabled Britain to smoothly transfer capital resource from non-white colonies to white ones and support industrial growth in the latter. By the above process, the United States became the wealthiest capitalist country by the end of nineteenth century and received the largest amount of capital and labour.

Uptil 1914, the mobility path of capital followed the trail of white migrants while countries with large non-white populations were left with more efficient exploitation through all precapitalist channels available to the European business community settlers and colonisers. The net capital inflow to underdeveloped countries was minimal. Above all, investments in white settling colonies were loose with minimum control over the funded projects while in underdeveloped countries investment was monitored under tight control. In Brazil, 'enterprises were conceived by Britons, constructed by British contractors' (Bagchi, 1972) while simultaneously a powerful British lobby acted against industrialisation of Brazil till the end of nineteenth century (Graham, 1968). Tying up of aid to such projects and industrial development of the metropolitan country operated in India with utmost efficiency exemplify an abject dependency to Britain.

Movement of capital and labour in the nineteenth century was not on the basis of complementarity as stressed by Nurkse (1959) but on the method of exploitation of the underdeveloped countries. Nurkse himself observed that British capital tended to bypass tropical economies and flowed mainly to regions of recent settlement. Further investments in the white settlements were in productive activities that led to development of resource and industries while in the non-white colonies these were in projects of the colonial governments that aided the centralisation in the exploitation of resources. On the other hand, the drain from such countries in the form of primitive accumulation formed a large part of this capital e.g. the drain from India formed more than 50 per cent of the annual capital export of Britain in the seventh decade of the nineteenth century (Bagchi, 1972).

Considering such discrete movements of capital as casual and not accidental to the world capitalist development, it can be suggested that the latter part of the nineteenth century was the period of mobility, concentration and centralisation of capital that led to an increasing size of firms in advanced capitalist countries paving the way for major changes in the structure and organisation of capitalist enterprises (Jenkins, 1987). Industrial capitalism of Britain was internationalised during this period and capital from its underdeveloped empires was transferred to European countries and other overseas offshoots to fructify through capitalist mode of production (Bagchi, 1972).

The crisis of disposal of profit was averted by the railway boom and the major characteristic of the century was an alternation in the troughs and booms in the advanced capitalist countries. With USA's emerging as a marginal creditor and Britain's changing position from the world workshop to an industrially unprogressive financier of the western world that the problem of reinvestment of capitalist profit became sever and mobility of capital to areas of cheap input cost became a necessity. Lenin's (n.d.) designation of 1900 as a watershed between colonialism and imperialism thus marked a differentiation between competitive capital from monopoly capital in advanced capitalist countries. Export of commodities, typical of a competitive state was replaced by the export of capital expressing typicalness of monopoly capitalism (Peet, 1987). This was also the period when cartelisation emerged as a major practice by monopoly capital to control the market. Electric cartelisation became internationalised and cartelisation of large cigarette manufacturing companies namely American Tobacco Comapny (ATC) of the United States and Imperial Tobacco Company (ITC) of Britain took place to form British American Tobacco (BAT). Established in 1903, this world cartel lasted till 1911 when US antitrust authorities required its dissolution (Newfarmer, 1984).

Lenin's focus on the end of the nineteenth century as the crucial phase of transition from competitive to monopoly capitalism was taken up by Baran and Sweezy (1968) who emphasised on monopoly arising from the tendency of falling rate of profit under capitalism. Sohn Rethel (1971) found this falling rate of profit promoting expansion of market on the one hand and opening new territories and field for capital investment on the other. While Palloix (1977) argued that internationalisation of the circuit of money capital that began with the stage of monopoly reached its ultimate stage of internationalisation of productive capital signifying international production by multinational firms and spread of capital as a social relation of production. Industrialists from Britain, Germany, Holland and America found production more lucrative in areas of cheap labour and raw material and moved their firms overseas to Latin America, Africa, Asia and Australia. Aided by development in transport, storage and communications, firms like Singer, ITT, General Electric, Dunlop, Lever Brothers, Nestlé, Bayer and Siemens established manufacturing plants overseas during the last quarter of nineteenth century. Singer was the first to manufacture and mass-market its product bearing the same name across the world. In 1867 it built its first overseas factory in Glasgow. Most of the investments of these companies were in Europe and North America (Jenkins, 1987). In 1902 F.A. Mckenzie commented, 'America has invaded Europe not with armed men but with manufactured goods... Our babies are fed on American foods and our dead buried in American coffins.'

By early twentieth century single-centred firms controlled by individual entrepreneurs were replaced by large corporations with numerous plants. Factors of size and efficiency prompted their growth. The organisation that developed to administer and control these corporations on a continent-wide basis were also well suited to operate plants and subsidiaries on cross-country basis. In Europe, the so-called Great Depression (1873-96) stimulated the growth of many consumer goods industries as food prices fell. Also increasing tariff protection introduced in Germany, France and the USA stimulated international production. Many of these early corporations such as British petroleum or Standard Oil made their investments in mining and petroleum sectors. The manufacturing multinational firms especially received stimulation during and after World War I when a number of nation states preferred foreign investment for export promotion of their products. At the same time and more importantly to maximise return and achieve self-sustained growth, control of marketing operations was required by the large firms. Given their development in communications and rapid growth of product cycle, more and more came to venture cross-country production. The product cycle was essentially prolonged by gaining control of marketing outlets, moving to places of cheap labour and reinvesting profit thus accrued to further research and development in home countries (Hymer, 1972). Manufacturing and merchandising MNCs like Singer, General Electric, Coca-Cola, Nestlé, Philips, Siemens, Lever Brothers and a number of European drug and chemical firms hence geared themselves to spatial expansion (Fig 1.1).

1.2.1. Multinationals' entry into the Third World

The first MNCs entering into the Third World at the turn of the present century were mainly engaged in primary activity like oil and mineral investment in Mexico, copper mining in Chile, Peru and Belgian Congo, bauxite in British and Dutch Guyana and oil in the Dutch East Indies. Significant companies were Royal Dutch Shell, Exxon, Anaconda, Copper and International Nickel, mainly dealing with oil and petroleum mining. Agriculture was the other significant sector. Much before World War I, United Fruit Company had entered Latin America, Mexico and Caribbean along with other American food processing corporations, while Dutch and British corporations like Unilever and Cadbury entered Africa in areas of vegetable oil and cocoa production. As an extension of colonial ties, British corporations like Dunlop entered in Malaya in rubber plantations and Brooke Bond set up tea plantations in India and Ceylon. In all the above cases the MNCs did not however, initiate the respective economic activities. Rather the MNCs monopolised and integrated these already existing economic activities in a carefully designed hierarchical network.

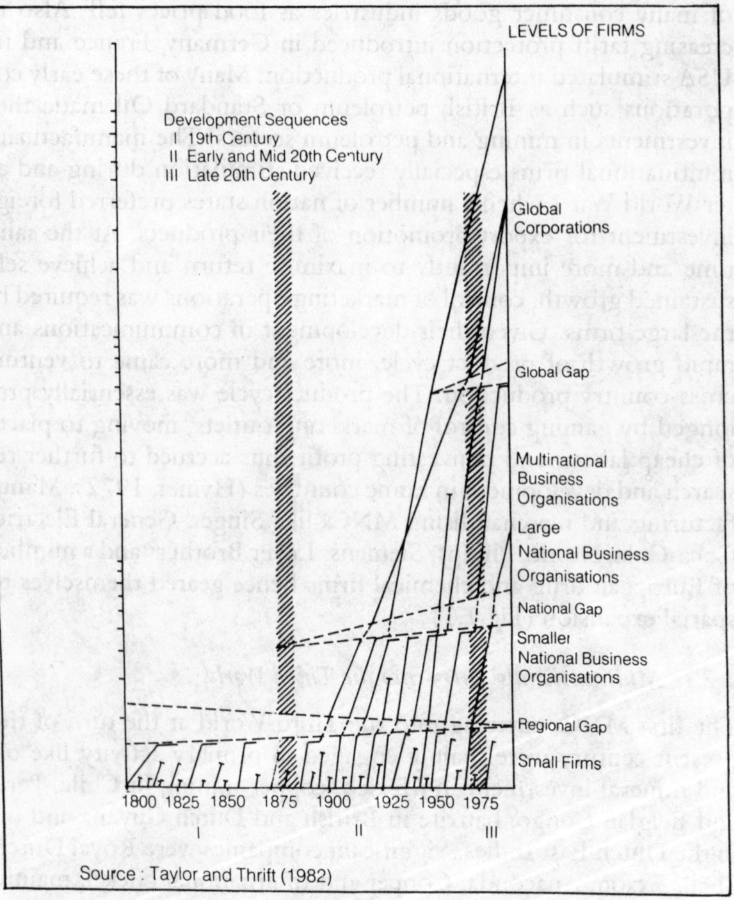

Fig. 1.1 Historical emergence of global corporations

During the First World War more than 60 per cent of the foreign direct investment was located in developing countries (Dunning, 1983). Of this, 55 per cent investment was in the primary sector and 15 per cent in manufacturing which were concentrated in the developed countries. Foreign direct investment made by the

United States during the period had the same pattern of investment. Of the total foreign direct investment 39 per cent was in mining, 18 per cent in agriculture, 13 per cent in oil. All these concentrated in less developed countries. Only 3 per cent of the total investment was in manufacturing.

It was during the inter-war period that multinational corporations started entering in manufacturing. The major region of expansion was Latin America where 200 firms from the US and Europe had set up plants as subsidiaries by 1940. Mentionable names were Ford, General Motors, Goodyear, Firestone, Singer, General Electric, Abbott and Parke Davis from the US, Nestlé from Switzerland, Unilever from Holland and UK, Philips from Holland, Siemens, from West Germany and Olivetti from Italy. In other Third World continents, nearly 100 manufacturing subsidiaries were set up before 1944 with India as the major destination country. During the Second World War MNCs were still concentrated in the primary sector. There was only a shift from mining to food-based items or plantation activity. In Africa and Middle East along with copper mines, oil and metal operations, coffee and rubber plantations were set up and more than 50 per cent foreign investment of the US during early forties was in this group (Fig 1.2). Gradually with passage of time multinational corporations entered manufacturing sector in a big way and achieved a further shift from food product items to products like chemicals, heavy engineering, electrical and electronics, etc. With their further spatial expansion, sectoral and geographical integrations were complete. In the seventies they emeraged as major determinant players of the international economy with substantial control over world production, trade and market operations.

1.3 Multinational Corporations in Post World War II Era: Fifties and Sixties

One of the salient traits of post-war economic growth was capital accumulation at world scale led by the developed countries in which multinational corporations played a crucial role. Ever since the end of the second world war, capital exports have helped shape the evolving global economy. The quarter century after World War II saw an unprecedented expansion of MNC activity initially led by the US capital when vanquished nations of Europe along with other countries were slow in competition. It was the vigorous expansion of

US multinationals in 1950, that led the way to a new stage of globalisation. By doing so, they created an environment in which giant corporations of all countries, for new accumulation opportunities, had to turn multinational and widen their international base. By the end of 1950 half of the world's foreign direct investment was accounted by US firms, comparable to the share of UK prior to World War I (Monthly Review, 1992).

Gradually the relative status of the United States dropped and European and Japanese firms surfaced as important competitors. Thus even though there was no lessening of interest by US capital in continuing to expand its overseas investments, the US share of foreign direct assets declined from 47 per cent in 1960 to 28 per cent in 1989 (Table 1.2). Especially significant was the speed with which Japan and Germany got into the scene.

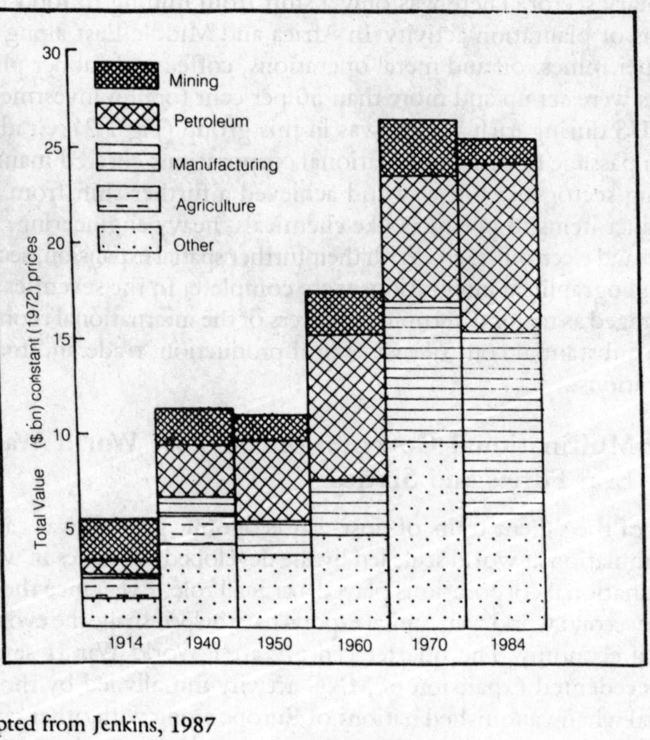

Adapted from Jenkins, 1987

Fig. 1.2 Sectoral distribution of US foreign investments in the Third World countries

Table 1.2 *Sources of FDI*

Countries of Origin	1960	1973	1989
	(Percentage of Total)		
USA	47.1	48.0	28.3
Canada	3.7	3.7	4.8
UK	18.3	13.0	16.7
Germany	1.2	5.6	9.1
Italy	1.6	1.5	3.8
France	6.1	4.2	5.3
Netherlands	10.3	7.5	6.1
Japan	0.7	4.9	11.5

Source : International Trade Administration, US Department of Commerce, September, 1989; July, 1991.

There were other reasons for the tremendous growth of MNCs during this time. Firstly, technological development. It accelerated geographical co-ordination of diverse and dispersed economic activities leading to a considerable reduction of operation and production costs. This also helped the MNCs to corner, control and trade technology at a world scale creating a serious technological gap evident especially in drug and pharmaceutical industries during post World War II era. Then, there was post war boom shrinking world market (added also by the separation of world market due to the operations of Soviet Union, China and other like countries) and the need to build and rebuild industries in the developed countries. There was serious impairment of foreign exchange resources in these countries and a natural need for resources. In certain cases earnings of the foreign companies were blocked and reinvested in infrastructure and industries. The USA, because of its physical distance from the theatre of war, was not affected much and did not have its economy or industries destroyed. During the war and after, it could, therefore, take the sole responsibility of supply and production which was further aided by a tremendous development in the field of transport, storage and communication. The second reason for the growth of MNCs lay in the Third World countries many of which became independent or decolonised during or around this period. These brought the issue of their economic development to the forefront. Differentials in the relations between the economic system and the system of power in these countries gave rise to various possibilities of development and autonomy where the character of the local bourgeoisie varied to a great extent from collaborative to comprador. Colonialism in all these countries had not created any sound base for capitalist development, but introduced, nevertheless, capitalist relations of production. Many of them, after transfer of power or decolonisation, retained the colonial politico-administrative structure by only nationalising it. The strong relation of dominance-dependency between the coloniser countries and their colonies thus instead of a decline got transformed into newer political economic relations. Instead of bilateral dependence it became multi-lateral interdependence wherein the underdeveloped countries led by their own elites looked for inspiration and financial support towards the west in the scientific and technological assistance in financial commitments, as well as in progressive ideologies. In place of the old colonial link, a neo-colonial link was thus established between the developed and the Third World countries at economic, political and cultural levels.

Third World countries bought the idea of development path from the west in the name of 'growth model' and wanted to increase their per capita income very rapidly along with the Gross National Product. In India 'with a poor population and a social structure dominated by a weak and far from homogenous capitalist class, the market for better types of consumer goods particularly durables remained extremely restricted. The state apparatus precariously balanced the interests of landlords, monopoly capitalists, professional class and collaborative elements in the upper classes. Government policy hence was never radical enough to release agriculture from conditions of semi-feudal bondage and lay a firm base for assured growth' (Bagchi, 1973). The various plans and public projects of the Third World countries had also the requirement of major inputs in the form of large-scale investments. From the very early years of their national planning era, these countries thus opened up their economies to foreign capital and technology investments for the aim of accelerating industrialisation process and attaining economic development (IDPAD, 1984).

Economically and effectively, these countries gradually became dependent on foreign capital. The large-scale industrialisation that was heavily leaning on 'import substitution' process involved large-scale import of foreign capital and technology which created a situation of entrapment. The dependent nature of industrial development in these countries did not create any diversification in the production sector and other productive fields like agriculture. Due to the prevailing underdevelopment thus there was no proper demand base for diversified industrial products nor was there a supply base. Further with heavy import of inputs and technology an imbalance of foreign exchange reserve was created leading to a simultaneous crisis of balance of payments. Almost all of them became dependent on aids (usually loans) from the advanced capitalist countries through international financial institutions for meeting their balance of payment requirements. In the process, they opened up their economy more to foreign capital and multinational corporations. Their economic development path was redesigned by the proponents of economic growth model with strong advocacy for export promotion industrialisation process. In Latin American countries this process had maximum saleability. In Southeast Asian countries like South Korea it was monitored by a substantially interventionist government which could put in foreign capital on check and generate development compared to others (Bagchi, 1987). India joined the line later but without any positive role of the government and therefore went more in a 'Latin American' way.

In the rigid framework of an international capitalism underdeveloped countries of Latin America experienced an industrialisation that was dissociated from progress and national development. Structure of industries in Argentina, Brazil and Mexico in the sixties showed 'deformations characteristic of a reflective development' (Galeano, 1973). A handful of concerns, mostly foreign owned or collaborated, controlled the industrial sector representing global industrial conglomerations. Growth of Latin American manufacturing was aided and initiated from outside and not from within, by any national development policy. Positioning itself from the beginning under protective customs barriers but with foreign control and close foreign ties through import substitution on the one hand and maintaining the semi-feudal agrarian structure intact—in order to strangle agricultural market and internal production—on the other, industrialisation in Latin America in post Second World War era largely represented a dependent development with large multinational corporations controlling the process. They had no obligation to develop the host Third World countries industrially or technologically and they held technology as a commercial item through patent laws while the poor host countries, in order to tide over the immediate crisis of balance of payment created by import-substitution policy, accepted these laws mostly recommended by IMF or GATT. Being caught in this they remained technically backward and failed to adapt suitable techniques through research and development. In India, Turkey, Pakistan and Trinidad, to take some examples from a 1964 United Nation's study, more than 89 per cent of all outstanding patents were owned by foreigners. In Chile patents owned by foreigners increased from 65 per cent to 95 per cent in 1937-67 while in Colombia foreign based MNCs who constituted 10 per cent of all patent holders owned 60 per cent of all patents of the country (Barnet and Muller, 1974).

It needs mention that the above 'development' path of the Third World countries was required by the MNCs for their own survival and growth. With diminishing profit, balance of payment in parent countries and increasing contradictions among themselves, the corporations had no other option than to make more sophisticated products with high input cost and therefore to mitigate it simultaneously to search for newer markets and newer productive operations. In the export-led industrial policies that they initiated in the Third World countries, their role as major exporters or contributors to value added from export was minimum. Helleiner (1976)has specially pointed to the limited extent to which MNCs have been involved in production for export in the Third World and the continued predominance of their manufacturing for local markets. Employments created by such exports also were minimal (Vaitsos, 1976) and concentrated mainly in unskilled categories for which benefits from training of labour and technology transfer were small (Jenkins, 1987). Also in terms of investments, these firms earned more than what they invested. Between 1950 and 67 US investments in Latin America (not including reinvested profits) totalled to $ 3.921 billion while profits and dividends sent abroad during the same period amounted to $ 12.819 billion, i.e. more than 3 times the capital invested (Galeano, 1974).

During this period, the most rapidly growing sector for MNC activity was manufacturing and the most favoured locations were the Third World countries. Even though a considerable section of the international trade was carried out between and among the developed countries themselves, the location decisions of MNCs to start subsidiaries or collaborations or direct manufacturing operations in the Third World were significant, thanks to the import substitution policies followed by these countries that made MNCs the major beneficiaries (Jenkins, 1987). The extraordinary competitive edge in using the technology of communications and market manipulation also went in favour of the MNCs in the form of transfer pricing and intra corporation transaction in capturing the market of the Third World countries. Following this the major industrial development took place in the developed countries with huge corporations as the centres while their branches and subsidiaries expanding with intense rapacity in the Third World. In pre-Allende Chile, 51 per cent of the largest 160 firms were effectively controlled by corporations located in developed countries. In each of its seven key industries foreign firms controlled at least 51 per cent of the production. Of the top 22 MNCs operating in the country, 19 either operated free of all competition or shared the market with other oligopolists. In Argentina, in early sixties, of the total sales of the 50 largest corporations, more than 50 per cent were transacted by MNCs. In 1962 Mexico's rubber, electrical machinery and transportation industries were already 100 per cent foreign owned, metal and tobacco industry were controlled by MNCs by 42 per cent and 17 per cent respectively. In 1966 MNCs in Brazil accounted for 64 per cent of the total net profit derived from rubber, motor vehicles, machinery, household appliances and mining sectors. By 1961 MNCs owned 100 per cent of automobile and tyre production, 59 per cent of machinery and 50 per cent of electrical appliance manufacturing (Barnet & Muller, 1974). Eighty per cent of the net financial investment of the US multinational corporations during this period was directed towards Latin America. Of these, five countries (of which the US was undoubtedly the supreme) were largely aided by the operation of the international banks (Table 1.3).

Table 1.3 *Geographic concentration of manufacturing subsidiaries in the Third World 1968–70*

Origin of Investment	Location of subsidiaries in the Third World: Latin America %	Asia and Oceania %	Africa and Middle East	Total %
USA	56	31	13	100
Japan	19	70	11	100
UK	10	47	43	100
West Germany	47	26	26	100
France	40	15	45	100

Source : C. Vaitsos (1976) in G. K. Helleiner (ed) *A World Divided*

This nature of industrial development that hence obtained led to a spatial separation of the production process and a resultant disintegrated operation of industrial manufacturing. The control of the entire cycle, from the purchase of raw materials right up to the sale of the finished products lay in the hands of the MNCs which decided to engage the domestic firms to undertake final stage jobs for some products requiring labour intensive inputs, e.g. textiles, toys and shoes. The direction and form of industrial development were thus primarily decided by these corporations (Bacha, 1983).

By the end of 1960s multinational corporations deepened their world-wide sourcing activities, particularly in the Third World. They expanded and extended their operations in different ways and forms right from the use of cheap, at times unskilled (female) labour to extremely sophisticated operations (e.g. in areas of electronics) with the basic decision of keeping productive knowledge, managerial control, marketing and other key elements of the organisational set-up confined with the parent firms. Such a development led towards a new form of international specialisation (Vaitsos, 1976) where capital was being raised at an international scale but controlled at equity level by the MNCs of the developed countries; considerable section of labour of the Third World by this association did not necessarily improve their skill as a class or enter into the proper cycle of social reproduction because development of skill occurred according to the demand of countries. Labour of the Third World countries thus represented a disjunction between industrial development and development of productivity.

1.4 Geographical Expansion of Multinational Corporations in Post Seventies :

The 1970s can be seen as a period in which major shift took place in the structure of the world economy that was getting precipitated since the 50s. Seventies can also be called a period of transition towards a new phase of internationalisation of production and labour. A major force in materialising the above changes were again the multinational corporations (Vernon, 1979). It was a period that saw the emergence of a truly global economic system with the MNCs at its centre (Table 1.4).

Table 1.4 *Foreign manufacturing subsidiary networks of 315 large MNCs* (in 1950 and 1970)

Number of Enterprises including Subsidiary Networks	180 US based MNCs		135 MNCs based in UK and Europe	
	1950	1970	1950	1970
6 countries	138	9	116	31
6 – 20 countries	43	128	16	75
20 countries	0	44	3	29

Source : Vernon, 1979 pp 258.

With a presence in almost all countries the spatial expansion policies that the MNCs started following since 70s were distinct from those years. Earlier they would set up subsidiaries first in familiar areas moving later to the unfamiliar ones based upon profit maximisation (Taylor and Thrift, 1981). The post seventy policies would assess the performance of the regions and select the best ones in terms of producing the highest returns. Fifty five MNCs received 66 per cent of the net profits of 100 largest private enterprises (Barnet and Muller, 1974) during late seventies (Fig 1.3).

The seventies also saw MNCs managing their environment and

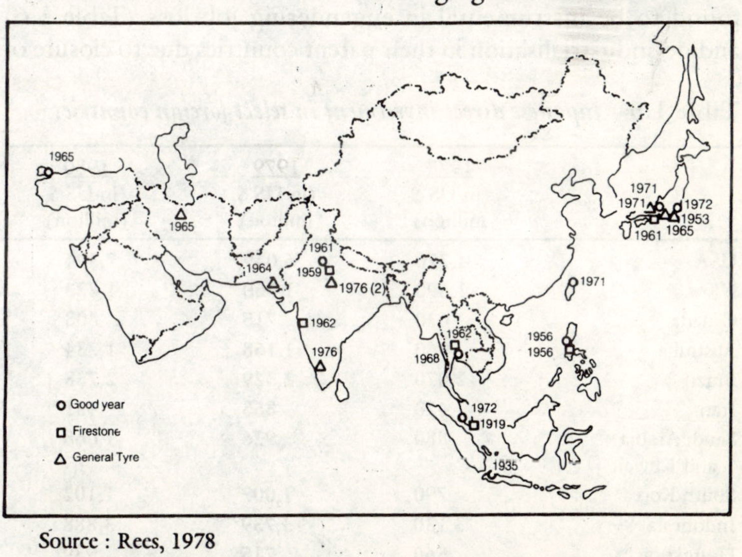

Source : Rees, 1978

Fig. 1.3 Spatial expansion of three major tyre corporations in Asia

managing it more efficiently. Due to increasingly efficient telecommunication, transmission of information became easier and quicker.

Further, the development of administrative science enabled information to be analysed and represented in all possible ways. This made it easier for the multinational corporations to centralise information (Aglietta, 1979) and control and decentralise operation. The matrix form of organisation of the MNCs, with a grid structure and vertical hierarchy also emerged during this period. This enabled the corporations to diversify their products and diffuse the operation more extensively. It also helped them plan and replan operations in response to the changing local situations. Multinational corporations during the seventies became more financially oriented and their fiscal measures became extremely adaptive. As money became more mobile MNCs became more powerful in finetuning the monetary operations. During the post seventy era the extreme dominance of the US based MNCs was reduced with various European (West Germany along with Dutch, Swedish and French) and Japanese corporations entering the scene. Since 1970s Japan's investment in foreign countries (Table 1.5) increased significantly (Nakase, 1981). Besides creating conditions for uneven and dependent development in the Third World countries, MNCs since seventies have also been found to be instrumental in engendering job loss (Table 1.6) and de-industrialisation in their parent countries due to closure of

Table 1.5 *Japanese direct investment in select foreign countries*

	1978 (in US $ million)	1979 (in US $ million)	1980 (in US $ (million)
USA	4,770	6,049	7,394
UK	1,690	1,750	1,823
Canada	630	715	808
Australia	960	1,168	1,734
Brazil	2,070	2,329	2,738
Iran	470	855	431
Saudi Arabia and Kuwait	880	926	1,068
South Korea	790	1,007	1,102
Indonesia	3,130	3,739	3,888
Hongkong	560	715	939

Source : Nakase, 1981, pp 64.

Table 1.6 *Percentagewise distribution of employment within Philips* (1964-76)

	1964	1970	1978
Netherlands	35	27	22
Europe	53	55	49
USA and Canada	12	5	10
Rest of the world	–	13	19

Source : Taylor and Thrift, 1981

plants (Tharakan, 1980; Thrift, 1980; Hansen, 1981; Massey and Meegan, 1982). The new international division of labour based on the 'relocation' of manufacturing, was primarily responsible for this. It should not be seen as a mere reaction to crude labour costs, but a result of technology and communication development and also for a need to control markets in developing countries. With their technological might the MNCs pick and choose locations for particular production processes, respond and react to prevailing political and fiscal conditions of the host countries and, in the process obviously use the wage differentials to earn more profit. This gave rise to a continuous process of 'locational rationalisation' by which the fixed capital of a particular production plant of a multinational

Table 1.7 *Comparative labour costs of the Coats Patons* (April, 1981)

Country	Single Shift		Double Shift	
	Total Cost per hour	Index	Total Cost per hour	Index
UK (Parent country)	2678	100	3186	100
Italy	3259	122	3499	110
West Germany	3561	133	3696	116
Canada	3596	134	3564	112
USA	3134	117	3134	98
Portugal	1076	40	1177	37
Colombia	0.950	36	1121	35
Brazil	0.840	31	1009	32
Peru	0.611	23	0.620	19
India	0.342	13	0.345	11
Philippines	0.276	10	0.276	9
Indonesia	0.166	6	0.169	5

Source: Financial Times, 29, June, 1981 pp. 11.

corporation got continuously checked against a more profitable investment elsewhere (Taylor and Thrift, 1981).

And with a worldwide production space, the most profitable locations for the capital seem to be found usually in the less developed countries (Table 1.7).

But this does not mean that the multinational corporations did not locate their plants or employ capital in other developed countries (Fig 1.3). In late seventies US capital in Western Europe controlled 80 per cent of the production of electronic computers, 50 per cent of the output of transistors and 95 per cent of the market for integrated circuits. In Canada their penetration was further deeper and complete. They held 50 per cent of the total assets of Canada's largest corporations, 90 per cent of the automobile industry, 80 per cent of the rubber corporations, 75 per cent of the chemical corporations and 65 per cent of electric apparatus industry. They also held more than 50 per cent of mining, smelting, petroleum and natural gas industries (Roy Chowdhury, 1981). Seventies was also an era when the MNCs went in for collaboration with local capital of the host countries in a big way. In this process, besides usual profit, they started earning from repatriation. In 1970, a foreign corporation operating in Colombia remitted annual profit nine times more than the original investment. In 1976, Colgate-Palmolive, a US based MNC in the consumer goods sector, remitted 88 per cent of their original capital as gross profit (Saini, 1981).

During this period free production zones or export promotion zones surfaced as an associative feature of MNCs. These industrial areas, separated off from the rest of the country and located at places of cheap labour, became sites for world market factories characterised by low wages, long hours of work, short holidays, high level of labour, intense working conditions and rapid rates of labour turnover (Frobal, *et. al.* 1980) and, therefore, became unique examples of super exploitation. In 1975, 79 free production zones were in full production in 25 underdeveloped countries. Eleven of these countries were in Asia, 5 in Africa and 9 in Latin America. During the same year 500,000 labourers were engaged in the free production zones world wide. Side by side in at least 14 other countries, a large number of world market factories were installed in sites outside these zones. In 1975, estimates of foreign employment amounted to a total of 800,000 employed by West German manufacturing industries in foreign countries outside the EEC. The number of subsidiaries abroad per company ranged from 1 to 40

(Frank, 1977). It needs mention that relocation of production to export processing zones in the Third World is not a general tendency of capital. In certain times and in certain branches when there occur major obstacles to increasing relative surplus value that such relocations take place. During sixties and seventies such conditions existed in clothing and electronics (Jenkins 1983). In mid sixties in at least 39 underdeveloped countries such factories were functioning; 15 in Asia, 8 in Africa and 16 in Latin America.

The tendency and ability to expand spatially was found to be more with the large size. In late seventies IBM operated in 80 countries, Siemens in 52 countries and Volkswagen in 12 countries. Many of these had major production bases outside their parent countries e.g. Exxon had 81 per cent of its production outside the United States, Unilever 70 per cent and Philips 67 per cent (Table 1.8).

Table 1.8 *Nature of multinationality*

Average size of MNCs (Value product in billions of dollars)	Percentage of production undertaken overseas
5.5	75
4.4	45
3.5	44
2.3	34

Source : D. Swamy, pp 91.

During the eighties expansion of the multinational corporations reached newer height. While distorting the economic policies and infrastructural development of Third World countries, international capitalism during this period became exceptionally systematic. For example, international organisations like IMF (International Monetary Fund) and World Bank openly came out in support of these corporations. Like any lending institution IMF requires changes in domestic economic policies of potentially borrower countries to make it essentially conservative. If a deficit less developed country refuses the latter's advice it faces the danger of refusal of not only IMF loan but also from World Bank or from other bilateral loans. In the name of helping the less developed countries in their economic development, during eighties these organisations in a big way therefore, started controlling their investment pattern, rate, areas, and technology positing the multinational corporations in the forefront of this process.

Despite a deceleration of world economic growth, MNCs grew and in a unique way. They started using a wide variety of institutional arrangements many of which involved little or no investment of capital as evident by a marked decline in the rate of foreign direct investment to underdeveloped countries.

The eighties also marked the era of intense competition among the MNCs. In the background of world wide recession and slower economic growth MNCs faced difficulty in diversification and spatial extension. To gain a bigger control over the market their behaviour turned to be more and more oligopolistic resulting in large scale mergers and acquisitions. In mid eighties alone several major US corporations or their subsidiaries were acquired by non US corporations e.g. Chesebrough-Ponds by Unilever, Celanese Corporation by Hoechst, Doubleday by West German Publishing Group, Bertelsman and the semi-conductor firm Fairchild by a Japanese firm (Clairmonte and Cavanagh, 1987). In a similar manner Japanese Nippon Mini Computer was taken over by Data General or Toyo Tire was bought over by Good Year of the USA. The increasing size of firms and the rise of coalesce groups also made the vertical and horizontal integration of plants a dire necessity leading to more efficiency that again made internationalisation of production and exploration of newer markets (UNCTC, 1988) a reality.

There has also been a change in the activity space of the MNCs of different countries. For the US based MNCs eighties were the era of saturation. From 1950 to late seventies US firms geographically expanded to an extent that in 1977 overseas employment of the US MNCs exceeded 10 per cent of the domestic employment (UNCTC, 1989). This trend declined in the eighties. But during the same time US military power rose as did the control of the US armament industry in political matters. Since eighties role of the US as a global political and military power aided by the support of major international organisations is discernible. For the MNCs from Western Europe, Japan, Australia and Canada, it was a period of both expansion and locational shift. MNCs of the Federal Republic of Germany this was a period of increase of expansion evident by the rise in their aggregate assets and share increase of foreign affiliates' employment. Increase of activity of British MNCs, however, cannot be, compared with those of the FRG as in the UK firms' spatial expansion was more due to unfavourable production conditions in the home market than by the exceptional competitiveness of the firms (UNCTC, 1989). Japanese and other European MNCs increased their practice of spatial expansion in eighties with a move towards diversification. Throughout eighties West European and Japanese MNCs increased production through their subsidiaries or collaborating partners and exported the items back to the international market through their sophisticated distributive network. This rise in the competitiveness of Western European and Japanese MNCs relative to the US ones decreased the attraction of foreign production for the US firms and increased the advantage of other foreign firms (Table 1.9). All these operations accounted for a large proportion of the international trade of the developed world. Actually trade between the principal units and their affiliates, between principal units and the subcontractors accounted for a major share of the international trade thus creating a detrimental effect on free competition and price differentials.

Table 1.9. *Foreign direct investment, national assets and national wealth: USA, Japan, UK and the FRG in late 1970s*

Country	Stock of FDI	National Stock of FDI			
			% of National		
		Assets	Wealth	Assets	Wealth
USA (1978) (Billions of dollars)	146.0	17887	9104	0.82	1.60
Japan (1977) (Trillions of Yen)	2.8	1792	894.2	0.16	0.32
UK (1977) (Billions of pounds)	20.1	13276	617.3	1.51	3.26
FRG (1977) (Billions of DM)	51.6	10172	5534	0.51	0.93

Source : UNCTC, UNCTC Current Studies, Series A, No. 8, 1989, pp 22.

All these led to extreme concentration of corporate power. The world's largest 200 corporations in 1985 recorded sales worth $ 3.06 trillion and only two countries accounted for 75 per cent of these corporations and 76 per cent of their sales. US firms accounted for more than 50 per cent of the firms (Clairmonte and Cavanagh, 1987).

Considerable expansion of the MNCs in the service sector was observed during this era when this sector became capital intensive. Expansion of the sector at an international scale thus owed much to the multinational corporations with their large markets that required considerable administration, much of which is carried out within the corporations either by the parent unit or by the regional headquarters. But for various reasons especially for their cheap availability outside, much of these services are externalised and bought in, stimulating thereby the growth of producer services (Noyelle, 1983). Although the service firms have fewer owner-specific advantages, investment in this sector of the MNCs is more efficiently regulated than in the manufacturing sector. Opening up of the service sector was apparent during the latter half of the eighties (Table 1.10).

Table 1.10 *Foreign direct investment*

Countries	Mining		Manufacturing		Services	
	1975	1990	1975	1990	1975	1990
USA	26	18	45	41	24	36
UK	11	7	69	23	29	41
Japan	28	6	32	43	36	68
Germany	4	2	46	41	42	57
Holland	26	33	39	17	15	31

Source : Clairmonte, 1991

Clairmonte (1991) suggests that since 1980s the world economy witnessed an industrialisation of the service sector and tertiarisation of the industrial sector which has had detrimental impact on the Third World economy (Table 1.11). By 1990 the same competitive trends that created proliferation of subcontracting and rise of unorganised labour force under the aegis of the corporate banner were seen in the service sector. The drive to quantitatively limit the inputs of labour and thereby its political potency became common in this sector also.

Table 1.11 *Economic situation of select Third World countries*

Countrie	Earnings per employee (Growth rate)		GDP (Growth rate)		Average annual rate of inflation	
	1970-80 %	1980-88 %	1965-80 %	1980-88 %	1965-80 %	1980-88 %
Mexico	1.2	-5.2	6.5	0.7	13.0	72.7
Brazil	4.0	0.0	9.0	3.0	31.3	227.8
Turkey	6.1	-3.3	6.2	5.1	20.8	41.4
Sri Lanka	N.A.	1.7	4.0	4.0	9.4	10.9

Source : Srinivas-Raghavan, 1991.

In the operational field, eighties saw the maximum collaboration in various forms. There was cross licensing of new technologies and products, joint ventures between MNCs as well as joint research and development programmes; shortening of the life cycle of both end products, need to innovate continuously in order to remain competitive and sharp increase for the corporations to seek collaboration and merger. In order to reduce risks involved in contractual arrangements, MNCs established closer ties with the subcontracting firms which often took the form of quasi-integration. In many cases they even entered into joint ventures with their suppliers. Subcontracting thus became an important source of exports of many Southeast Asian countries especially in consumer electronics, textiles and clothings and toys.

A series of economic, technological and institutional factors can be identified to have played significant role in shaping the international economy during the eighties. There has been a general decline in the rate of world economic growth added with growing inequalities among the Third World countries with collapsing commodity prices, spiralling debt service burdens. There has also been an intensification in living standards of the vast sectors of the Latin American and Caribbean population (Clairmonte and Cavanagh, 1987). The less developed countries gradually slided down through the path of 'structural adjustment' and liberalisation prescribed by World Bank and IMF. The fundamental gap between them and the developed countries thus continued to widen. In 1960 the per capita GDP of the underdevelped countries combined was a minimal 8.7 per cent of that of the developed ones. Even this percentage fell to 7.4 per cent in the seventies and then to an abysmally low of 6.1 per cent in late eighties. Excepting the oil producing countries of the Middle East whose relative position improved between 1970–1987, situation of the remaining Third World countries was dismal. In 1987 during the decades of intensified globalisation by the multinational corporations the per capita GDP of Africa (other than South Africa) as a per cent of the per capita GDP of the core countries became half of what it had been in 1960 (Table 1.12) and for Latin America it was three-fifth of the figure of 1960 (Sweezy *et. al.* 1992).

Table 1.12 ***Gap between developed and underdeveloped market economies***

Gross Domestic Product Per Capita : Underdeveloped Countries as a percent of Developed Countries

	1960 %	1970 %	1987 %
All Underdeveloped Countries	8.7	7.4	6.1
Africa*	6.0	5.6	3.5
Latin America**	22.2	17.9	12.5
Oil Producers	31.3	26.3	12.0
Others	20.0	15.3	12.7
Asia-Middle East	16.7	14.9	19.6
Oil Producers	18.9	16.7	27.8
Others	15.2	13.5	11.8
Asia-East and Southeast	5.3	4.5	3.8

* Excluding South Africa

** Including Caribbean region

Source : Monthly Review, vol.43(10), pp 10, 1992

As a natural consequence, the universe of the MNCs in the nineties became highly concentrated. The largest 100 corporations (ranked by the size of their foreign assets) had about 3.2 trillion in global assets in 1990 of which nearly one-third was outside their own home countries (UNCTD, 1993). Even within these 100 corporations a sizeable number from some few countries, viz. the USA, UK, Germany, Japan and France is seen accounting for almost three quarters of the largest 100 MNCs (Table 1.13). Simultaneously there has been a major intensification of FDI cross investment beween the industrialised economies especially in the triad regions (Dicken, 1994) and reduction of flow to developed economies.

Table 1.13 ***Degree of concentration of the largest 100 multinational corporations by foreign assets and foreign sales***

Corporations	Share in the largest 100 in %		Share in the largest 100 in %	
	Total Assets	Foreign Assets	Total Sales	Foreign Sales
Largest 10	25.8	33.5	23.2	29.4
Largest 25	50.0	54.4	46.0	49.2
Largest 50	70.9	76.3	68.7	70.9
Largest 100	100.0	100.0	100.0	100.0

Source : World Development Report, 1993, United Nations

In the early nineties 25 largest multinational corporations of the world by sales were found to dominate in textiles, chemicals, computers and electronics, food, beverages, apparel, automobile and transport, mining, petroleum and pharmaceuticals, industrial and farm equipment, machinery and building materials and last but not the least, soaps and cosmetics (Hammes and Teitelbaum, 1991). In 1990 the US topped the list having 40 per cent of the world's biggest 25 companies, followed by Japan. Japan accounted for the maximum number of corporations with the highest sales. Besides, a clear pattern of Japan's moving into the race was distinct since 80s. In 1980, 23 US multinationals made the top 50 compared with only 5 Japanese. In 1990 there were 17 American corporations and 10 Japanese. Of the 46 biggest corporations in electronics, 16 were US and 15 Japanese. With globalisation speeding ahead, US and European multinationals were also busy in mergers and acquisitions in 1990s. Smithkline Bickman of the US and Beecham Group of Britain merged to become Smithkline Beecham, the third largest pharmaceutical company of the world. Nippon Mining, a metal and petroleum company, entered into electronics by acquiring Gould Inc. of the US. Asea Brown Boveri, the Swiss-Swedish joint corporation making heavy electrical equipment acquired a major part of Westinghouse of the US and Ford of the USA bought Jaguar of Britain. The world looked more like an industrial village for the MNCs. *Fortune* (1990) suggested to order clothes from Levistrauss, the largest apparel maker of the US with material brought from Japan. In an international economic space of 1990 according to Pak and Solo (1990), an individual could build a house with British building materials and buy tyres for the car from a Japanese Bridgestone. The multinational corporations have completed their great circle.

2

Organisation and Operation : Sector and Space

2.1 Organisation, Structure and Operation

Recent Analyses on foreign investment have discarded pure economic theory and turned to the explanation of industrial structure, production locations, nature of technology, market imperfections as well as regional inequality to understand the complex phenomenon of multinational corporations.

Organisational aspects of multinational corporations need to be analysed with the above perspective. At the outset, it should be pointed out that the power of the MNCs grows from (a) their vertical and horizontal integration, (b) their important share in the overall trade among the developed countries, (c) their share and control over the economies of the Third World countries, in particular, (d) their dominating status in the key industries, (e) their control over the international pricing mechanism and finally, (f) their oligopolistic nature. All these are closely associated with knowledge, power and development policy of these corporations (Vaitsos, 1976). Thus both size and internationality play an important role in the MNCs' strength and ability. The earlier organisational modes of single product or single plant firm have undergone enormous changes and, therefore, analytical norms also need modification. It needs to be kept in mind that the MNCs in pursuit of their profit maximisation may not only locate the plants in countries, regions or areas of cheap labour and resource, they may also accordingly orient their organisation to achieve product diversification and larger control over the market. In the evolution of the large size corporations Chandler identified three major stages, namely (1) The Marshallian firm, organised at the factory level with functioning oriented round a single firm and a single product. The decision-making power at this stage rested in the hands of a few who actually were the decision makers on almost all fronts. (2) The second stage arrived with rapid growth and merger movement among firms in the late 19th century especially in the United States and noticeably not in the UK for reasons explained in Chapter one. As capitalism had its uneven development, following it the development of the organisations of MNCs was also uneven bringing in its wake a need for an efficient vertical integration to deal with a much wider production and marketing space. At this stage the family firms were replaced by modern corporations with more complex organisational structure. One of the basic features of this phase was the growth of innumerable units of one large corporation. (3) The following stage experienced corporations with multidivisional organisation that came around early 20s. At this stage the corporations became multinational and started crossing the national frontiers and facing international competition. As a natural corollary to this, the firms responded by continuous innovation, decentralising into several divisions which became almost autonomous units, at times as large as national level firms (Hymer, 1979). With deepening of the root of control in this multidivision and multiplant structure, the corporations, however, developed a highly flexible form that could operate in several industries and adjust quickly to changing demands. After the World War II, the corporations with the above nature of organisation became very large.

Conceptualisation of the above corporate structure has been deftly taken up by organisation theory. Most of the authors have considered environment as the guiding force in shaping the structure and organisation of the business organisations (Clarke, 1985). Pfeffer and Salancik (1978) contended that through feedback the corporations can also at times influence the forces of environment thereby enacting their own environment and bring about some stability and operational certainty. Several levels of the environment have, therefore, been conceptualised, the broadest of which are the global and societal environments. Levin and White (1971) and Thompson (1967) had earlier argued that business organisations, in the process of their becoming larger, establish an environmental 'domain' and identify the areas which can influence their operations and vice versa. Dill (1958), on the other hand, had identified a 'task' environment consisting of customers (users and distributors, suppliers of material, capital, labour, equipment and space), competitors and regulatory groups. The above ideas are pertinent for understanding the structural differences within organisations. These authors have also argued that the simultaneous structure of differentiation and integration which the organisations at a later stage adhere to, actually arise out of a need to serve the homogeneous segments of the environment especially through horizontal differentiation by establishing various departments and through vertical integration. The latter is achieved by dividing the organisation into various levels of control in the form of a hierarchical network. These basic building blocks of the corporations are constantly co-ordinated for an efficient functioning.

The most significant feature in the organisation structure of the multinational corporations is thus the horizontal differentiation and vertical integration. Any increase in the organisational size will lead to structural differentiation. On the other hand, structural differentiation at a later stage will create a need for vertical integration. Thompson (1967) had critically discussed the integration aspect. His concept of 'internal interdependence' within the organisation elaborated how the differentiated structure utlimately helped in unifying the decision process. Thompson identified three forms of interdependence in the hierarchical network of the MNCs: (*i*) pooled interdependence with simple functional divisions, e.g. marketing, production of research co-ordinated by standardised methods of communication; (*ii*) sequential interdependence in which each sub-unit in the organisation would readjust with alteration and result in planned co-ordination. This actually would lead to a separation of the technical core from the general functions while (*iii*) in reciprocal interdependence, actions of any one sub-unit must be adjusted to all other units for making a policy of mutual adjustment. When this system is made extensive, the technical core and peripheral functions are segmented but clustered. Each cluster may constitute a self-sufficient unit. In contrast, Franklin (1977) observed a lagged effect in some corporations regarding diffusion of information and order down the hierarchical structure due to which direct control over the sub-unit would ultimately be lost (Ouchi, 1977). Alternatively Hirsch (1975) has pointed out the potent importance of sub-units in terms of performance due to decentralisation as it happened with the pharmaceutical industries of the United States in early seventies.

Like the models of firm growth which consider large-sized firms as the end of a continuum (Taylor and Thrift, 1982), models of corporate development also consider multinational corporations as the end point of a single development continuum. This is because both the models are closely related to the more general theories of firm. The related theories also try to identify a set of motivations that explain why firms move from national into multinational sphere and their oligopolistic behavioural patterns. Bambrick (1979) and Fitzgerald (1974) have identified export oriented corporations in the primary resource sector as well as manufacturing sector (Fieldhouse, 1978) that explore resource market or other production factors of a foreign country. However, these expositions still do not unfold the complexity of the entire gamut of the organisational diffusion and operational coverage.

The primary fall-out of the above organisational set-up of the MNCs is its vertical and horizontal stratification and integration. This multi-tiered structured firm has different levels of operation achieved through the set-up of parent corporations, subsidiaries, collaborations and franchisees (Chandler and Redlich, 1961). This has been elaborated in the following section. In brief, parent corporations always operate at Level I and represent the parent country while the subsidiaries, collaborations and franchisees can operate at both Level II and Level III according to their nature of operation or decision-making status. MNCs through Level II and Level III operations may decentralise and adapt to variegated circumstances, laws, customs and culture and also co-ordinate their activities vertically and horizontally and achieve integration.

Different forms of organisational structure in this arrangement relate to a specific spatial characteristics that is integral to the overall organisational structure. Organisation theory has been most successful in tackling the vertical dimension, i.e. the hierarchical arrangement. A geographical perspective would emphasise, in addition, the spatial, i.e. horizontal aspect of the division of labour. It characterises a fusion of ideas relating to horizontal differentiation from industrial geography together with those on vertical differentiation from organisation theory featuring spatial form and structure respectively (Fig 2.1). In addition industrial geography also stresses on the locational aspects of the sub-units within an organisation (Clarke, 1985). There are also significant behavioural

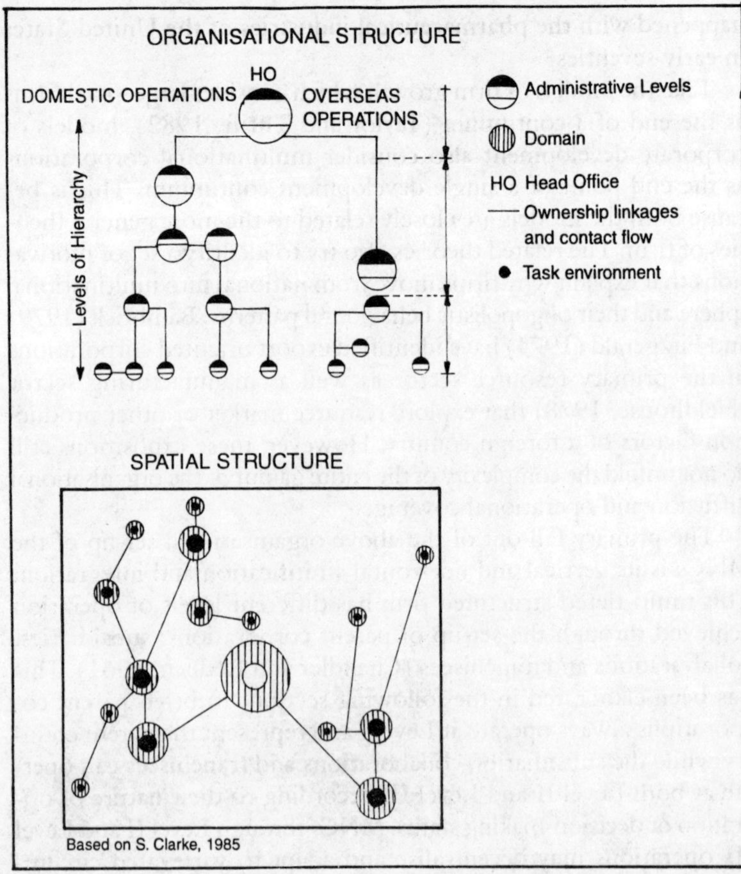

Adapted from S. Clarke, 1985

Fig. 2.1 Organisation of corporate space

patterns involved in the international operation of the MNCs. With a division of market and technology, they create a division of labour between countries that correspond to the division of labour between various levels of the corporate hierarchy. These complex divisions and behavioural patterns are a part of their intricate operational network. With this efficient organisational set-up, a wide spatio-sectoral operation at an international scale is planned which exhibits the shrewdest business acumen of these corporations. Further, with changing needs, they make considerable change in their strategies and mode of operation depending on the economic and sociocultural norms of different countries and regions. Power, knowledge and the resultant development strategies of the multinational corporations are, therefore, vital while discussing their organisation and operations. Since eighties, with drastic changes in international economic relations, MNCs reoriented their organisational structure by extending the geographical scope of production. The recent change in the organisation of MNCs is an outcome of the strategies adopted for achieving it. The three strategies are : (*i*) multicountry strategy, (*ii*) regional strategy and (*iii*) global strategy. In multicountry strategy, there is a clear division of market control between the parent corporation and the affiliates. While the respective affiliates serve their home markets, the parent corporation controls the affiliates operating in all such markets. To achieve greater cross-national integration, especially in industries like retailing and food production where problems of trade barrier, economy of scale and national tastes and habits prevail, this strategy, at times, also incorporates acquisition of national firms as Unilever acquired Boursin to operate in a speciality food area of France with a strong national base. Similarly, while Unilever organised its detergent business on a regional basis in Europe and North America, it kept a national structure in Asia, primarily to meet divergent consumer tastes (Maljers, 1992). Following this strategy, Nestlé manufactures chocolate in 23 countries for local distribution (Yip and Coundouriotis, 1991). The multicountry strategy has also proved helpful for incremental transport cost of raw material supply by organising simultaneous production in different countries at different standards. The operational pattern is closely associated with the recent spatial reorganisation of MNC activity discussed elaborately in this section.

Regional strategy includes production organised simultaneously by affiliates located in various host countries within a single region and non-affiliated companies acting as suppliers and sub-contracters. Final assembly in this case is a regional operation while market also is regional. Unilever in the late seventies (1973–89) rationalised its toilet soap manufacturing in Europe by reducing the number of factories from nineteen to thirteen and since then its four key units located in Austria, France, Italy and UK supply the entire European market but each with separate line of products (Howelles and Wood, 1991). Similarly, French MNC Thomson manufactures three different types of televisions in Germany, France and Spain. In Germany it is high feature, large screen, in France it is high volume and in Spain, low cost, smaller sets. All are done in association with regional affiliates and non-affiliated companies. Global strategy is actually a combination of multicountry and regional strategies which involves increasing geographic spread of economic activities across national boundaries especially to have a command over the world's largest markets *paripassu* increasing regional and sub-regional networks. This means global strategy is met through regional organisations and cross regional operations as well.

With the help of the above strategies, MNCs could further reduce export of finance capital to less developed host countries. Even earlier substantial percentage of their investment in host countries came from their profit in the latter including repatriation fees, technology prices, etc. (Muller, 1973). For example, from late sixties to early seventies in India, more than two-thirds of the local finance of the MNCs came from domestic sources (Chowdhury, 1979) (Table 2.1). Thus the volume of capital exported from developed countries to less developed countries came down from 88 per cent in 1970 to 68 per cent in 1977 (IDPAD, 1984). Even this reduced investment was well protected by multi-pronged strategies.

Table 2.1 *Source of financing of 50 MNCs in India*

Year	Domestic source Rs. in lakhs	Foreign source Rs. in lakhs	Domestic source in proportion to foreign source
1969 – 70	8,119	765	91.4
1970 – 71	9,547	84	99.1
1971 – 72	12,031	780	93.9
1972 – 73	8,698	892	111.4
1973 – 74	30,883	– 233	100.8
1974 – 75	9,859	– 467	95.5

Source : Chowdhury, EPW, August 18, 1979.

However meagre, MNCs always undertook multi-pronged strategy to protect all kinds of investments (*i*) by forming protective clauses in bilateral and multilateral agreements in favour of foreign investments; (*ii*) by encouraging collective capital investments from large corporations of more than one developed countries, thus tying the interests of collective capital powers, or (*iii*) by initiating joint ventures or collaborations in the Third World, at times preferring it over subsidiary firms to facilitate access to local economy. Parent state's support in such cases is always assured. The western Europe multilateral treaty for Africa, drawn up on the basis of old colonial ties for expansion of foreign capital and implemented through the Lome Convention, or United States' bilateral treaty (NAFTA) with Latin American countries are noteworthy examples (Rao, 1994)

A number of schemes has been developed to explain the structure of the MNCs based on these aspects. These are broadly identified as three types. In reality, however, MNCs incorporate more than one structure, if needed. The first type is parent dominant subsidiary subservient type of enterprises. International activities of such firms have a motivation to increase the business in the parent country or of the parent corporation in the international market. Good examples are US MNCs like Procter and Gamble with authoritarian parent units controlling overall money flow strategy and job descriptions for the affiliates.

The second type is enterprises with high degree of autonomy for subsidiaries. In other words here the parent company has very little control over the goal-setting or operational phases of the subsidiaries' business, as it happens in Japanese MNCs.

The third type is the integrated enterprise in which operations of the parent company and that of the subsidiaries are incorporated into an overall managerial effort. The aim of the enterprise is to advance global activities. Unilever is a good example of this type. In this structure clashes between the parent company and subsidiaries are not uncommon but the reason is different from that of the first type (Blake and Walters, 1976). The above three structures can also be explained by Barlett and Ghoshal's (1989) typology of three different organisational models of MNCs. The first, international organisational model involves formal co-ordination and control by corporate headquarters; the second model is characterised by a decentralised federation of activities and simple financial control by the parent corporation whereas the third type i.e. the global organisational model is based on centralisation of assets and responsibilities.

Increasingly, MNCs are adhering to the third structure. Firms like Procter and Gamble or Coca-Cola, which had a tighter control of the parent company, have opted for more integration since the late eighties by co-ordinating their affiliates in Europe and setting up Euro Brand teams controlled by affiliates themselves (UNCTD, 1993). First, it can be achieved through hierarchy, secondly through administrative and control systems and thirdly, through voluntary activities. This means the process of capital accumulation gets more and more specialised and develops elaborate system of internal division of labour, a more efficient centralised control and power to command accumulated capital and investment. World production thus gradually becomes more integrated (Hymer, 1979).

More and more MNCs are opting for complex organisational structure This multiplies linkages within a firm and despite greater geographical dispersion of activities, there remains a high concentration of decision-making. That may occasionally rest with affiliates but only on the basis of corporate wide mandates for particular functions. Along with the concept of integrated structure, MNCs are establishing headquarters, especially product-line headquarters outside home countries. Examples are IBM, AT & T, Monsanto and Nestlé. All have set up headquarters in Europe and other countries for specific products. Regional headquarters are also established in response to the need for regional integration such as General Electric's regional headquarter in Asia for its main product lines of power generation, aircraft engines and plastics. This system illustrates a geographically based organisation of activities. In contrast, functional headquarters—again an off-shoot of integrated enterprise structure—are responsible for a specific activity of the MNCs which would otherwise have been undertaken separately in home and host countries. This system enables the parent corporation to reduce extra responsibility and thereby focus on the overall co-ordination, strategic planning and finance.

To achieve all these, the configuration of MNCs' activities and the flow of information require matrix forms with vertical and horizontal integration (UNCTD, 1993). As complex integration covers cross-border transactions not only between companies under common ownership but also between unrelated firms, international partnership or alliances have become increasingly popular with MNCs. This forms a part of corporate organisation that spreads risks and adds newer advantages over firm specific advantages. These alliances can take place at various points of the activity chain ranging from research and development, production, raw material sharing to marketing and even after sales service. For example, IBM (USA) has alliance with Thomson-CSF (France) for marketing microprocessor chips, Renault (France) and Volvo (Sweden) have an alliance to produce automobiles and trucks, Nestlé (Switzerland) and Coca-Cola (USA) for distributing canned hot drinks through vending machines. Such alliances guarantee increased access to high value-added resources like technology, complex manufacturing processes, skilled labour, marketing etc. Interestingly, MNCs seldom strike alliance in areas of their respective core strength. Finally, strategic alliances across countries affect national regulatory policies of state governments (Graham and Krugmen, 1991).

Multinational corporations thus enlarge their domain as a centrally planned world production space and reduce the scope of a decentralised one. Competition that had increased in the wake of monopoly capital also considerably decreases with the level of concentration growing higher. The worldwide organisation of production is achieved primarily in two ways : (*i*) by controlling international sources of raw material and labour, and (*ii*) by controlling international market. Because of their size, international network and especially for their accumulated production knowledge, MNCs can procure inputs from any distance, engage labour at any location and cost, both high and low, get easy access to capital and research and development (Gabriel, 1972). Due to the regional network MNCs also can disaggregate their research activities to strengthen respective regional markets. Fujitsu of Japan has developed its computer systems business from its R & D facilities in the UK and has strengthened its functions in that country (Warrant, 1991).

Application of centralised control in decision-making enables the MNCs to operate as major non-market forces in the world economy. This stems from their ability to shape the demand of their products worldwide and influence both economic and cultural environments through planning and exercise of power. With their rising share in the world trade and production, by which they exchange products with affiliated or collaborative firms, the MNCs easily bypass the direct market considerations. Such tied-up trade has a far-reaching effect. The trade of MNCs with their subsidiaries and affiliates at times exceeds the total trade of the Third World countries. These are again associated with the conditionalities of collaboration or acquisition of technology or purchase of intermediate products and capital goods from the MNCs.

The detrimental effect of such MNC operations can be identified in their firm control over the planning of the raw material, transport and marketing sectors in the Third World countries. Their entry into various industries of these countries increases economy of scale and thus increases the barrier of entry for indigenous firms. Instead of increasing production, they, thus, substitute it (Lall, 1980; New farmer and March, 1981).

Do the MNCs increase the export of Third World countries?

Even parent MNCs have been found prohibiting subsidiaries to export. Moreover, export and import between MNCs and their subsidiaries are based on transfer price which is different from market price and thus deprives the Third World countries of higher export earnings and hastens devaluation of their currencies. On the other hand, through transfer pricing, these corporations evade taxes and affect the balance of payment position. During monetary restraints, MNCs use external financing to follow expansion policies and, during monetary expansion, they use lower rates of interest to transfer funds, thus affecting the balance of payments of host countries (Ghosh, 1985).

Finally the lobbying tactics of MNCs and their financial support to political parties for influencing the government machinery in parent and host countries also need to be mentioned as their operational norms. In 1975, Exxon contributed $ 27 million for election in Italy and got its falsification record condoned. Similarly, in early seventies, the prospective Jamaican President was cautioned by the US ambassador not to make bauxite nationalisation an election issue. Interference of Firestone in Liberia, Shell's participation in the operations of the Nigerian government, and United Fruit Corporation's involvement in Latin America are known examples (Deo, 1986). Political intervention by MNCs may be much direct as it happened in Chile with the overthrowing of Allende by the collaborative efforts of International Telegraph and Telephone Corporation, Kennecott and Anaconde and the US government. The Bedak revolt of Sumatra was also linked with the nationalisation of Royal Dutch Shell's holdings (Deo, 1986).

All these operational methods reflect a steady rise in the economic and political power of MNCs. They tend to operate in a world environment that they create, recreate and mould for their growth and expansion. Due to enormous control and power to plan economic activity at a very large spatial and sectoral scale, with a formidable impact on society and culture, MNCs enjoy a considerable geographical advantage. By their propensity to operate anywhere they wish to, they do create a system of universal interdependence and an increasing integration of the world economy. This, however, broadens the economic and social gap between rich and poor countries, simultaneously creating a dominance-dependency relationship between them. The capitalist processes they perpetuate accompany a related ideology and spread beyond production processes in using people as resources, involving not only the aspects of production and economy but also a sophisticated diversionary ideology. MNCs essentially act as carriers of these ideologies, By nature hegemonic (Gramsci, 1968), through which they sell their products. The capitalist system, in its turn, strongly supports corporate capital as a mode of social organisation, projecting consumption as an alternative to other basic models of change and thereby mitigating class contradictions and antagonisms.

All these phenomena work on space–time convergence and incorporate space specific as well as time specific organisations and consequences. Spatial dynamics of multinational corporations, therefore, assumes increasing significance in the analysis of internationalisation of capital and production.

2.2 Spatial Organisation of Multinational Corporations and the Changing Spatial Division of Labour

Enlargement of the geographical sphere of operation of large monopoly organisations across countries and a resultant shift in the organisational structure are both cause and effect of the increasing power of multinational corporations. The worldwide industrial relocation that it ultimately led to was also made possible due to a qualitative change of the conditions for capital expansion and accumulation. It was first evident in the sixties in relocation of manufacturing in only labour intensive industries where technology could be stabilised with cheap labour. Due to conditions created within this system—by earning greater profit from relocated sites and simultaneous crises in home countries relating to higher input cost including wage differentials, slackening home market for specialised products and problems of respective life cycles of products—it became imperative for large corporations to relocate capital-intensive operations also to alternate regions. The spatial organisation of multinational corporations which underwent consequential change and the spatial division of labour that emerged due to this change were thus associated with long-term cyclical recessions. At the initial stage of this reorganisation, worldwide supply of disposable cheap labour was a significant factor (Clairmonte and Cavanagh, 1978). Given the inherent contradiction of capital, there was also a simultaneous effort to discover capital-intensive devices for producers' goods and new product lines for consumer goods.

So far as spatial organisation is concerned, industrial corporations with this modified structure started operating at well-defined hierarchical order with clear-cut levels of operations. This segmentation of production space was associated with a geographical distribution of roles with different regions having different developmental experiences. As an analytical framework for this stage, Chandler and Redlich (1961) distinguished three levels of business administration, three horizons, three levels of task, three levels of decision-making and three levels of policies. Following this, the highest office of a multinational corporation with Level I activities will always be located in the largest cities of the parent countries completely isolated from the other levels and concentrating on the specific function of planning strategy and formulating development goals. These activities, also with associated services, are extremely concentrated on space as they need to be located close to the capital market and the primary seat of power and thus are expected to be found in the world's major cities in the developed countries like New York, London, Paris, Frankfurt and Tokyo. Later, with improved communication, Level I had locations in medium cities too having sophisticated communication network. The Level II activities first evolved due to the separation of head office from field offices. In national corporations, this level is not completely separated from Level I whereas in multinational corporations the separation is more complete and Level I is completely detached even from Level II. Level II activities of large corporations, because of their need to have white collar workers, communications system and information network, tend to be located in large cities of host countries. As Level II activities in general want to share the economy of scale, many corporations tend to locate such activities in the same cities and form a cluster on space. Thus, like Level I activities, Level II activities are also concentrated on space, although their location can be found in many more cities compared to the fewer locations of Level I activities. Throughout the world, the larger cities in the host countries contain regional headquarters of foreign multinational corporations (Hymer, 1971).

Level III activities include day to day plant operation at the grassroot level of production operations. According to location theories (Walker and Starper, 1981), Level III activities would spread over the earth, depending on the supply and availability of manpower, resource, raw materials, markets as well as other necessary infrastructure in given conditions. With this locational spread is associated the global command of the multinational corporations over capital, technology, price and finally, a rationalised use of labour power. In the host as well as in parent countries, this spatial organisation of the MNCs follows the settlement hierarchy to a considerable extent with having larger and important cities higher level offices and the smaller cities or settlements having plant offices or production units. Geographical specialisation thus tends to reflect the hierarchy of corporate decision-making which again reflect the hierarchy of settlements and countries (Fig. 2.2).

It should be mentioned again that head offices are not automatically located in the city at the top of the urban hierarchy and the effects of decisions to adopt innovations also do not 'trickle down' from larger to smaller centres in a traditionally accepted way. For example, in the chemical business of the Shell group, an innovation may be made at the department laboratory at a Level III unit, but the decision to introduce it to the market will be taken by the head office located at Hague and the trial may be actually carried

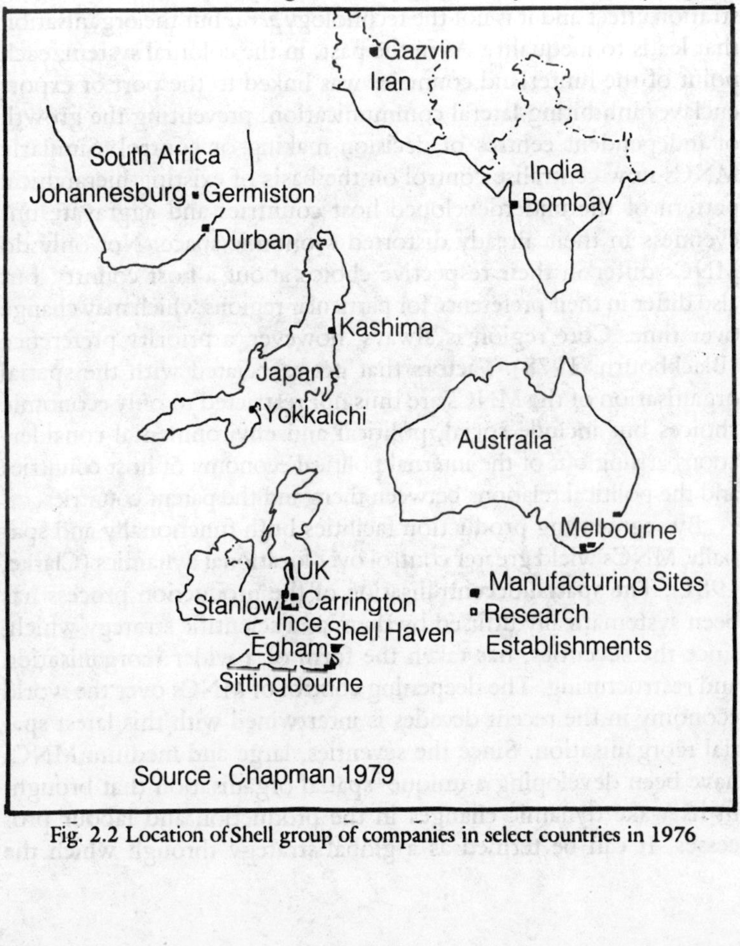

Fig. 2.2 Location of Shell group of companies in select countries in 1976

out in Bombay (Chapman, 1979). And on this matter, the hierarchy concept has a validity only in an organisational sense rather than in a locational one. Level III activities of MNCs are thus found to be geographically the most mobile, at times located at interior centres of the host countries. Union Carbide plant at Bhopal in India is a good example.

The structure of income and consumption thus tends to parallel the structure of control and authority (Hymer, 1971) and the occupational distribution of labour depends on its functional placement in the international hierarchical economic system. In the process, there emerges a sharp contrast between the growth rates of core and peripheral cities of the host countries, perpetuating uneven spatial development. In Third World host countries, Level II and Level III activities are largely influenced by international demonstration effect and it is not the technology *per se* but the organisation that leads to inequality. As in the past, in the colonial system, each point of the hinterland countries was linked to the port or export enclaves inhibiting lateral communication, preventing the growth of independent centres of decision-making or control. Similarly MNCs now centralise control on the basis of existing hierarchical pattern of the underdeveloped host countries and aggravate unevenness in their already distorted economic space. Not only do MNCs differ in their respective choice about a host country, but also differ in their preference for particular regions which may change over time. Core region is always, however, a priority preference (Blackbourn, 1978). Factors that get associated with the spatial organisation of the MNCs are thus not restricted to only economic choices but include social, political and environmental considerations arising out of the internal political economy of host countries and the political relations between them and the parent countries.

By segmenting production facilities both functionally and spatially, MNCs wield greater control over locational dynamics (Clarke, 1981). The spatial decentralisation of the production process has been systematically utilised by them as a scientific strategy which, since the seventies, has taken the form of a wider reorganisation and restructuring. The deepening control of MNCs over the world economy in the recent decades is intertwined with this latest spatial reorganisation. Since the seventies, large and medium MNCs have been developing a unique spatial organisation that brought in its wake dynamic changes in the production and labour processes. It can be termed as a global strategy through which the prevailing international hierarchy of decision-making, production and consumption could be strengthened, but in a diametrically different manner. Spatial division of labour under this reorganisation no longer featured division of work but got intrinsically associated with international pricing system, wage differentials and the relative immobility of labour. It also brought a change in the erstwhile relocation process from cores with highly skilled and highly priced organised labour to peripheries with skilled but cheaper organised labour which got associated with reduction in input cost, higher profit and labour aristocracy in host countries. The newer spatial reorganisation evolved an altogether different perspective in the concept of spatial division of production of labour. Thrift (1986) argues that this new spatial division of labour has its roots in the breakdown of traditional economic and social structures in many developing countries. But the more important reason was that the production process of the multinational corporations due to their transport and communication technology could become more fragmented, more homogenised and suitable to many sub-processes that could be spatially separated and carried out by even less skilled workers. This partial production process distributed at various points became a hallmark of the newer spatial organisation of the MNCs (Thrift, 1986).

Massey (1984) has identified three major types of corporate organisation associated with the above shift, viz. (*i*) intensification, (*ii*) rationalisation, and (*iii*) technical change and investment. They are necessarily not exclusive to each other; rather they arrive as a package strategy. Ettlinger (1990) argues that such strategies are nothing but non-traditional manipulations on the part of the multinational corporations in a typical non-Fordist manner. More broadly, these moves of the MNCs represent a perspective relationship between production and consumption systems (Aglietta, 1979).

The earlier relocation was associated with Fordism that evolved as a system of mass production in manufacturing in the heyday of monopoly capital that tended to associate rigid division of labour between management and production as well as division among different types of workers with different specialisation. It gave considerable importance to labour skill and quality control. Consequently, plants operating under principles of Fordism, oriented their activities to large-scale, high-volume production and achieved efficiency through internalisation of economies of scale, increase in the size of production, specialisation and sophistication. It created agglomeration economies and, as a natural consequence, uneven development. Large urban areas with skilled labour became points of higher firm activities and immigration, while production that could run with comparatively less skilled labour got located in areas with less wage and low safety regulations. Since the mid-seventies, multinational corporations started restructuring their production that differed qualitatively from Fordist spatial organisation. The newer strategies involved large-scale and simultaneous small-batch production, similar to craft production of the late nineteenth century, achieving efficiency by externalising economies of scale. Ettlinger (1990) has preferred the term 'non-Fordist' than 'post-Fordist' for these strategies due to their simultaneous accommodation of modern and pre-modern production systems than a unilinear, evolutionary progression of the Fordist one. The non-Fordist type externalisation is achieved through sub-contracting unorganised labour and giving rise to non-capitalist territorial production complexes that can coexist with capitalist Fordist production complexes. This drastically brings down the cost of production more importantly of reproduction—and works towards an absolute exploitation of surplus (Chandoke, 1991) and therefore reaps profit. It also saves the associative cost of organised large-scale production and, therefore, becomes handy in times of product change or production relocation as it does not involve dismantling of plants or factories or retrenching of organised labour. Gradually, large-sized MNCs have been opting more for non-Fordist strategies and an associated spatial reorganisation and spatial division of labour, leading to shrinking of jobs in the organised sector in both home and host countries.

The series of plant closures and contractions which started since the second half of the seventies are nothing but a fall-out of these strategies. Examples are the closures of Massey and Ferguson, Chrysler, SKF, Kodak, ITT and Firestone with huge job loss. The trend continued unabated in the eighties and in the nineties. Between 1986 and 89, General Electric's employment fell from 3,73,000 to 2,92,000, but its revenue increased from $ 42 billion to $ 55 billion. AT&T restructured its production method and trimmed 42,000 jobs while its revenue went up by $ 3 billion. Around the same time, IBM retrenched 13,292 organised workers. During 1987-89, Fiat reduced employment by 14,578 workers while its revenue increased by 12.4 billion lire (Lowe, 1992). The effect of this spatial reorganisation in populous Third World host countries is disastrous. In Unilever, cost per worker in Asia during 1980-87 was brought down by retrenching workers while profit per worker rose by 50 per cent (Elshof, 1988). In 1984, due to its acquisition of Brooke Bond, employment in Africa rose while in Europe during the same time, 60,000 workers were displaced (Elshof, 1989). In North America, Unilever's sale increased by 50 per cent while employment increased by 30 per cent. ILO studies (1981) note that in MNCs operating in Asia, Africa and Latin America since the seventies, there has been an increase of unskilled workers at the cost of large-scale displacement of production workers. In Danish enterprises, the employment of managerial staff increased by nearly two and a half times while production workers increased by one and a half time. For any single plant of any MNC, therefore, the ultimate form of labour process in the above spatial reorganisation would not necessarily be sequential; it would, instead, follow local labour market conditions and accordingly reorient the labour force (Storper and Walker, 1983). It also reflects an ongoing recomposition of local social relations by the foreign corporate sector's infiltration through market and not through organised employment, creating high degree of demonstration effect (Hirschman, 1958) even in interior and backward areas.

The new international spatial division of labour evolving from the above process is actually a spatial division in labour. The uneven mosaic of capitalist development becomes a premise for such reorganisation (Teulings, 1984). Essentially it consists of three elements (Clarke, 1981) : (*i*) capital product strategy based on the best options open to the firms for investment including labour cost, (*ii*) methods of production that include division of labour and specific forms of labour processes, and (*iii*) geography of resources including spatial variations of labour along with a given social structure. In totality, the above spatial reorganisation forges the international capital to differentiate its organisation of production, consumption, sale and control on geographically divided lines of culture, society and economy (Hymer, 1972) and perpetuates a segmented labour market.

From simple functional and geographical links to a complex spatial organisation with optimum geographical spread thus has been the basis of growth and power of multinational corporations. This evolution continues as these corporations seek to protect their existing comparative advantages and develop new ones. In this background, it seems imperative to develop a scheme of space–time convergence to understand the complex phenomenon of MNCs.

2.3 Industrial Geography and Multinational Corporations

The interest of industrial geographers in the phenomenon of the multinational enterprise is of comparatively recent origin. Reluctance on the part of geographers to catch up with the wider dynamics of spatial economic operations can be traced to two opposite situations. One hand, it was their preoccupation with regional economic problems that kept them busy with macro-level analysis, on the other, extensive related works in economics, especially industrial economics, resisted their entry into this field (Smith, 1985).

However, increasing integration of regional, national and world economies clearly warranted explanation from geographers on industrial change at various spatial scales that gradually brought the geographers in the field of international industrial restructuring. The body of literature already developed in industrial geography since the sixties on the spatial behaviour of large firms at national levels (Hamilton, 1974) also aided to a considerable extent.

In developing an understanding of the multinational corporations in industrial geography, researchers have concentrated on three main areas. These are : (*i*) the regional economic environment and industrial corporation, (*ii*) structure of an industry, and (*iii*) the behaviour and spatial ramifications of corporate activity. Wood (1980) argues that although the foci of industrial geography research during the seventies had already shifted considerably to areas of regional economic change and implications of multinational activity on regional policy, most works developed as isolated areas and no plausible interlinkage could be forged. These three approaches attempt to bridge this gap and link up the research areas into a comprehensive integral body. In the process of developing this research base, industrial geography has also shared and borrowed thoughts from industrial economics, business studies, regional science and other social science disciplines like sociology and political science. The body of literature that has ultimately emerged, is of an interdisciplinary nature. The following sections briefly examine the thrust areas of relevant research in the above disciplines.

The general characteristics of multinational corporations, their operations and effects have been extensively explored in recent literature in economics. At the same time, due to the changing relationship with economics and geography, considerable researches have also been done on spatial dimension of industrial operations. Increase in research, improvement in methodology and growth of information in disciplines of sociology, social anthropology, psychology, social administration, international studies and political science provided new conceptual frameworks, hypotheses and theories, leading to the growth of corporate studies of a much wider nature. A review of the entire related literature in economics (Caves, 1983) is not within the scope of the present work. Contributions in economics that are most relevant to the development of spatial approaches and from which the three above-mentioned approaches in industrial geography have benefited are discussed in brief.

Theories concerning 'why' and 'where to' of multinational corporations have generated a wide range of explanations in the mainstream of economic studies. Existing literature indicates that the modern economic theory on MNCs has shifted largely from the established neo-classical viewpoint of foreign direct investment and comparative advantage. Literature, in general, is concerned more with the organisation and operation of MNCs with special emphasis on the advantages enjoyed by them, e.g., ownership-specific advantages are generally associated with conditions of oligopoly including proprietory technology, product differentiation, managerial and marketing skills, economies of scale and favoured access to inputs. Here, specially mentionable are the seminal works of Hymer (1960, 1972) that incorporated the space–time dialectic to a large extent. His views were further developed by Kindleberger (1969), Kindleberger and Andrestch (1983), Vernon (1971, 1978), Wolf (1977), Aliber (1970), Dunning (1973, 1981) and Lall (1980). The traditional theory of industrial location that long time back had been developed in economics based on neo-classical approach (Weber, 1929, Losch, 1954; Hoover, 1948; Isard, 1956), primarily focused on the economic principles of industrial location with a regional perspective. It studied the spatial distribution of economic activity with respect to given or static distribution of factors of production and market, either supply-oriented (Weber, 1929) or demand-oriented (Losch, 1954), with a profit maximisation motive. It did not thus explain the locational dynamics that command a broad set of spatial choices both in terms of factor supply and demand conditions. A comprehensive theory of international location needs to incorporate not only (production) cost and market factors but also the revenue factors and national regulations derived from the systematic advantages of global production, marketing network, financial markets and currency areas. Contemporary works of industrial location theory, which have focused on the role of capital and market, initially concentrated on firms operating within national boundaries (Massey, 1977, 1979; Walker and Storper, 1981; Storper and Walker, 1983). Later works focused on the effects of foreign corporations on employment and economies of host countries (Massey and Meegan, 1982; Goyal, 1980; Saini, 1981; Deo, 1986; Sau, 1986; Swamy, 1986; Ghosh, 1985).

There also exists a considerable amount of literature in economics and economic geography on specific industry or country (Vaitsos, 1976; Lall and Streeten, 1977; Newfarmer, 1983; Nofal, 1983; Schoenberger, 1984). Most of them concentrate on the effects of foreign corporations on either the host or home countries. Besides Clarke (1985) and Jenkins (1987) take up home and host countries simultaneously.

Special mention should be made of the development of models of corporate growth in industrial economics and organisational science that consider MNCs as the end point of a single development continuum. These models are closely related to the more general theory of firm locations. The oligopolistic behaviour of corporations in terms of location specific resources has been analysed by Reuber (1973) and Fieldhouse (1978) in general and in specific countries by Mckern (1976), Fitzerald (1974) and Smith (1978). Explanations on the 'why' of internationalisation of production have thus generated theories of multinational growth (Thomas, 1980; Buckley and Casson, 1976).

Models of corporate growth have also been developed by Human geographers especially on spatial expansion of multinational enterprises. While Blackbourn (1974), Taylor (1975) and Hakanson (1979) take up individual industrial organisations as their examples, Rees (1978) and Watts (1980) concentrate on inter-relationship between several organisations and their impact on spatial developments. Following these models, questions of spatial expansion of MNCs and the reorganisation of spatial structure of economies have been worked out in developed countries by Wilkins (1974), de Smidt (1966) and Martin (1973), including locational preferences of MNCs in peripheral regions (Keeble, 1976) or the impact of political influence on locational choice (Ardagh, 1977). Similar works on underdeveloped countries are also considerable (Rogerson, 1981, Forbes, 1986, Fujita and Ishigaki, 1986, Abumere (1981) Newfarmer et al. 1981).

Despite certain amount of common ground with the above studies on MNCs, industrial geographical studies have largely overlooked the internal workings of the multinational corporations and have preferred to work on the linkage analysis. On the other hand, the organisational theories in sociology and economic theories do not consider the spatial aspects of the MNCs as vital. A fusion of geographical and organisational theories in order to solve the above problem, has also been attempted by the enterprise approach in industrial geography.

Three broad approaches on firms and their behaviour that have consequently developed in industrial geography take up a wide range of spatial effects that the MNCs can induce. The industrial systems framework developed by Hamilton and Linge (1979) is the foremost approach focusing on the relationship of enterprises with the regional environment, encompassing a wide variety of topics of industrial studies and regional studies like traditional locational analysis, spatial forms and implications of growth, changing organisational forms, firms' decision-making process and their adaptation to the regional economic environment, changing size and scale of operations and their diverse spatial behaviour, industrial organisations in contrasting economic and social systems as well as in diverse cultural environments.

It has contributed considerably towards studies of linkage analysis and spatial behaviour of firms. Although, because of its coverage of a diverse variety of topics, it has been argued (Malecke, 1982) that the approach lacked an explicit structure of analysis.

The second strand that offers a much integrated framework is the structuralist form of analysis developed by Massey and Meegan (1979). They develop three distinct analytical steps to examine the industrial structure denoting a movement from general to particular: (*i*) national and international economic trends, (*ii*) implications of these trends for each firm, and (*iii*) evaluation of their effects on the form of production and employment. Marshall (1982) argues that this framework stands opposite to the functionalist concepts and shows that in this approach firms have been classified on the basis of their process of economic change rather than on the basis of their organisational characteristics which, he feels would have been more appropriate. However, Clarke (1989) suggests that the first two do not contribute much in providing a tangible analytical focus for industrial geography separately. The third framework, according to Clarke (1989), is a much useful mechanism to link the aspects of new international division of labour. Developed primarily by McNee (1958) as the enterprise approach, it generated a stream of researches on the behaviour and spatial dynamics of corporate activity (Watts, 1979, 1982; Dicken, 1976; Rees, 1972) and hence, provided a central theme of investigation on industrial corporations and their role in spatial change. This approach, however, is not very useful in understanding the principles of corporate organisation (Clarke, 1989).

These three approaches, developed within the sub-disciplines of industrial and economic geography, do not offer insight into the geographical aspects of international division of labour and underdevelopment of the Third World countries. They focus more on the regional question without positing the latter in the background of international production and consumption space. Hence Marshall (1982) argues that organisational approaches in industrial geography need to be based more on social theory. Conventional industrial studies have also been criticised for their failure to place organisation in the national and international economic context (Massey, 1979). Industrial Geography, in studying organisations had also given more stress on the managerial approach. A number of authors (Massey, 1980; Walker and Storper, 1981) developed a more radical perspective to studying industrial change and restructuring of the national and regional economies.

One of the crucial areas in which these authors have provided stimulating insight is the control of the production system and the relative distribution of costs and benefits associated with that operation (Dickens, 1994). The concept of production chain developed by Walker (1988), characterising the connecting filament among technologically related activities or Storper's (1992) concept of commodity chain in a global context or Hopkins and Wallerstein's (1986) concept of commodity chain, exemplifying the historical evolution of a capitalist world economy, focus on transactionally linked sequence of functions of large firms in which each stage in the sequence adds value to the process of production (Dicken, 1994). Common to the entire chain is the technological process of production and the physical movements of the constituent elements. This characterises the entire production system as a complex input-output chain with vertical, horizontal and diagonal links. The segmented functions in the production chain, although physically separated, are actively integrated for which flows of material and information are regulated along with a systematic regulation of the labour process. Storper and Harrison (1991) have further developed a core-ring concept of network-power structure to identify the organisation or governance of the production chain in different development trajectories. In developing these concepts, a need for an integrated approach to study industrial operations in geography with a political-economic framework has emerged.

We will now analyse the political-economic approach in brief in relation to the field of development geography that has considerably helped in developing a spatial perspective in the studies of multinational corporations. By political-economic approach, we mean an approach where an explanation is derived through the interaction of various class forces within a given production system. The technology possibilities determine the outer boundary of this interaction while the balance of class forces, however imperfectly defined the classes are, essentially determines the choice or decision for a specific political, economic and social system (Bagchi, 1984).

2.4 Political Economy Studies and Development : Approaches towards MNC Studies

Political economy approach emphasises the role of the interaction between production specific requirements (demand based) and the geographical variations in the labour factor (supply based characteristics) in shaping industrial location outcomes. Labour supply differentials in space are seen not only in terms of price (wage) or quality (skills) but also in terms of conditions of labour control and reproduction. The political economy approach, in spite of its potential to handle international issues like division of labour and production at world scale, has not focused much attention to the spatial dynamics of the above phenomena. This critical gap is reduced if there is a fusion between political economic approaches and geographical analysis. An idea of the development so far achieved in this line will be in order.

From the political economy angle, although we lose perspective of the firm and markets, we gain a deeper understanding of the underlying web of economic forces and social relations which produces concentration and centralisation of capital and its geographical expansion beyond the national frontiers (Nofal and Schoenberger, 1984). Originally it was Marx who had clearly stated that the rule of the monopolies which inevitably resulted from the concentration of capital and the merger of banking with industrial capital, gave rise to finance capital. In the wake of monopoly capitalism, the latter could alter relations between different capitalist countries to a considerable extent. While these relationships, prior to the epoch of monopoly capitalism, were mainly determined by the mobility of goods, in the period of monopoly capitalism they got increasingly dependent on the mobility of capital and technology and created a need for control over a larger space in the form of market and production complexes. Thus conditions changed, so did the different kinds of capital. Internationalisation of capital was represented chronologically by the movement of commodities and gold, steadily supplemented by the movement of money capital as credit as well as finance capital. Interventions of fictitious capital and the state also created conditions to liberate production capital from rigid constraints. Direct investment thus became more feasible, accompanied by newer organisational forms like multinational corporations ensuring the complementarity of money, commodity, production and labour movements (Harvey, 1982. The above dynamics reveals a concrete pattern of extension of spatial and temporal horizons by capital due to over-accumulation. The rhythms of capitalism's development in space thus acquires greater significance.

This spatial dimension of capital and capitalist development, a major base in the studies in political economy, was not identified as a geographical phenomenon for quite sometime. Historical materialism appears to have produced studies on historical transformation, ignoring the creation of specific geography by capitalism. Priority of time over space led to *ad hoc* concessions on spatial questions by Marxian theorists and the processes of production of space integrating into capitalist dynamics and contradictions were never taken up with proper weightage (Harvey, 1985). Thus, various aspects with spatial dimensions such as urbanisation, industrial development, inter-regional relations, international division of labour and regional restructuring, development and underdevelopment, territoriality and state functions were considered in dissociation from space relations by most political-economy researchers, excepting a handful (Myrdal, 1957; Hymer, 1972; Bagchi, 1972). Geographers have argued that space relations and geographical phenomena were fundamental material attributes and 'active moments' in the contradictory dynamics of capitalism, making analysis of space or, for that matter, control of space an integral part of social theory. Thus any analysis of capitalist accumulation, such as global operations of multinational corporations, would require an integration of space-time convergence as a conceptual framework which is not possible to achieve by industrial geography alone.

Lefebvre (1973) perhaps expressed it most directly when he noted that capitalism found itself able to alternate (if not resolve) its internal contradictions and succeeded in achieving growth by occupying and producing space. Lefebvre has been in the forefront of the recent endeavours to understand the interrelation between geographical space and capital accumulation. Taking the benefit of the integrated framework Palloix (1973, 1975) and Harvey (1982) have delved deeply into the structural forces underlying the internationalisation of capital in the form of money, commodity and production. Palloix, like Mandel (1975) and Amin (1974, 1976), pays special attention to the historical stages in the evolution of capitalism to changes in the international division of labour and operations of multinational corporations. Two phases in the process of internationalisation of productive capital, depending on whether the branch plants are placed in (*i*) integrated or (*ii*) fragmented types of manufacturing processes have been identified by Palloix (1977) while Harvey (1982) abstracts from concrete history but integrates space and time in a powerful analytical framework of the spatial dynamics of capital. The centralisation of capital, he argues, within the organisation of the MNCs is accompanied by a simultaneous process of decentralisation of space and hence experiences the contradiction of fixity and movement between local environmental considerations and global interest. He builds an explanation of changes in the organisational structure of capital, in technology and location as the base of capitalist competition and draws association between locational aspects and technological advantages in the competitive search for excess profit by different multinational corporations. Like Adyalott (1976) he reiterates the need for understanding the political economy of the MNC operations in the background of spatial configurations to view development in space and specific location in a relational as well as a part dynamic process.

Castells (1983) has also stressed on the contribution of communication and technology towards delocalisation of places of production and consumption at both national and international levels. Analogy can be drawn with Hymer's (1975) formulation on hierarchically integrated set-ups of MNCs depending on the development in communication technology and a simultaneous spatially expansive production operation. This worldwide geographical dispersion of the erstwhile routine manufacturing activity, according to the pull of manpower, resources and markets and the spatial concentration of Level I central functions (as mentioned in the previous section) in a few major cities of the advanced industrial countries, reflects the need for a combinational outlook between space and sector. At the root of spatial specialisation of production and international division of labour and the resultant uneven development of space lie the technological and organisational set-ups of these large international corporations and their global outlook.

In a similar manner, although not specifically in the context of MNCs, theorists like Baran and Sweezy (1968), the dependency theorists (Frank, 1969, 1978; Wallerstein, 1974) and especially Amin (1974, 1977) have explored the spatial aspects of the hierarchical network of the world capitalist system (Brewer 1980). Bagchi's (1972) analysis of underdevelopment has also highlighted the need for a spatial perspective.

In all these works, spatial dialectic of an interdependent world system shaping and reshaping macro and micro regions (Peet, 1978) through interregional flows at various scales has been focused. But such coincidence of economic and spatial approaches are characteristically rare. In the internationalisation process of capital by concentrating power and wealth at the centre and creating hierarchical relationships (Lenin, 1950; Frank, 1969; Wallerstein, Emmanuel, 1972) among nations, the MNCs have played a formidable role since the early twentieth century. Banana and sugar empires in Central America and the Caribbean, British tea companies in India and Sri Lanka and Dutch and British endeavours in West Africa in the early part of the present century are good examples. The larger part of the population in the peripheral countries by this process is excluded from the capitalist sector where precapitalist mode of production is not totally eliminated (Amin, 1974). Thus bipolar economic structure of 'peripheral capitalism' becomes a choice of the MNCs for profit maximisation. This is closely associated with the idea of the superficial nature of technological modernisation and demonstration effect in the Third World countries without any parallel increase of income (Hirschman, 1974; Dasgupta, 1964). Emphasis on the totality of the world system of social formulations is very significant in the analysis of MNCs as it highlights the synthesis between the institutional system of multinational corporations and the world economic systems, with the latter being interpreted in modes of production formulation (Brookfield, 1975). Development geography also suggests that the study of MNCs cannot only be sectoral or institutional; it must place its growth and spatial extension through a system framework in the development of the mode of production. Drawing from these works, three major periods that can be identified for MNC analysis are: (*i*) the earliest period when the centre drew commodities produced in use-value dominated modes in the periphery and transnational companies operated in a merchantile capacity; (*ii*) a second period of export of capital characterising the monopolisation of central economies in which MNCs got involved in the primary extraction and production, and (*iii*) the contemporary period of internationalisation with an integration of the world's labour forces in the process of self-expansion of capital.

Peet (1981) suggests that these periods are not exclusive to one another. The earlier ones continue to the present and there is no uniform presence of features of one period all over the world at a point of time. Uneven development can thus be seen as an outcome of different capitalist moves in the context of the spatial contradiction between the mobility of capital and labour.

Continuing this framework, we can approach a scientific explanation of the recent changes in the geography of the changing mode of industrial production, especially the internationalisation of capital. For geography it offers the possibility of integrating philosophy and history, thereby opening up a whole new world of ideas and analysis. Hypermobility of capital can be seen as a reflection of greater exploitation of labour force on an internationally expanding scale (Damette, 1980) pointing, however, to an overall domination of organised manufacturing employment by the industrial heartland of Europe, North America and Japan followed by Mexico, Brazil and Argentina (Peet, 1981). The recent restructuring and relocations, argues Landsberg (1979), have been thoroughly detrimental to the indigenous capitalist development of Third World countries as through this process surplus value is appropriated more by the largest firms in the competitive sector, creating a dynamic change in dominance-dependence relations between giant firms and conglomerates and relocation of various related economic activities.

All industrial regions irrespective of their country of origin, become vulnerable to the remote control of some multinationals by this process and become sensitive to the movement of capital that moves most rapidly (Susman and Schutz, 1983). A unique regional crisis thus emerges, signifying exploitation of regions by regions.

Existing literature on industrial restructuring in geography has already highlighted the relationships between different MNC organisations, their location and operation in a given temporal and spatial setting. With political economy insights such works have gone beyond casual empiricism or descriptive analysis and place the phenomenon of multinational corporations in a proper space-time context. Works of Massey and Meegan (1982), Storper and Walker (1983), Harrison (1984) and Markusen (1983) point out towards a successful combination of the twin approaches in producing an integrative theoretical analysis on industrial location, relation and mobility of capital with empirical understanding. Such works act as models for the present analysis.

3

Foreign Direct Investment in India : Sector and Affiliation

This chapter seeks to explore the dynamics of foreign direct investment in India during the post 1947 period. The first section, in brief, gives an overview of the history of foreign capital in India and the related policies and attitude of the Indian government towards foreign capital in this period. The following two sections examine the nature of MNC operations in India and identifies the significant parent countries during the early years of planning till 1970.

3.1. History of Foreign Capital in India : Policy and Perspective

The present pervading role of foreign capital and multinational corporations in India is associated with the colonial past and the post 1947 policies as well. At the time of transfer of power in 1947, presence of foreign capital was marked in most of the areas and later it was present in all the key sectors of the Indian economy which expanded to some more crucial areas. During 1949-50, it was noticed that though British and other foreign capital was getting replaced by Indian capital in traditionally important industries like cotton and jute, new plants were being set up by American and British capital in heavy industries sector like machinery, engineering, chemicals and automobiles. The precolonial ties with foreign capital actually provided a conduit for its flow during the later period (Bagchi, 1972).

Foreign investment is of two types : foreign direct investment (FDI) and portfolio investment. The former is primarily undertaken by corporations rather than individuals and includes a package of complementary inputs—of both tangible and intangible assets and services. It consists of equity capital, technical and managerial services, capital equipments and intermediate inputs. It also includes legal rights to patented and secret products, processes or trade marks. Portfolio investment consists of investment in shares and debentures of local firms by foreigners which is of rentier category and need not imply management control over the firms (Swamy, 1980). The analysis done in the present work is on the FDI in India in the manufacturing sector with special reference to foreign collaborations and subsidiaries.

In 1950 out of the total foreign investment in India—both direct and portfolio investment— 72 per cent was British investment. On the other hand, out of the total British investment, 82 per cent was direct investment. USA had a share of around 6 per cent of which nearly 99 per cent was direct investment. This amply reflects the colonial control of Britain in the matter of foreign direct investments in India during that time. On the other hand, 20 per cent of the total direct investment of Britain was in manufacturing while nearly 30 per cent was in trading. Essentially plantations, mining, and trading were the favoured areas of FDI in early years which reflected vestiges of a colonial economy. This is further clarified by the sectoral investment in manufacturing. Foreign capital virtually dominated in eastern India in traditional activities and industries. Foreign control was total in tea, overseas shipping, in wool and hides (80 per cent) and in coal and other mining (70 per cent) operations. More than 66 per cent import and export trade was financed by foreign banks and about 50 per cent of non-life insurable business was in foreign hands.

During the pre-Independence period, the national attitude towards foreign investment was hostile commensurate with the anti-colonial national liberation movement. During the years after Independence, this attitude started getting diluted with a growing ambivalance towards foreign capital. Gradually, there was a change in the approach and realignment of attitudes towards foreign capital started taking shape from opposition to neutrality to warm welcome (IDPAD, 1984). The industrialist class of India due to its collaborative attitude towards the colonial imperialist power, had also always suffered from the misgivings in going against the foreign capital.

Thus the softening of attitude since the fifties was a natural phenomenon. Foreign capital was invited in the form of both direct investment and portfolio investment. The latter was for helping in the planned development of the country. No rigid rule was framed for control of foreign capital that contradicted the explicit anti-foreign stand of the Indian National Congress or the industrialists during the thirties and the forties. Whatever small opposition came from the Indian industrialists was expressed in an inconsistent manner (DID, 1969) while some had no hestitation in collaborating if the need arose.

Thus the industrial policy resolution of 1948 and 1950 highlighted the need for state control over commanding sectors of the economy in black and white. Actually those industries were reserved for the public sector in which the private sector was unwilling to commit its resources (Bettelheim, 1971), but keeping enough loopholes and room for a loose implementation in order to offer concessions to foreign capital and Indian monopoly houses. Nehru had made repeated anouncements during this time, reassuring private capital, both domestic and foreign (Mukherjee, 1988). Actually, the industrial policy resolution of 1956 guaranteed existing facilities against nationalisation and permitted public-private co-operation in the development of some reserved sectors (Planning Committee, 1958). Consequently, licences for industries scheduled 'A' under the 1956 resolution and earmarked entirely for the public sector were issued to the private sector too (Table 3.1).

Table 3.1 *Statement showing issue of licenses in some industries in schedule A of the Industrial Policy resolution, 1956*

As in the Schedule	Product category	PSU	Private (Others)	Total
1. Iron and Steel	Pig Iron	2	15	17
2. Heavy castings and forgins of Iron and Steel	Steel Billets and Ingots. Iron and Steel castings and forgings and stampings	6	306	312

As in the Schedule	Product Category	PSU	Private (Others)	Total
3. Heavy Part and Machinery required for Iron and Steel production for mining, machine tool manufacturing and for such other basic industries as may be specified by the Central Government.	Mining Machinery	1	30	31
	Metallurgical	1	5	6
	Cement	–	9	9
	Chemical	1	59	60
4. Coal and lignite	Coal, lignite, etc. and other by-products	46	343	389
5. Mineral Oil	Aircraft Fuel oil	3	7	10
6. Aircraft		2	2	4
7. Ship-building	Ships and Vessels	–	12	12
8. Telephone and Telephone cables, Telegraph and wireless apparatus (including radio receiving sets)	Other items of telecommunication equipments	3	17	20

PSU – Public Sector Units.

Source : Department of Industrial Development, Government of India, Industrial Policy Resolution, 1956.

The contradiction in the attitude of the Indian government towards foreign capital was no doubt rooted in the historical nature of the Indian state and Indian capitalist class. The Fabian principles upheld by Nehru did not have any firm footing in the official policies of the government as Nehru himself did not recognise them officially. In support of the second plan proposals, he had strongly criticised the concept of equalitarianism, labour intensive devices and the demand for nationalisation (Nehru, n.d). Despite the socialist rhetoric, therefore, the Indian Government was proven to be extremely close to the business class (Kochanek, 1974). During the food crisis occurring after Independence, the resultant deficit in the country's balance of payments was met by the Government by devaluing the rupee and attracting foreign capital. Simultaneously Indian capital which had always cherished a desire to collaborate with foreign capital in the post-Independence period, pressurised for a favourable official attitude towards the latter (Kidron, 1968).

The official policy gradually swung unreservedly towards a dependence on direct foreign investment, imported technology and foreign collaboration. Increased foreign dependency was explicitly recognised in the formulation of the third plan in the form of increasing foreign aid. The policy got fructified with the devaluation of rupee in mid-1966. In 1958, the Associated Chambers of Commerce and Industry—an organisation dominated by foreign capital—had already expressed its willingness to create favourable conditions for foreign private investment (ASSOCHAM, 1956). ASSOCHAM, however, was primarily an organised means through which foreign capital in India formulated its demand, and developed a response to policy initiatives of the Indian Government (Kochanek, 1974). But, side by side many local industrialists also started demanding more liberal policies. One of the significant characteristics of the Indian planning process since then has been a close collaboration between Indian and foreign capital (Table 3.2). An increase in the number of agreements for financial credit and technical borrowing was noticed during this period (Bagchi, 1963).

Table 3.2 *Balance of payment estimates for the Third Plan as indicated in the Third Plan document*

(Rs. crores)

A.	Receipts :	
	1. Exports	3,700
	2. Invisibles (net)(excluding official donations)	Nil
	3. Capital transactions (net) (excluding receipts of official loans and private foreign investment)	550
	4. External Assistance	2,600
	5. Draft on Foreign Exchange reserves	Nil
	Total 1 to 5*	6,850
B.	Payments :	
	1. Imports of machinery and equipment for plan projects	1,900
	2. Components, intermediate products etc. for raising production of capital goods	200
	3. Maintenance imports	3,650
	Total 1 to 3*	5,750

Source : India, Planning Commission, The Third Plan, Mid-Term Appraisal, Delhi, 1963, p. 41.

*P.L. 480 imports are excluded from both sides.

The move towards liberalisation in the late fifties obviously necessitated the Indian governments disowning its earlier commitments, e.g., while nine indigenous medium-scale industries were not allowed to enter the manufacturing operation of electric motors, General Electric was permitted to start operation in this field. In the national interest, foreign capital was also invited to invest in fields which had hitherto been reserved for the public sector, viz. aluminium, drugs, heavy electrical equipments, fertiliser and synthetic rubber (Bettelheim, 1971). Collaboration agreements were approved where already an indigenous production line existed, such as sewing machines in the small-scale sector. During this period, several tax concessions were announced, reduction in the taxes on royalties received by foreign collaborators was introduced and the processing of foreign investment further streamlined by establishing a Foreign Investment Board (Table 3.3). External pressure was marked in the sphere of inter-industry priorities. It is interesting to note that some spokespersons of the United States were consultants during the Third Plan (IDPAD, 1984). Industrial licencing was not the only way through which foreign capital entered the economy during this time, it interfered with the country's agriculture, exchange rate and trade policies as well.

Table 3.3 *Private sector: Long-term foreign business investment (country-wise)*

(Rs. Crores)

Country	Outstanding investment as on end-March 1963	Outstanding investment as on end-March 1967
France	14.3	31.3
Germany (West)	24.2	61.7
Italy	9.6	27.0
Japan	15.2	45.4
UK	493.2	587.0
USA	119.8	309.8
Other	129.8	168.4
Total	806.1	1,230.6

Source : Reserve Bank of India Bulletin, August 1969, pp 1129.

With rupee devaluation, import duties were also reduced and fifty-nine priority industries, accounting for 80 per cent of industrial production, were granted import licences for bringing components and raw materials. Towards the end of 1969, the Monopolies and Restrictive Trade Practices (MRTP) Act came into practice under which an undertaking which controlled more than one-third of the manufacturing of a product had to get itself registered. But such restrictive acts, incomplete by their very structure (Kumar, 1982), could not be of much use. Further, the already curtailed mass consumers' market and an expanding affluent 'elite' market, however, exclusive it might be, paved the way for more foreign collaborations (Bagchi, 1963). Hence those were the years when foreign capital penetrated deep into the Indian economy especially in its key sectors and increased their profitability margin which is reflected in the large remittances abroad (Table 3.4).

Table 3.4 *Remittances by foreign companies (milions of Rupees)*

Year	Profits	Dividends	Technical knowhow	Royalty	Interest Private	Interest Official	Total
1963–64	128	188	–	46	108	624	1086
1964–65	156	220	36	44	62	720	1238
1965–66	135	194	70	30	94	860	1383
1966–67	214	288	104	51	176	1353	2186
1967–68	172	327	147	43	194	1542	2425
1968–69	130	302	180	47	199	1672	2530
1969–70	127	314	131	57	193	1763	2585
1970–71	132	435	206	51	202	1857	2083
1971–72	99	389	139	59	182	1827	2695
1972–73	156	390	114	73	212	1979	2924
1973–74	219	375	141	62	215	2128	3140
1974–75	72	183	126	85	463	1789	2718
1975–76	204	248	256	105	321	1743	2877
1976–77	131*	485	378	159	347	1936	3436

Source : IDPAD, 1984, pp 130.

* Provisional

Between July 1948 and December 1961, net transfers of private capital were estimated at only Rs. 10 crore per year—in total, approximately Rs. 123 crore only (Kidron, 1965). Chaudhuri (1979) has shown that during 1956-75, foreign sources contributed only

5.3 per cent to the growth of the 50 multinational corporations. Thus 94.7per cent of their growth was attributed to domestic and internal sources. The Reserve Bank of India sources have also shown that more than 50 per cent of the net inflow from foreign private sources was actually accounted by reinvestment of profits while fresh capital flow was small. In other words, profit that was generated from within the country and remained undistributed got reinvested, which, according to an estimate of United Nations, was to the extent of 75 per cent (RBI, 1978). Thus 60 per cent of the increase in private foreign investment during the second and third plan periods has been argued to have come from undistributed profits (Roy Chowdhury, 1981). In eight leading foreign drug companies, the actual capital inflow through subscription of equity was only 13.51 per cent of the share capital whereas their parent companies held 64.32 per cent. The rest was raised through bonus shares or subscriptions by local public sector financial institutions (Kumar and Chenoy, 1982), which became a regular practice with foreign corporations (Table 3.5). Subrahmanian (1972) states that the part played by private foreign investment in India in augmenting capital formation and in smoothening foreign exchange constraint was negative. From 1965 to 1970, tax ratio of inflow to outflow of foreign capital increased from 1 : 2.4 to 1 : 3.3 (Table 3.6).

Table 3.5. *Total inflow and outflow (1964-70) on account of foreign investment*

	Selected Items Rupees (in crores)		
Imports	–	1600.2	
Exports	+	727.9	
Dividends, royalties, technical fees, etc. remittances	–	253.7	
Net inflow of investment	+	491.2	(1968-69)
Total	–	634.8	

Source : Mukherjee, et al., 1977

Moreover, the foreign-controlled corporations started draining financial resources from within the country in collaboration with public sector financial institutions (Table 3.7).

Table 3.6 *Sources of finance for industrial expansion by MNCs and their associates (an illustrative list)*

(Rupees in lakhs)

Sl. No.	Company	Associate Equity	Additional Equity	Loans from IFCU, UTI, ET: Rupee	Loans from IFCU, UTI, ET: Foreign Exchange	Other Public Institutions	Internal accruals	Total
1.	Hindustan Lever Lever (1977)	Lever (UK)	803.20 (29.06)	1,040.00 (37.62)	285.00 (10.31)	364.89* (13.20)	217.91 (.80)	2,764.00 (100.00)
2.	Peico (1979)	Philips (Holland)	224.00 (5.38)	1,862.00 (44.78)	50.00 (1.20)	– –	2,024.00 (48.65)	4,160.00 (100.00
3.	International Computers (1979)	GEC (UK)	130.00 (46.43)	150.00 (53.57)	– –	– –	– –	(280.00) (100.00)
4.	Welcome Hotel	BAT (UK)	65.00 (34.03)	32.50 (17.01)	–	85.00** (44.50)	8.50 (4.45)	191.00 (100.00)

* Includes : Interest free unsecured loan from WBIDC (Rs.334.89 lakhs) and Central Government subsidy (Rs. 30 lakhs)

** Includes : Term loans from Rajasthan Financial Corporation (Rs.30 lakhs), Rajasthan Industrial and Mineral Development Corporation (Rs.25 lakhs) and Central Bank of India (Rs.30 lakhs)

Bracketed figures show percentages.

Source : Goyal, 1979, pp 5.

During the sixties and the seventies, thus, despite contrasting tendencies in policy formulation, the Indian state did not face any serious opposition to its basic attitude towards foreign capital. During late 1969, the department of industries stressed on the importance of large industrial houses and foreign dominated sector and eulogised them as rightfully controlling the key sectors of the economy. New Industrial Licencing Policy of February, 1970, states that large industrial houses and foreign capital would enter into the core sectors while maintaining their existing investment in other sectors. Bagchi (1986) raises strong objections about this statement while Subrahmanian (1972) questions the vague reasoning presented by the government in support of its decision and points at the high price—financial and social—that India had to pay for it. Even in sectors earlier earmarked for promoting small-scale industry, such as tooth paste, paint, household electric gadgets, leather footwear etc., foreign capital with active support from the Indian government entered into sectors for which a large domestic market had already existed.

The new Industrial Policy of 1970 expressed its hope to augment technological development and export in the core sector with the help of foreign capital and hence permitted foreign financial participation in such industries, despite a strong observation made by the National Committee on Science and Technology that foreign equity participation was not essential for procurement of technology (Gaurishankar, 1980). Independent researchers have also shown that parent corporations (such as Philips) in many instances have even disallowed Indian subsidiaries to copy the design of machinery or instrument supplied by the parent company while preparing drawings even after the expiry of contract period (MRTP, 1974). In the name of developing technology, Indian counterparts of MNCs were found to be purchasing technology, borrowing brand and trade names and paying a heavy price in the process (Goyal, 1979). However, the above change in the industrial policy during 1970-73 brought in the Foreign Exchange Regulation Act (FERA) with much fanfare in January, 1974, before which no legal definition of foreign companies existed in official documents, excepting for the branches. In brief, the Act (*i*) placed an obligation on all foreign branches operating in India to register themselves under the Companies Act, 1956, and (*ii*) directed all foreign subsidiaries and other foreign controlled companies to reduce their percentage of shares held abroad. By this Act, all branches of foreign companies were required to convert themselves into rupee companies with Indian participation ranging between 20 and 60 per cent, depending on the nature of their activities. They were also to be guided by Reserve Bank of India guidelines. Only three categories of companies were permitted to remain foreign majority companies (i.e. with foreign equity ranging upto 51 per cent or 74 per cent. These were : (*i*) companies operating in specified high priority areas, (*ii*) companies whose activities involved use of sophisticated technology and (*iii*) companies exporting more than 40 per cent to 60 per cent of their own production. The Industrial policy of 1973 restricted fresh foreign investment to non-core industries but the guidelines issued under FERA kept possibilities open (Chaudhury, 1979) for such investment. Actually FERA was found not actually harmful to the foreign companies. Corporations that left India following the introduction of FERA were trading companies or firm like IBM or Coca-Cola who did not intend to share their secrets in high-tech area in the formula of soft drinks. Firms engaged in dominant and dynamic sectors of manufacturing did not leave. Because, after floating separate rupee companies and sharing dividends with Indian share capital, they still had alternative sources of profit like transfer pricing and royalty earnings. According to some, (Chaudhuri, 1970) the Act actually benefited foreign capital at the cost of subverting the Indian interest, as a result of which, foreign exchange outflow increased. The fallacious nature of the FERA strategy that was supposedly designed to reduce the level of foreign exchange remittances by foreign companies, actually helped it. It is clearly reflected in the utilisation pattern of foreign exchange by 133 foreign subsidiaries in the following years (Table 3.7).

Table 3.7. *Pattern of foreign exchange utilisation by foreign subsidiaries (1975-76)*

(Rs. in thousands)

Sl.No.	Head	Foreign exchange spent	Percentage
1.	Capital good	65,401	2.95
2.	Raw materials (of which oil imports)	1,092,793 (717, 019)	85.71 (32.29)
3.	Spares	47,612	2.14

Sl.No.	Head	Foreign exchange spent	Percentage
4.	Interest	13,616	0.61
5.	Dividends	110,398	4.97
6.	Know-how	19,581	0.88
7.	Royalty	7,991	0.34
8.	Travelling	2,457	0.11
9.	Commission	17,075	0.77
10.	Others	33,320	1.50

Source : Goyal, 1979, pp 18.

The Industrial Policy of 1970–73 also had a positive view about the multinational corporations' contribution towards increase in export. Although by then the United Nations Centre in Transnational Corporations already stated that FDI had oriented primarily towards producing abroad for the domestic markets of host countries rather than towards exporting from foreign sites (Shekhar, 1992). Between 1964–65 and 1969–70, operations of MNCs in India had resulted in a net outflow of Rs.684 crore worth of foreign exchange on account of imports exceeding exports and other payments. Wholly or majority-owned foreign firms (IDPAD, 1984) affected the trade balance negatively to a greater extent than firms with only minority foreign participation. During 1975–76 in case of 133 foreign subsidiaries, (Goyal, 1979) there was a net deficit of Rs. 984.34 million while in case of 184 foreign-controlled companies, the loss was Rs. 139 million. Further, during 1970–78, when there was a spurt of export activity in India, it was found that the value added by MNCs in export was minimal and foreign collaboration agreements, by and large, acted as vehicles for increasing imports in the economy (Bagchi, 1986). During 1977–78, exports as a proportion of total production did not change much while there was a substantial increase both in the absolute amount and in the relative proportion of imports (RBI, 1985). During the same period, foreign exchange balance and value added by foreign corporations also declined. While Bagchi (1973) and RBI (1974) in the seventies identified restrictive clauses prohibiting MNC subsidiaries to export in regions of the parent units' operation, researches in related areas showed instances of lowering of export as a proportion of the total sales in foreign-owned companies in engineering goods (Subrahmaniam and Pillai, 1978). Table 3.8 shows the long-term trend of foreign exchange loss incurred through the transactions of large foreign-controlled corporations in India. Much later, Nagesh Kumar (1984) observed that affiliates of foreign corporations, set up in response to the import substitution drive of the India government, contributed very little to export and remained largely confined to the domestic market. Same observation was put forward by Newfarmer and Marsh (1981) and Jenkins (1987) on the negative role of foreign-controlled corporations inaugmenting export in Latin American countries. Despite the above observations and findings, in the late seventies the official goal of self-reliance and import-substitution-based economic development were systematically replaced by a new emphasis on export related industrialisation. Numerous concessions were offered to the private sector in augmenting exports. During the brief change in the government from Congress (I) to Janata in 1977, the sporadic attempts to curb the expansion of a few MNCs did not, however, change the real trend which remained positive towards foreign capital. In 1978–79, the import policy was further liberalised, especially in the case of capital goods, raw materials and components. Interestingly enough, during the Janata rule, entry of foreign capital in the small-scale sector continued unabated while the scope and items of this sector were restricted. Abolition of managing agencies also did not affect the foreign capital much as interlocking directorships, secretaryships and other favourable legal practices continued.

Table 3.8. *Foreign exchange loss through transactions of large foreign controlled corporations*

Year	Foreign exchange earning	Foreign exchange utilisation	Net earning of F.E.
1975–76	173.73	179.95	– 6.22
1976–77	220.54	207.54	13.00
1977–78	216.32	234.32	– 18.01
1978–79	213.88	263.56	– 49.68
1979–80	232.20	362.72	– 130.52
1980–81	280.36	406.13	– 125.77

Year	Foreign exchange earning	Foreign exchange utilisation	Net earning of F.E.
1981–82	355.87	488.42	–132.55
1982–83	396.27	533.03	– 136.76
1983–84	366.19	528.58	– 162.39
1984–85	381.22	592.04	– 210.82
1985–86	434.70	731.09	– 296.39
1986–87	463.10	851.19	– 388.09
1987–88	521.63	911.32	– 389.69

Source : Chandrashekhar, 1992, pp 61.

From the 1980s, the shift of policies towards export-led industrialisation became clearer (UNI 1981). A ready response came from the US, West German and other European countries and India was adjudged a less risky developing country for investment. MNC collaboration was hailed by none other than the Indian finance minister and MNC penetration in both domestic and foreign markets was welcomed. Various concessions were also given to foreign capital through a new industrial policy introduced in 1980, wherein the role of public sector was drastically reduced. Some leading MNCs like Hindustan Lever, Union Carbide, Pfizer, E. Merck and Johnson and Johnson were allowed to maintain majority foreign equity and two foreign banks were allowed to set up branches—a novel feature since the bank nationalisation of 1969. Even RBI (1985) stated that foreign investment was being viewed by the Government of India as a vehicle for development of technology and promotion of exports. The government simultaneously allowed higher percentage of equity for export-oriented units. For 100 per cent export units, 100 per cent foreign equity was allowed, paving the way for further growth of export promotion zones.

In the eighties, the final negotiations on the massive IMF loan to India provided a further conducive atmosphere for foreign capital (Table 3.9). Following IMF guidelines, anti-labour laws like the Essential Services Maintenance Act were enacted, subsidies for food and fertilisers reduced, price of public sector products increased, import and industrial policies were further liberalised and the rupee devalued (IDPAD, 1984). In 1985, the Indian government openly invited foreign investment and assured further liberalisation. But the real headway came in the nineties. With the need for fresh IMF loan, ground for which was created during the eighties, India had to opt for structural adjustment in its economy at the behest of

Table 3.9 *Foreign investments approved during 1976-1989*

Year	Approved Foreign Investment (Rs. Cr)	Year	Approved Foreign Investment (Rs. Cr)	Year	Approved Foreign Investment (Rs. Cr)
1976	7.26	1981	10.87	1986	108.95
1977	4.00	1982	62.80	1987	107.70
1978	9.40	1983	61.87	1988	239.75
1979	5.63	1984	113.00	1989	316.67
1980	8.92	1985	126.06		

Source : Ministry of Industry, Government of India, 1990.

the IMF. After the budget of 1991–92 and 1992–93, the economy was made fully open. MRTP and FERA restrictions were scrapped and foreign equity upto 51 per cent was permitted without the firms requiring any permission from the RBI. Licensing was almost dispensed with, except in 18 industries. The faulty implementation of the Industrial Licensing Policy was corrected by totally doing away with licensing. Many public sector units were sold out to the private sector and basic infrastructure areas were handed over to the private sector, mostly foreign. Ironically 24 per cent foreign equity was allowed in small scale units. Between 1983 and 1989 in the organised sector, employment increased only by 1.7 per cent while within the private sector, employment fell (Table 3.10). The 20.6 lakh growth of employment was only in the public sector (RUPE, 1991). New proposals for setting up firms with 51 per cent foreign equity henceforth did not require any accompanying foreign technical collaboration proposal and foreign firms could now acquire any Indian firm without any restriction. The new economic policy and structured adjustments completed a circle. Also the balance of class forces that determined the political and economic choices (Bagchi, 1984) was drawn more clearly.

Table 3.10 *Employment in private sector industry, 1983-88 (in lakhs)*

Year	Employment in Manufacturing
1983	46.56
1984	44.73
1985	44.21
1986	44.48
1987	44.10
1988	43.95

Source : Economic Survey, 1985-86 and 1990-91.

3.2 Structure and Organisations of Multinational Corporations in India :

Multinational corporations are not recognised as any particular class of companies in India. Actually, there is no legal definition of MNCs in India. During the post-Independence era till 1990, multinational corporations' operations in India have shaped around four definite forms : (*i*) branches of multinational corporations, (*ii*) subsidiaries, (*iii*) joint venture firms with majority or minority foreign equity with or without technical collaboration, and (*iv*) only technical collaborations or licencees. Branches of MNCs are the companies registered abroad having business interest and operations in India. They constitute the most direct form of MNC investment in India. During the mid-seventies, the largest foreign branches, according to assets, were Burma Shell (Rs. 70.27 crore), Calcutta Electric (Rs. 66.05 crores), EID Parry (Rs. 45.85 crores), Caltex (India) Ltd. (Rs.36.92 crores). Many foreign branch companies following the enactment of FERA got converted into foreign subsidiaries or Indian companies (Goyal, 1978). Quite a few tea gardens in India, which were formerly branches of British companies, merged with Indian companies or acquired new identities under the Indian Corporate Statute. Mcleod Tea, Williamsons, Macneill Magor and Warren Tea are pertinent examples. Many branches now also operate as liaison or agency offices or service companies like airlines or banking institutions and do not have a big role to play in the manufacturing activity. However, the decline of branches of foreign corporations largely due to FERA regulations does not suggest any reduction of the importance of dominance of MNCs in the Indian economy.

Under section 4 of the Companies Act, 1956, a subsidiary of a multinational corporation is an undertaking which is registered in India and in which more than 50 per cent of the voting right should rest with the corporate identity. If the majority rights are shared by more than one company—even by two—the undertaking cannot be treated as a foreign subsidiary (Dhar, 1984). In Zuari Agro-Chemicals, nearly 64 per cent of equity shares were held abroad. But the company was never termed as a foreign subsidiary. Prior to FERA, these were companies with 51 per cent of the share with effective management control held abroad with one company. The enactment of the FERA had its impact on these subsidiaries. Although the resultant decline of such undertakings, was not of the same order as that of the foreign branches. As the FERA put a stipulation on the percentage of foreign equity holding of a company registered outside India to 40 per cent, most of these firms were obliged to dilute their foreign equity. At the same time, the FERA left some special category companies out like those (*i*) engaged in manufacturing activities under priority industry groups, (*ii*) predominantly manufacturing for exports (minimum exports being 60 per cent of the total production. Subsequently, in 1976, companies exporting 40 per cent of their total production were also allowed 51 per cent foreign equity share); (*iii*) using sophisticated technology; (*iv*) tea plantations; (*v*) trading companies with distributing expertise and communication network not indigenously available in India, and (*vi*) branches of foreign companies engaged in shipping or airlines etc. Examples are Cadbury India (Cadbury Schweppes), Colgate India (Colgate-Palmolive), ITC (British American Tobacco), Food Specialities Ltd. (Nestlé), Peico (Philips), Imperial Chemicals, Wimco (Swedish Match), and Indian Oxygen Limited (British Oxygen). The bracketed names are those of the respective parent companies.

Dilution of foreign equity to 40 per cent, however, did not reduce the control of the foreign corporations holding majority share earlier. Instead, it helped the multinational corporations in many ways. They could now get 'Indian citizenship' by virtue of which they could bypass restrictions applied to foreign corporations. Some of the important foreign subsidiaries which became Indian were ITC Vazir Sultan Tobacco, Godfrey Philips, Hoechst Dyes and Chemicals and Macneill Barry (Table 3.11). Actually, 40 per cent was a high cut-off point. Due to wide dispersal of shareholding, it was not even necessary to have upto 40 per cent of equity for the parent firm to have absolute control. With not more than 2 – 4 per cent equity shares, Tatas have an overall control over TISCO. The more significant test for corporate nationality lies in the location of the centre of management control (Goyal, 1980). Monopolies Inquiry Commission (MIC, 1964), however, assumed that 50 per cent equity would be considered as a majority equity which, however, was challenged by the Industrial Licensing Policy Inquiry Committee (ILPIC, 1969) and fixed the equity criterion at one-third of effective equity. This was done mainly with the consideration that many important shareholders like public financial institutions, insurance companies and trusts might be non-voting ones. MRTPA initially had adopted an approach similar to that of the

ILPIC. Initially, the former took one-third of the total equity and later changed it to one-fourth (Chalapati Rao, 1985). The FERA approach was more liberal than the general approach of MRTP and ILPIC (Dhar, 1984). Further, it was also inconsistent with the business realities of the present day (Dhar, 1984; Goyal, 1980). An Interna-

Table 3.11 *Select foreign companies which became 'Indian' after equity dilutions under FERA*

Sl. No.	Name of the Indianized Company	Name of the Parent Company	Percentage of Foreign Equity after Dilution	Assets in 1981 (Rs. Crores)
1		2	3	4
1.	Bata (I) Ltd.	Leader, AG, Switzerland	40.00	47.07
2.	BritanniaBiscuit Co. Ltd.	Control Nominees, UK	38.00	25.88
3.	Brooke Bond (I) Ltd.	Brooke Bond Liebig, UK	39.90	75.41
4.	Cadbury (I) Ltd.	Cadbury Schweppes Overseas, UK	40.00	17.06
5.	Colgate-Palmolive	Colgate–Palmolive Co., USA	40.00	18.11
6.	Crescent Dyes & Chmls. Ltd.	Imperial Chemical	40.00	13.82
7.	Food Specialities Ltd.	Nestle Holdings, Bahama Islands	40.00	17.86
8.	HMM Ltd.	Horlicks Ltd., UK	40.00	27.14
9.	ITC Ltd.	British American Tobacco, UK	39.00	181.65
10.	Indian Oxygen Ltd.	British Oxygen, UK	39.90	65.48
11.	Intl. Computers Indian Mfrs.	Intl. Computers, UK	40.00	17.57
12.	Parke Davis(I)Ltd.	Parke Davis & Co. USA	40.00	8.79
13.	Peico Electronics Electricals Ltd. (Philips)	Philips, Holland	39.70	96.49
14.	Reckitt & Colman (I) Ltd.	Reckitt & Colman, UK	39.90	11.23
15.	Sesa Goa Ltd.	Finsder, Italy	40.00	16.39
16.	Tube Invt. Co. (I) Ltd.	Tube Investment, UK	39.92	31.00
17.	WIMCO Ltd.	Swedish Match Co., Sweden	39.50	50.21

Source : Goyal, 1982, pp. 81.

tional Business Directory of London had to acquire only 10 per cent share in an Indian company to classify it as an associate. IMF suggestion (1964) of 25 per cent or more stake by a single share-holder or an organised group to denote control over the undertaking was later reduced to a meagre 10 per cent of rating rights or equity share (IMF, 1927).

The Reserve Bank of India (1950) only for research purposes used to consider an undertaking as a foreign controlled company if (*i*) 40 per cent or more of its shares were owned abroad; (*ii*) it was a branch or subsidiary of a foreign company; (*iii*) 25 per cent or more of its share were owned by foreign-controlled Indian joint stock company which was not a managing agent or (*iv*) it was a company managed by a foreign-controlled managing agency company (Dhar, 1984). After 1961 the RBI (1973) started publishing data and information on branches and subsidiaries of foreign companies as well as on selected companies having foreign equity capital. It then pragmatically considered 25 per cent or more of foreign equity in a company as a basis for designating it as under foreign control. However, this classification, as mentioned, was not used to control the foreign firms.

Most of the industrially advanced countries take into account a much lesser share of foreign equity to identify foreign control over an undertaking. It needs to be kept in mind that in a country where there is no restriction on foreign equity holding, foreign corporations may have 100 per cent equity holding in many undertakings. But with regulatory laws, the percentage of foreign equity will naturally be brought down by the parent corporations in an optional pragmatic manner. MNCs in such cases forego exclusive ownership rights but ensure a hold over the management by non-equity forms of participation, e.g., long-term legal contracts. In many Indian companies, where the foreign equity share holding is less than 40 per cent, a new clause in the company articles is introduced which allows the management control of the company to continue under the specified MNC. Similarly, firms having technical collaboration agreement with a foreign corporation can also be effectively controlled through various laws and by-laws.

An IDPAD (1984) survey of 28 MNCs with less than 40 per cent foreign equity reveals that many companies included clauses which gave their parent companies the right to appoint chairman/ managing directors on the boards of the Indian counterparts. Pfizer, Indiacarb and Philips had a clause giving right to the parent company—even with 26 per cent equity holding — to appoint a board of directors. Restrictive clauses on trade name enabled the parent company to exercise technical and business controls. For example, Abbott Laboratories was allowed to use the word ABBOTT in its corporate name so long the parent company held 40 per cent of the equity. Piaggio, the Italian parent company of LML-Vespa, filed a legal suit asking for disallowance of the Indian collaborator to sell in the European market even after the expiry of technical contract period. There are numerous examples of effective control by the parent company through various clauses and rules. Also, the extent of shareholding is ultimately decided on the nature and extent of spread of shareholders. The spread-out ownership of shares in MNCs rules out any practical possibility of the emergence of a major contending block of shareholders.

During the post-Independence era, the absolute number of MNCs that have entered in India is not very high. In many cases the entry has been made in the form of collaborations with Indian business. For example, Daimler-Benz of West Germany has collaborated with Bajaj Tempo while Ciba collaborated with Lalbhai House, Kaisers and Ford have found their collaboration in Birla. Utilising the political and administrative contacts of the local business houses and their rapport with the Indian consumers, the MNCs could make serious inroads into the Indian economy.

Moreover, in India, for a number of reasons, foreign companies, subsidiaries or other closely-related companies have never been grouped together to reflect the extent of their international operations. Even if companies are under common control and management and actually represent conglomerates, they are always treated separately. Actually, to understand the linkage and co-ordination of international groups, more importance should be given to common control status than their separate legal identity. For instance, to consider Lintas a foreign branch of Unilever, as different from Hindustan Lever, Unilever's largest subsidiary in India, would be an analytical error (Goyal, 1980). Subsidiaries are allowed to maintain separate legal identities from their parent units for remaining out of restrictions applicable to large industrial houses under MRTPA. Hence many large international conglomerates in India are not covered by anti-monopoly provisions as each branch or subsidiary of that conglomerate is treated as a separate entity independent of its corporate associates, viz ITC and Vazir Sultan or Polydor and Siemens-Philips. Occasionally, for the same reasons, affiliates of MNCs are

Table 3.12 *An illustrative list of companies which diluted foreign equity under FERA, 1973 with rights to appoint directors held by the parent units*

Sr. No.	Indian Affiliate	Parent Company	Minimum share holding needed to exercise	Right to appoint or remove
	1	2	3	4
1.	Abbot Laboratories (I) Ltd.	Abbot Laboratories, USA	25	One third (including Managing Director) of the total Board of Directors.
2.	Colgate Palmolive (I) Ltd.	Colgate-Palmolive Co.,USA	20	- Do-
3.	Corn Products Co. (I) Ltd.	CPC Internatioanl Inc. USA	–	Chairman and Vice-Chairman.
4.	Davy Ashmore (I) Ltd.	Davy Ashmore Ltd., UK	26	One third (ncluding Managing Director) of the total Board of Directors.
5.	E. Merck (I) Ltd.	Chemitra-Gmbh	26	One third (non-retiring including Managing Director of the Board.
6.	Furford (I) Ltd.	Schering-Plough Holding Ltd., UK	10	One third (including Chairman) of the Board of Directors.
7.	Lipton Tea (I) Ltd.	Unilever Ltd., UK	26	Managing Director.
8.	Malayalam Plantations	Malayalam Plantations (Holding) Ltd., UK	26	One third (including Managing Director) of the total Board of Directors.
9.	Mather and Platt (I) Ltd.	Mather & Platt Ltd. UK	26	Chairman & Managing Director.
10.	May & Baker (I) Ltd.	May & Baker Ltd., UK	26	One third (including Managing Director) of the total Board of Directors.
11.	Nicholas Laboratories(I) Ltd.	Aspro-Nicholas Ltd., UK	..	Chairman and Vice-Cairman.
12.	Parke-Davis (I) Ltd.	Park-Davis & Co. Ltd., USA	..	Chairman and Vice-Chairman.
13.	Pieco Electronics & Electrical Ltd.	Philips, Holland	26	Managing Director.
14.	Pfizer Ltd.	Pfizer Corporation, Panama	..	Managing Director.
15.	Sesa Goa Ltd.	Finsider, Italy.	26	Chairman.
16.	Thomas Cook (I) Ltd.	Thomas Cook Overseas Ltd., UK	..	Chairman & Managing Director.

Source : S.K. Goyal, 1980.

controlled through another subsidiary located elsewhere and not directly by the parent company. British paints controlled by Hoechst's UK subsidiary Berger-Jenson is an example. In reality, British Paints, is a member of the Hoechst group of companies.

The question is, therefore, not the actual percentage of foreign equity holding, but the actual control of the foreign corporation over the operational, financial and administrative functions of any undertaking. In Japan, an undertaking with 20 per cent or more foreign equity is treated as foreign controlled. In France also, the dividing line is 20 per cent while the United States has decided on a much lower cut-off point—10 per cent (Dhar, 1984). Thus, it becomes obvious that control over an enterprise can be exercised with small percentage of equity holding and minority of votes (Table 3.12). With a large number of shareholders combined with intercorporate investments and non-voting institutional shareholders, a very small group of shareholders with a marginal stake in the overall risk capital can exercise control over the management. When other countries officially and legally recognise this reality, India does not. A more realistic way to understand the control of multinational corporations over the Indian undertakings will be to consider a much less foreign equity holding as well as other business links and collaborations beyond equity participation (Table 3.13). Following this, if one accepts that an MNC would be a company that operates in more than two countries and has large assets or sales to be accredited as a leading industrial concern at international level, it can be safely said that foreign capital in India is essentially an issue of multinational corporations (Goyal, 1978). The policy of concessions, in foreign direct investment has been effectively used by a handful of foreign corporations, large in size and flexible in operations. At the same time, a mere statistical survey of the equity share of multinational corporations in Indian manufacturing will also not reveal the true picture of their growth and expansion. Their gradual penetration and relative presence in key manufacturing sectors have to be carefully examined.

On the eve of Independence, the pattern of foreign investment of India reflected the colonial interests of Britain. The latter then owned 80 per cent of the total foreign stock which was in commercial sector and not in industries. With Britain's declining status in the international economy, direct investment from other developed countries specially the OECD countries,

Table 3.13 *Pattern of foreign exchange utilisation by foreign subsidiaries (1975–76)*

Sl. No.		133 Foreign Subsidiaries	% of Total (col. 2)	189 Foreign Controlled (Rs. Thousand)	% of Total (Col.4)
1.	Capital Goods (Machinery)	65,401	2.95	2,14,900	8.26
2.	Raw Materials (of which oil imports)	19,02,793 (7,17,019)	85.71 (32.29)	20,47,400 (7,17,019)	78.26 (27.55)
3.	Spares	47,612	2.14	1,09,400	4.20
4.	Interest	13,616	0.61	16,300	0.63
5.	Dividends	1,10,298	4.07	1,23,800	4.76
6.	Know-how	19,581	0.88	21,800	0.84
7.	Royalty	7,991	0.34	8.400	0.32
8.	Travelling	2,457	0.11	2,700	0.10
9.	Commission	17,087	0.77	20,800	0.80
10.	Others	33,320	1.50	37,000	1.42

Source : S.K. Goyal, 1982.

became significant. The attitude of the Indian state and the bourgeoisie towards foreign capital also underwent significant change from hostility to favourable disposition to cordiality frequently marked by preferential treatment. The rationale behind this change of attitude, however, got modified from time to time with changing economic scenario. During the late forties, it was argued that foreign investments would complement the limitation of natural resources and achieve higher rates of investment, bring advanced technology and capital equipment without straining the foreign exchange reserve (Goyal, 1980). In the mid-fifties foreign investment was invited to promote import substitution which, however, was neither associated with increase in saving nor with industrial efficiency and development. With balance of payment deficiency as a natural consequence, India started depending on loans from advanced capitalist countries. Over the years, the proportion of grants to total public foreign aid declined while the proportion of India's export earnings pre-empted for debt repayments (Bagchi, 1973).

By 1966, there were 112 companies, each with assets of Rs. 10 crore and more. Of these, 48 were either branches or subsidiaries. Besides, 14 other Indian companies were dependant on heavy loans from foreign companies and were virtually foreign controlled. These 62 corporations together controlled 53.7 per cent of the total assets of the Indian joint sector. During the mid-sixties, there were many Indian companies with technical collaborations with foreign firms for mainly transfer of technology (Table 3.14) and were either sacrificing equity ownership or creating captive market for spareparts and machinery of the latter (Swamy, 1980).

Table 3.14 *Position of MNCs among India's giant companies (1966)*

	Number of Companies	Assets (Rs. crores)
Foreign companies	48	973.25
Foreign controlled companies	15	397.60
Indian controlled companies	50	1181.44
		2552.29

Source : Indian Licencing Policy Enquiry Committee, Vol. II Appendices.

During this period, the foreign domination was the most pronounced in the drug sector. Within 25 years since 1947, this sector increased its turnover from Rs. 10 crore to Rs.370 crore while its production was largely controlled by the MNCs. In 1973, 66 MNCs controlled 80 per cent of the total production of drugs and their annual repatriation of profit was more than 50 per cent of their initial investment. Among them Glaxo, ACCI, Ciba, Pfizer, Hoechst and Bayer were the largest. Actually, the FERA provisions, however superficial they were, could not be applied to the pharmaceutical multinational corporations as India was then considerably dependant on them for supply of several bulk drugs, drug intermediates and even essential formulations. It was only in 1981 that these corporations agreed to dilute their foreign equity (Martinussen, 1988) once they realised that it would bring them gain and not loss. Seven FERA companies did it even as late as 1984.

Following the devaluation of rupee in 1966, domination of MNCs in India's industrial sector increased. It attracted a fresh bid of foreign capital and during 1966–70, MNCs experienced a considerably high growth rate in their capital, sales turnover and obviously in profit. Their capital stock increased by 12.56 per cent per year while the sales experienced an increase of 9.32 per cent per annum. Subsidiaries of the MNCs during 1969–79 also experienced large-scale expansions (Table 3.15).

Out of a total of 39 foreign subsidiaries, six expanded their assets by more than 200 per cent in ten years and 18 doubled their assets. In terms of sales, 28 subsidiaries could use local resources to the extent of nearly three times their share capital. As their foreign equity participation was diluted to less than 40 per cent they could procure huge financial assistance from local financial institutions and even from the Union and State Governments. During 1969–73, these firms repatriated about Rs. 26 crore to their parent countries by way of payment of royalty, technical fees and dividends (Hathi Commission, 1975). At the same time, on many occasions, they have issued liberal bonus shares to avoid hostilities (Table 3.16), in the host country (Nair and Kasbekar, 1975). During this period, the special concessions given to foreign capital was primarily for ensuring its assistance to sell Indian goods in international market. These Indian goods were, however, manufactured by subsidiaries or collaborative firms.

Seventies was also a period when the number of branches and subsidiaries of MNCs in India declined but the total MNC assets rose (Table 3.17). Average assets per reporting unit rose from Rs. 3.7 crore in 1972–73 to Rs. 5.4 crore in 1976–77 for branches as against from Rs. 6.5 crore to Rs. 10.3 crore for subsidiaries. From Table 3.18, it also becomes clear that during the mid-seventies, branches continued to dominate in commerce, i.e., trade and finance as well as agriculture and allied activities, while subsidiaries dominated in processing and manufacture. This is borne out by the fact that 45 per cent of the branches were engaged in agriculture and allied activities and 70 per cent of the subsidiaries undertook processing and manufacturing works. The concentration areas of MNCs in industry types were tea (processing and manufacturing), copper mining and quarrying, machinery, footwear, iron and steel, automobile and parts, electrical goods, basic industrial chemical and fertiliser, medical and pharmaceuticals, toiletries as well as cigarette manufacturing.

Table 3.15 *Growth of foreign subsidiaries during 1969-77*

Sl. No.	Company	Year of incorporation	Assets (Rs. crores) 1969	Assets (Rs. crores) 1977	Percentage	Turnover (Rs. crores) 1969	Turnover (Rs. crores) 1977	Percentage Change
1.	2.	3.	4.	5.	6.	7.	8.	9.
1.	Hindustan Levers	1933	31.82	122.02	283.5	108.79	261.50	140.4
2.	Dunlop	1926	39.78	99.78	149.2	81.70	166.85	104.2
3.	Brooke Bond	1912	23.21	55.00	136.9	75.36	186.30	147.2
4.	Union Carbide	1934	35.24	68.18	93.5	44.13	106.85	142.1
5.	Indian Explosives	1954	51.05	79.96	56.6	15.13	91.59	505.4
6.	Indian Aluminium	1938	59.03	96.18	63.0	27.29	117.17	329.4
7.	Ashok Leyland	1958	22.30	61.51	175.8	29.11	97.41	234.6
8.	GKW (1972+1977)	1931	41.99	70.98	69.0	53.37	88.73	66.3
9.	Bata	1931	27.10	50.02	84.6	48.33	83.05	71.8
10.	Siemens	1957	18.02	47.95	166.1	19.98	77.74	289.1
11.	Goodyear	1962	14.08	23.98	70.3	28.84	52.16	80.8
12.	Philips	1930	24.18	55.64	130.1	32.23	82.04	154.5
13.	Metal Box	1933	21.82	32.58	49.3	25.97	54.20	108.7
14.	MICO	1951	15.85	40.90	158.0	14.59	61.14	319.1
15.	GEC	1911	23.87	34.72	45.5	17.98	58.60	225.9
16.	Alkali & Chemicals	1937	14.64	35.36	141.5	15.18	53.89	255.0
17.	Glaxo	1927	16.24	35.25	117.1	24.42	56.51	131.4
18.	WIMCO	1923	12.61	17.60	39.6	26.63	41.63	56.3
19.	Indian Oxygen	1935	15.73	33.75	114.6	15.86	48.10	203.3
20.	Ciba-Geigy	1947	–	21.16	–	–	34.64	–
21.	Pfizer	1950	12.51	25.09	100.6	15.89	41.29	159.9
22.	Britannia	1918	7.32	17.40	137.7	16.87	44.13	161.6
23.	Parry (1966+1977)	1975	7.44	46.05	518.9	–	108.88	–
24.	Chemicals & Fibres	1961	12.79	23.05	80.2	25.05	39.18	56.4

1.	2.	3.	4.	5.	6.	7.	8.	9.
25.	Chloride (I) Ltd. (1969+1973)	1947	7.57	9.25	22.2	6.77	16.76	147.5
26.	Bayer (I) Ltd 1958	8 .61	23.46	172.5	5.76	35.95	524.1	
27.	Sandoz	1947	8.66	16.50	90.5	7.60	36.45	376.6
28.	Tube Investment (1966+1977)	1949	11.38	19.62	72.4	–	26.20	–
29.	Colgate Palmolive (1966+1977)	1937	2.88	18.17	357.3	–	32.62	–
30.	Asbestos Cement (1966+1975)	1934	5.93	10.32	74	–	17.02	–
31.	Hindustan Milk Food (1966+1975)	–	1.46	6.48	343	–	16.67	–
32.	Cynamid	1947	5.72	12.80	123	–	16.89	–
33.	Associated Bearing	1961	9.25	18.18	107.4	5.05	19.88	293.7
34.	Lucas TVS (1966+1975)	1961	4.74	14.74	210	–	15.14	–
35.	Food Specialities	1959	5.72	12.38	115.4	7.87	20.79	164.2
36.	Sandvik Asia	1960	5.85	17.25	194.8	4.81	14.65	204.6
37.	Goodlass Nerclac (1969+1976)	1920	3.41	8.07	136.6	5.39	18.29	239.3
38.	Otis	1953	5.77	12.01	108.1	2.63	8.07	206.8
39.	India Tyre (1966+1975)	–	1.11	2.80	152	–	12.38	–
40.	Abbot Laboratories (1966+1975)	–	0.60	4.89	715	–	1.19	–
41.	Tribeni Tissues	1946	19.63	19.13	2.6	4.41	12.86	191.6
42.	Cadbury (1973+1977)	1948	6.45	13.40	107.8	9.79	16.89	74.1
43.	Reckitt & Colman	1951	6.23	8.28	32.9	7.17	11.86	65.4
44.	EEC	1957	6.01	11.69	133.3	2.15	16.58	671.2
45.	Atlas Copco	1960	2.75	6.79	146.9	3.75	11.61	209.6
46.	Hindustan Ferodo	1964	5.26	8.54	62.4	5.28	15.76	198.5
47.	Gramophone Co.	1946	3.60	10.94	203.9	3.97	11.34	185.6
48.	Merck Sharp (1966+1977)	–	2.98	6.73	123.8	–	11.60	–
49.	Boots	1944	2.51	5.10	103.2	3.49	11.98	243.3
50.	Shalimar Paints (1972+1977)	1902	4.37	6.77	54.9	6.85	12.00	82.5
51.	Roche (1966+1975)	–	3.81	6.70	75	–	9.84	–

Note : 1. Figures in brackets indicate the relevant years for which the data have been given.
2. * represents the figures for 1975.
3. – represents not available.

Source : S.K. Goyal, 1980.

Table 3.16 *Extent of bonus share in the total equity of 20 large MNCs in India, 1979*

Sl. No.	Name of the company	No. of Bonus Shares	Total No. of Equity Shares	% of Bonus Shares of total equity
1.	Hindustan Lever	208,61	291,62	71.53
2.	Dunlop	102,67	149,97	68.46
3.	Brooke Bond	80,40	151,22	53.17
4.	Union Carbide (1978)	133,61	217,22	61.51
5.	Indian Explosives	85,53	289,84	29.44
6.	Indian Aluminium	158,44	296,99	53.35
7.	Ashok Leyland	124,62	330,00	37.76
8.	GKW	113,10	145,99	77.47
9.	Bata	30,50	37,50	81.33
10.	Siemens	48,00	72,00	66.67
11.	Goodyear	46,77	74,83	62.50
12.	Philips (PEICO)	127,66	172,96	73.81
13.	G.E.C.	38,30	71,92	53.25
14.	Alkali Chemicals	12,40	48,12	25.77
15.	Glaxo	72,00	108,00	66.67
16.	WIMCO	42,50	84,50	50.30
17.	Indian Oxygen	54,91	82,13	66.86
18.	Pfizer	73,48	100,46	73.14
19.	Britannia	43,62	63,15	69.07
20.	Chemicals & Fibres	24,00	53,45	44.90

Source : S.K. Goyal, 1979.

During this period, the majority of the MNCs operating in India were UK based. Not many hailed from the US (Kochanek, 1980), Japan, West Germany and other European countries. Following the enactment of FERA, the number of wholly-owned subsidiaries declined, with a continued marked dominance of British corporations (Table 3.18).

Table 3.17 *Branches and subsidiaries of multinational corporations—distribution by industry*

	Branches				Subsidiaries			
	Number		Assets (Rs. crores)		Number		Assets (Rs. crores)	
	1972-73	1976-77	1972-73	1976-77	1972-73	1976-77	1972-73	1976-77
1. Agriculture and allied activities	115	112	211.5	299.6	4	4	35.8	68.80
2. Mining and quarrying	7	7	35.7	37.3	4	4	8.3	20.9
3. Processing and Manufacture	82	79	201.7	219.0	141	144	1164.8	1495.0
4. Construction and utilities	33	29	61.0	126.9	2	2	18.3	31.2
5. Commerce (Trade and finance)	162	121	1128.0	1452.0	31	27	30.3	25.8
6. Transport communications and storage	38	39	6.4	7.3	4	2	4.1	0.3
7. Community and business services	87	82	24.7	30.6	7	6	5.9	6.6
8. Personal and other services	14	13	3.8	5.6	2	2	0.2	0.3
Total	538	482	1672.8	2178.4	195	161	1267.7	1649.6

Source : Jain and Savara, 1981.

Table 3.18 *Wholly owned subsidiaries of MNCs before and after the enactment of FERA*

Parent Country	1972	1976
UK	62	40
USA	14	10
Italy	3	2
Sweden	2	1
Switzerland	1	1
Hungary	1	–

Source : Jain and Savara, 1981

In the early eighties, the Indian government openly announced its decision to invite multinational corporations as a policy. As a result, giant corporations like Siemens, GEC Guest Keen William, E. Merck, Johnson and Johnson were allowed to retain 51 per cent equity on their Indian counterparts which they had earlier diluted to 40 per cent under FERA.

A study conducted by the Indian Chamber of Commerce covering the activities of 34 foreign controlled undertaking during 1977-1982 showed that the sales of these companies during the period grew at an annual rate of 18 per cent, profit after tax grew at 20.3 per cent, dividends grew at 15 per cent, retained earnings increased at the rate of 22.8 per cent, equity capital grew at 21.5 per cent and total assets grew at the rate of 17 per cent (Maini, 1990). During the eighties MNCs operating in India went in for large-scale diversification of an unrelated nature that gradually became a characteristic feature worldwide. ITC entered into the business of luxury hotels and Chloride India started exporting shrimps.

By the early nineties, MNCs started using indigenous names while collaborating with Indian firms, e.g. Brindaban (a Lipton-Unilever Company) or Tribeni (British American Tobacco) as they would be more acceptable. Ciba focused on an advertisement drive where it highlighted the company's effort drawing knowledge from India's rich heritage. Through the Indian collaborators, MNCs also successfully entered many other Third World countries as well as the erstwhile Soviet Union where they were earlier not allowed to operate directly. The main suppliers of goods to the former USSR from India were Bata, Hindustan Lever and Nestlé. In addition, in the name of technology more and more brand names were introduced by these corporations while their inter-company transactions helped them to maintain overall profit at a global level.

MNCs in India command huge technical, financial and natural resources as they do in all Third World countries. They have access to a variety of crucial information within the government machinery to carry out business in the most efficient manner. They also represent a culture, a philosophy, and a powerful economic system (Goyal, 1980) which they manipulate to expand their market and increase their profit subverting the possibility of a healthy economic and cultural development. Their various types of operations, various shades of control are reflected in the nature of their various undertakings such as, branches, subsidiaries or collaborations. It is in this perspective that the multinational corporations operating in India have to be understood and analysed. The following section attempts a spatio-sectoral analysis of 435 foreign controlled corporations in India working as branches, subsidiaries, or units with majority or minority foreign equity.

3.3. Parent Country Affiliation, Status and Control : 1990 Scenario

The analysis of 435 corporations in India is based on data and information as of 1990. All the 494 corporations initially listed could not be included in the study due to the absence of uniform information, especially on their spatial dimensions. Corporations finally retained for analysis, besides being branches and subsidiaries of MNCs, are also companies with foreign equity ranging from 5 per cent to 50 per cent. Reasons for which firms with small foreign equity have been included for analysis has been explained in section 3.2. All firms having 5 per cent to 50 per cent foreign equity have been classified into various sub-groups depending on the range of foreign equity. However, with the process of buying out speeded up, it later became very difficult to say which country or corporation actually controlled (Table 3.19.) the Indian unit.

Out of the total 435 corporations, eight are branches which are registered in the parent countries. Almost all of them were born during the colonial period and were primarily British-owned. Available statistics on multinational corporations all over the world has revealed old colonial ties as a basis for their operations. More than 40 per cent of the UK based foreign firms in 1973 were located in the erstwhile colonies while in 1971 more than 50 per cent of the foreign controlled firms in former French colonies were having French parentage. Similarly, the branches of MNCs operating in India in-

Table 3.19 *Organisational distribution of FDI in manufacturing, 1990*

Country	Total Units	Branches No.	Subsidiaries No.	FE* 41% – 50%	FE* 31%–40%	FE* 21%–30%	FE* 11%–20%	FE* 5%–10%
Australia	3	–	–	1	2	–	–	–
Austria	1	–	–	–	–	–	1	–
Bahama Islands	2	–	–	–	2	–	–	–
Belgium	3	–	–	1	1	1	–	–
Brazil	2	–	–	1	1	–	–	–
Bulgaria	1	–	–	1	–	–	–	–
Canada	2	–	–	–	2	–	–	–
Denmark	1	–	1	–	–	–	–	–
Finland	1	–	–	–	1	–	–	–
France	8	–	–	1	2	3	1	1
Gulf	1	–	–	–	–	–	1	–
Holland	5	–	–	1	2	2	–	–
Hundary	1	–	–	–	–	1	–	–
Italy	16	–	–	–	5	6	4	1
Japan	27	–	–	1	8	13	4	1
Mexico	1	–	–	–	–	1	–	–
Panama	1	–	1	–	–	–	–	–
Singapore	1	–	–	–	1	–	–	–
Sweden	16	–	5	–	6	2	3	–
Switzerland	25	–	4	3	5	4	6	3
Turkey	1	–	–	–	–	1	–	–
U.K.	161	7	43	15	62	22	8	4
U.S.A.	101	1	16	11	46	12	9	6
W. Germany	50	–	9	5	20	13	3	–
UK/Holland	3	–	1	–	2	–	–	–
UK/France	1	–	–	1	–	–	–	–
Total	435	8	80	42	168	81	40	16

* FE – Foreign Equity
Source : Computed from Primary Data

cluded in the analysis are primarily British (87 per cent). Only one firm is the branch of an American multinational operating in the electronics sector. A good number of foreign branches also function as liaison offices, agency houses of air or water transport corporations or consultancy concerns or even banking and financial institutions without any manufacturing activity. Such firms have been excluded from the present analysis. Branches of the British MNCs included in the study operate in sectors of machinery, mining and tea plantations.

In 1990, the proportionate number of foreign subsidiaries having 51 per cent or more foreign equity is also much lesser compared to firms having less than 51 per cent foreign equity. In fact, the number of subsidiaries also declined considerably, especially since the mid-seventies following the institution of FERA regulations. From 243 in 1966, the number of subsidiaries declined to 171 in 1976. But their assets grew at a very fast rate showing a high degree of concentration in the hands of a few large subsidiaries. In 1976, the largest five accounted for 30 per cent gross income of the total 171 subsidiaries. These were Hindustan Lever, Dunlop, Brooke Bond, Union Carbide and Indian Explosives. Effectively less than 50 per cent subsidiaries accounted for nearly 90 per cent of the gross income of all foreign subsidiaries. Following the enactment of FERA, many corporations of this group diluted the proportion of their foreign equity, brought it down to below 51 per cent and became Indian. In the present analysis, the number of foreign subsidiaries is 80. They are primarily British (54 per cent), American (20 per cent) and West German (12 per cent). Firms with parent countries in Sweden and Switzerland also account for 6 and 5 per cent respectively. Some of the firms included in this group are subsidiaries of well known multinational corporations such as Hindustan Lever of the Unilever group; Alkali Chemical Corporation of the ICI Ltd. of the UK; Goodyear India Ltd. of Tyre and Rubber Corporation Ltd. or Johnson and Johnson India Ltd. of the Johnson and Johnson Company Ltd. of the USA; E. Merck India Ltd. of E. Merck Company Ltd. or Siemens India Ltd. of Siemens AG of West Germany; Flakt India Ltd. of Flakt AB of Sweden or Sandoz India Ltd. of the Sandoz AG of Switzerland. A number of British subsidiaries are engaged in tea and coffee plantations in eastern and southern India. Goodricke group under this head is the subsidiary of the Lawrie group of the UK which happens to be the world's largest private tea producing corporation. It owns two tea estates in Assam. As subsidiaries they represent giant MNCs. Giant rubber corporations, pharmaceuticals, cosmetic and toiletry manufacturers, chemical corporations and food product manufacturers are found in this group. Diversification of products of each individual firm is also considerable.

Following the enactment of FERA, a majority of the subsidiaries diluted their foreign equity participation rate and brought it down to less than 51 per cent. In the present analysis, 76 per cent of all the companies have foreign equity between 5 per cent and 50 per cent. However, a number of firms in 1990 still had foreign equity between 41 per cent and 50 per cent. They constitute the next group and are 42 in number out of the total of 422 companies. Again UK (36 per cent), USA (26 per cent) and West Germany (12 per cent) control the largest number. Some of the important ones are Tata Burroughs Ltd. tied up with Burroughs Corporation; Geoffrey Manners and Company in a tie-up with American House Products of the USA; Guest Keen Williams Ltd. tied up with Guest Keen Nettlefolds of Britain; BASF India Ltd., with a tie-up with BASF AG of West Germany; Xerographic Systems Pvt. Ltd. with Xerox Corporation of Switzerland. Engineering, electronics and machinery are the significant areas of this group.

Following FERA regulations, the range of foreign equity stake that became favourite with the MNCs was 40 per cent and less but more than 31 per cent. There are 168 companies in this group out of the total of 435, constituting a considerable 39 per cent. Many erstwhile subsidiaries were regrouped under this head, such as ITC with a turnover of Rs.325.00 crore in 1975, Vazir Sultan Tobacco with a turnover of Rs.89.68 crore, Godfrey Philips (Rs. 57.61 crore) Macneill Barry (Rs.30.69 crore) and Hoechst Dyes and Chemicls (Rs. 45.68 crore). Some other famous corporations that fall under this group are Colgate Palmolive, Procter and Gamble, Parke Davis, Pfizer, Pepsi and Rank Xerox Corporation (Modi Xerox) of the USA, May and Baker and Organon of the UK, Atlas Capco of Sweden, Ciba-Geigy (Hindustan Ciba-Geigy), and BOC Intl. (Indian Oxygen) of Switzerland, Matsushita (Lakhanpal National Ltd.) and Toshiba Corporations (Toshiba Anand Batteries) of Japan and Total CFP (Coates of India) of France. Last but not the least are Nestlé of the Bahamas and Brooke Bond of the Unilever (UK) group. Besides the dominance of UK, USA and West Germany, Japan is significantly present in this group. A large number of giant MNCs from the USA are found in this group. Giant pharmaceuticals, consumer goods, cosmetic and food product manufactures are members of this group. This is the most dynamic and diversified group in terms of products.

Companies that are included in the next group are those with foreign equity between 21 per cent to 30 per cent. Eighty-one companies that are included in this group have tie-ups with some well-known MNCs from Japan which dominates this group together with British, American and West German corporations. Significant names are SRF Nippon Denro (Nippon Denro), Goodlass Nerolac (Kansai Paint Corporation), Kinetic Honda and Hero-Honda (Honda Motor Corporation), DCM Toyota (Toyota Motor Corporation) or TVS Suzuki (Suzuki Motors) of Japan. Other well-known MNCs of this group are JC Gammon of the UK, Bewer Teppichfabrik (Transasia Carpets) of West Germany, Arora F. (Modi Carpets) of Switzerland, Astra Pharma (Astra India Ltd.) of Sweden, Piaggio of Italy (LML Vespa), Teodur NV (Berger Paints) of Holland, etc. Major products of the giant MNCs in this group are automobile, consumer items, electrical goods, petro-chemicals and textiles.

It is well known that for exercising control over a company it is not necessary to have majority equity stake. Management control can be effectively exercised with very little share holdings—as little as 10 per cent or even less—with technical collaboration agreements (Table 3.20). In the present analysis, therefore, companies with 5 per cent to 20 per cent foreign equity have been included. Fifty-six companies come under this group constituting 13 per cent of the total. Of these, 40 have foreign equity of 10 per cent and above. Countries such as USA (22 per cent), UK (20 per cent), Switzerland (15 per cent) have almost equal presence in this group followed by Japan (10 per cent), Italy (10 per cent), Sweden (8 per cent) and West Germany (8 per cent). Well-known Indian companies in this group are National Cereals Products and Kelvinator India with their parent corporations from the USA, Asian Cables (tie-up with Wilkinson Sword of the UK), Eicher Motors (with Mitsubishi of Japan), Bharat Seats (with Suzuki Motor Corporation of Japan). In the following group with less than 10 per cent foreign equity, Mahindra and Mahindra Ltd. is a well-known Indian firm in tie-up with Chryslers Corporation of the USA having 8 per cent of equity hold. Bharat Berg is the other mentionable name in tie-up with Berg AG of Switzerland having 6 per cent equity holding. USA, UK and Switzerland are the prominent parent countries in this group controlling 37 per cent, 25 per cent and 19 per cent of the units respectively. Major products of the giant MNCs in these last two groups are primarily consumer goods including light vehicles.

Table 3.20 *Organisational distribution of FDI in India (1964-80)*

Year	Foreign branches		Foreign controlled majority owned (51%)		Rupee companies minority owned (51%)	
	Value	%	Value	%	Value	%
1964	259.7	49.92	239.9	42.42	65.9	11.65
1974	241.6	26.45	470.4	51.50	201.4	22.05
1980	60.4	6.47	454.6	48.71	418.2	44.81

Source : Reserve Bank of India Bulletin, July 1975, March 1978, December, 1984, April 1985 and Nageshkumar, 1990.

Let us look at the distribution of foreign controlled companies countrywise. In all, 24 parent countries have been identified. Of these significant are the UK (with 38 per cent of the total corporations), the USA (23 per cent) and West Germany 12 per cent). Many of their assets or share holdings had been existing in India since the fifties or the sixties. Countries that have assumed significance later are Japan (with 6 per cent of the total companies), Switzerland (6 per cent), Sweden (2.5 per cent and Italy (3 per cent). France has equity stake in 2 per cent of the companies. Other countries that have also equity holding in India are Bahama Island, Belgium, Brazil, Canada, Holland, etc. Because of cross-country parentage (Holland/UK) Hindustan Lever with other companies of Unilever group has been kept a separate entity. Similarly, as Britannia is owned jointly by an alliance of UK, France and Singapore, a separate entity has been kept for its parent country (Fig. 3.1).

The UK owns the largest number of branches (7), while USA has only one branch in the electronics sector (Apple Industries). British branches, however, do not constitute large proportion of the total units controlled by Britain. It is a meagre 4.40 per cent. These branches mainly operate in machinery and engineering sectors. For example, Blackwood Hodge (I) Ltd. of British Steel Piling Company. Subsidiaries (41 in number) of British corporations are the largest in number compared to those of other parent countries and they constitute 26 per cent of the total British asset and interest companies. A number of famous tea processing and manufacturing units owned by British corporations fall

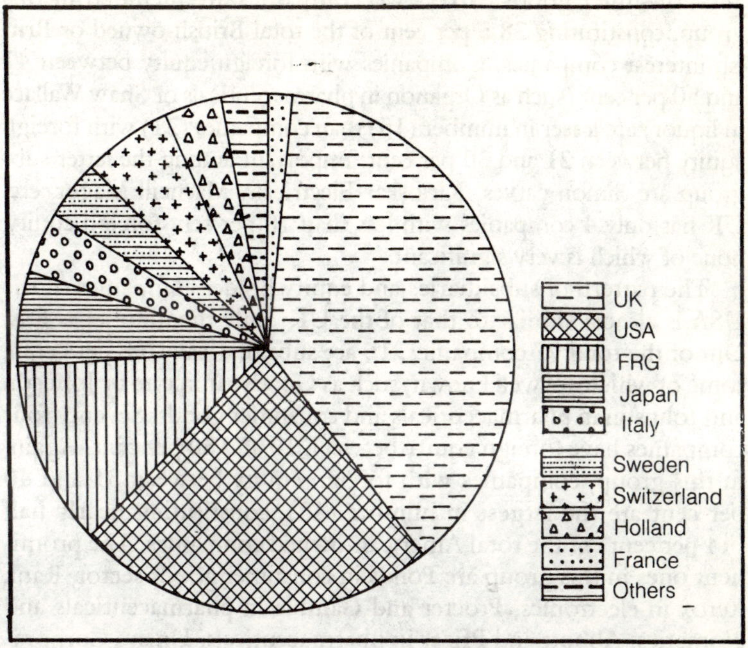

Fig. 3.1 Parent country affiliation of MNCs in India

in this group. Mention has been made earlier about the Goodricke group. Besides Goodricke, there are Assam Company, Assam Frontiers or Darjeeling Consolidated etc. Other well-known corporations in this group are Boots India in the pharmaceutical and consumer goods/sector, Glaxo in pharmaceuticals, Tribeni Tissues in paper and Alkali Chemicals in chemical and petrochemical sectors. Britain has the maximum stake in companies with foreign equity between 10 per cent and 50 per cent—105 in total. It constitutes 65 per cent of its total asset companies. Within this group again, the largest number of companies are found with foreign equity between 31 and 40 per cent wherein many of the erstwhile branches or subsidiaries of giant MNCs following the enactment of FERA regulations have slipped in. Some of them are worth mentioning : Dunlop in tyre and rubber products, Metal Box in engineering, Madura Coats in textiles, Harrison Malayalam in consumer goods, May and Baker and Smith and Nephew in pharmaceuticals, Vazir Sultan (BAT Industries) in tobacco and Reckit & Colman in pharmaceuticals and consumer goods. Sixty-two companies are included in this group, constituting 38.5 per cent of the total British-owned or British-interest companies. Companies with foreign equity between 41 and 50 per cent (such as Organon in pharmaceuticals or Shaw Wallace in liquor) are lesser in number (15) than companies (21) with foreign equity between 21 and 30 per cent. Important among the latter sub-group are Simon carves, Kirloskar Electricals, Macneill Magor, etc. UK has only 4 companies with less than 10 per cent foreign equity, none of which is very significant.

The pattern of subsidiaries and equity holder companies of the USA is almost similar to that of the UK; only the number is less. Out of the total 97 companies, 16 are subsidiaries (16.5 per cent), some of which are well known, such as Goodyear in tyre or Johnson and Johnson in pharmaceuticals and consumer goods. Seventy four companies have foreign equity between 10 and 50 per cent. Again, in this group, companies with foreign equity between 31 and 40 per cent are the largest in number (43), constituting nearly half (44 per cent) of the total American-owned companies. The prominent ones in this group are Ponds in consumer goods sector, Rank Xerox in electronics, Procter and Gamble in pharmaceuticals and cosmetics, Abbott and Pfizer in pharmaceuticals, Unisys Corporation in engineering or Pepsi in consumer food. Companies with foreign equity between 41 and 50 per cent (a few important ones being Tata Burroughs in machinery and electronics or Coromondal Fertilisers in chemicals) and 21 and 30 per cent constitute 11 per cent each. Two well-known multinational corporations in the last two groups are Hindustan Aluminium (tie-up with Kaiser Corporation) in engineering and Kelvinator in electrical sectors. Firms with less than 20 per cent foreign equity are only 15 out of 97. Both UK and USA based corporations are found to prefer controlling stake through joint ventures and not directly through subsidiaries.

West Germany does not have any branch operating in India. Nine Indian subsidiaries are wholly owned by West German multinational corporations. Important ones are Bayer India and E. Merck India in pharmaceuticals and Siemens India in diversified operations in electrical, machinery and consumer goods sectors. They account for 18 per cent of the total. Share of companies with West German equity between 10 and 50 per cent is, however, very large—82 per cent. Forty-one firms fall in this category. Again, 50 per cent of them are in the sub-group with foreign equity between 31 and 40 per cent. Significant are Hoechst and German Remedies in

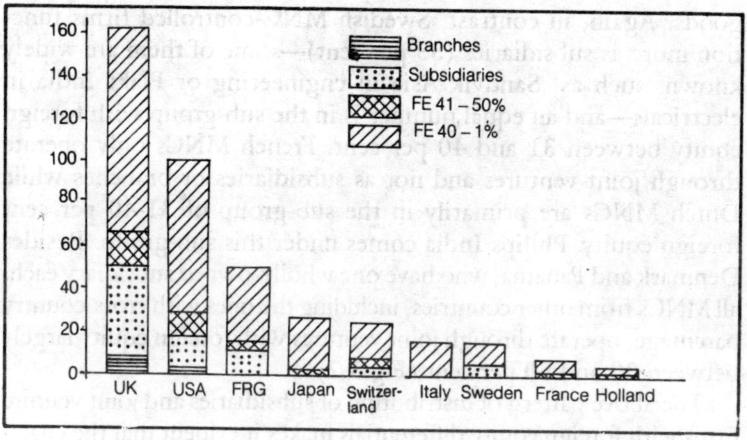

Fig. 3.2 Status of foreign controlled enterprises of various countries (foreign equity)

pharmaceuticals and chemicals, Starwall Volkmann in machinery, NOCIL and Colourchem (both joint ventures with Hoechst) in chemicals and petro-chemicals. There is no firm in India where West German equity is less than 10 per cent. In other words, in equity participation West German multinationals do not believe in very low equity participation. The organisational pattern of Japanese controlled firms is a little different. Japan does not have any wholly-owned subsidiary in India, 96 per cent of the firms with Japanese equity holding are in the group of 10-50 per cent foreign equity. But within this group a large contingent (50 per cent of the total) is in the sub-group of 21-30 per cent foreign equity while 27 per cent have foreign equity between 31 and 40 per cent. Some well-known Indo-Japanese joint ventures fall in this sub-group. Hero-Honda, Kinetic Honda (with Mazda Motors) and TVS Suzuki (with Suzuki Motors) in automobiles, Goodlass Nerolac (with Kansai Paints) in paints and varnishes or SRF Nippon Denro (with Nippon denro Co.) in electricals, etc. In contrast, among the companies controlled by Swiss MNCs, 16 per cent are subsidiaries and 72 per cent have 10-50 per cent Swiss equity. The total number in this sub-group is 18 out of 25. Within this group the sub-group that has the largest share of companies is having foreign equity between 11 and 20 per cent. The famous Swiss multinationals are, however, found in the sub-group with foreign equity between 40 and 51 per cent such as Roche and Sandoz in pharmaceuticals or Bata in leather goods. Again, in contrast, Swedish MNC-controlled firms function more as subsidiaries (33 per cent)—some of them are widely known, such as, Sandvik Asia in engineering or Flakt India in electricals—and an equal number is in the sub-group with foreign equity between 31 and 40 per cent. French MNCs only operate through joint ventures and not as subsidiaries or branches while Dutch MNCs are primarily in the sub-group of 31-40 per cent foreign equity. Philips India comes under this sub-group. Besides Denmark and Panama, who have one wholly-owned subsidiary each, all MNCs from other countries, including the ones with cross-country parentage, operate through joint ventures with foreign equity largely between 30 and 50 per cent (Fig 3.2).

The above pattern of distribution of subsidiaries and joint venture firms with foreign equity differentials makes it evident that the enactment of FERA in fact had an impact on their structure.

Analysis of the equity structure of the above corporations including branches, subsidiaries and majority as well as minority equity companies has been taken up together. The purpose of the analysis is to unravel the spatial dynamics of the multinational corporations in India and develop a spatial perspective. Differential in foreign equity holding hence does not surface in as a feature as the general locational policy of the MNCs is applicable to all grades of foreign-controlled companies.

4

Spatial Dynamics of Multinational Corporations in India

4.1 Product Specification and Diversification : Parent Country Preference

Prior to Independence foreign investment in India was primarily meant to exploit natural resources without any consideration to the development of the country. During the initial two decades after Independence, the pattern of foreign investment did not show any fundamental change in its essential character (Roy Chaudhury, 1981). It remained typically colonial in character by specialising in the extraction of primary products. The thrust of foreign investment then was to develop commerce rather than to develop modern industries.

During the fifties, the major share of foreign business was concentrated in plantations and oil fields. In the manufacturing sector, foreign participation was prominent in food, beverages and textiles rather than in machinery, transport or chemicals. By the sixties, foreign participation in sectors such as chemicals and metal manufacturing increased considerably, almost at a matching rate with the growth in consumer goods and textiles. Britain's share was maximum during this period. Finance participation by the US was much less. The ratio of UK and US participation was almost 7:1 although the US was the second collaborator in the rank order. Switzerland, Canada and West Germany had very little share. From the sixties onwards, the trend started changing, with the USA slowly increasing its share (Negandhi, 1962). The sectorwise breakup of foreign participation in manufacturing industry during 1957–64 indicates a growing bias on machinery and chemicals. After 1957, substantial foreign investment started flowing even in non-essential items. During 1957–63, 45 per cent of the consents for new capital issues involved foreign investments showing 11 per cent increase from that of 1951–63 (Kidron, 1965). This was the period when most of the foreign drug firms set up their establishments in India (Kumar, 1990).

The most fundamental change that emerged from the sixties, right up to the eighties in terms of sectoral distribution of foreign direct investment was the increasing importance of manufacturing sector. This increase was, however, at the cost of decreasing the share in plantations, mining, petroleum and services. Over the period from 1964–80, the total stock of foreign investments, both in absolute and in relative terms, declined from the mid-sixties to 1980. A detailed look at the changing pattern of foreign direct investment brings out the emerging importance of the manufacturing sector. During 1964, petroleum mining and plantations accounted for 25 per cent and 18.7 per cent of the total stock of foreign direct investment respectively, while manufacturing accounted for 40.5 per cent. Within ten years the relative share of manufacturing increased by more than 25 per cent and in 1974 it accounted for 68 per cent of the total foreign direct investment in India. The percentage share in petroleum industry by then had fallen to 14.7 per cent and in plantations to 11.7 per cent. Three years later, in 1977, manufacturing accounted for 81 per cent of the total stock while the share of plantations and petroleum industry got reduced to a minimum of 8.13 per cent respectively. By 1980, the trend was explicit. Manufacturing became the singlemost sector of foreign direct investment in India, accounting for 87 per cent of the total stock of FDI (Table 4.1).

Table 4.1 *Emerging trend of FDI investment sectors in India (1964-80)*

(in %)

Industry Group	1964	1974	1980
Plantations	18.7	11.7	4.12
Mining	0.9	0.8	0.8
Petroleum	25.3	14.7	3.94
Manufacturing	40.5	68.4	86.97
Services	14.6	4.4	4.12

Source : Reserve Bank of India Bulletins, 1975, 1978, 1984 and Nagesh Kumar, 1990.

However, in a large number of financial collaborations, what appeared as foreign capital inflow was no more than title to equity in lieu of technical knowhow and supply of machinery and equipment. Subrahmanian (1979) opines that the multinational corporations, which acquired majority of the total equity ownership of the manufacturing firms, contributed only a fraction of the total foreign exchange required for import of plant and machinery. On the other hand, the imported plant cost in joint ventures amounted to a large sum and accounted for a large proportion of the total cost.

Within the manufacturing sector also, there was a change in the stock pattern. During the sixties, food and beverages used to account for a considerable percentage (13.2) of the total foreign investment which was reduced to 4.82 per cent in the early eighties. Similarly in textile, the share declined from 7.2 to 3.94 per cent. Increase was perceptible in chemicals and allied products from 26 to 37 per cent and in electricals from 7 to 12 per cent (Table 4.2).

The new investments were directed more towards technology-intensive sectors. Chemicals, petrochemicals and pharmaceuticals dominated the scene, followed by electrical goods, machinery and machine tool products. Countrywise, there was a considerable reduction in the relative share of the UK. From 77 per cent of the total FDI stock in 1964, its share came down to 54 per cent in 1980. The United States emerged as the major contender, increasing its share from 14.5 per cent in 1964 to 21 per cent in 1980. The Federal Republic of Germany, Switzerland, Canada and Sweden also increased their stock considerably.

Table 4.2 *Distribution of FCI in India within the manufacturing sector (1964-80)* *(in %)*

Industry	1964	1980
Manufacturing	40.5	86.97
Food and beverages	13.2	4.82
Textile products	7.2	3.94
Machinery and machine tools	6.8	8.75
Transport equipment	6.5	6.34
Metal and metal products	14.4	14.62
Electrical goods	7.9	12.01
Chemicals and allied products	26.2	37.18
(a) Chemicals	7.1	16.09
(b) Medicines and pharmaceuticals	10.9	13.02
(c) Others	8.9	8.07
Miscellaneous	17.6	12.32

Source : Nagesh Kumar, 1990

As multinational corporations prefer operation in those sectors where they enjoy a competitive edge over existing or potential local competitors, their share in different sectors shows an uneven distribution. And this also necessitates an analysis of their comparative presence in individual sectors of industries. Work done by Nagesh Kumar (1990) on 1,334 medium and large non-government public limited manufacturing companies in the private sector—in spite of limitations of sample size—gives a detailed picture of the comparative presence of foreign direct investment between 1975 and 1980. The range of foreign share is classified into three groups: low (0-33 per cent), medium (34-66 per cent) and high (more than 66 per cent). Eleven industries are identified with high foreign investment share. These are processed food products, cigarettes, leather and leather products, aluminium, automobile components, dry batteries, metal products, plastic raw materials, drugs and pharmaceuticals, toilet preparations, other chemical products and safety matches.

Fifteen industries, where foreign investment share is in medium range, are non-ferrous basic metals other than aluminium, transport equipment other than vehicles, electric lamps, electrical machinery and appliances, machine tools, other non-electrical machinery, steel tubes and pipes, steel wire ropes, fertilisers, basic industrial chemicals, paints and varnishes, asbestos, cement and related products, sheet and speciality glass, automobile tyres and tubes, industrial and medical gases. A few estimates, such as, in machinery (electrical and non-electrical), machine tools or fertilisers were possibly exaggerated due to the presence of public sector units (Kumar, 1990). Industries with low foreign investment share but with considerable presence of foreign-controlled enterprises (with more than 10 per cent share) were edible oils, automobiles, electric cables, dyes and dyestuff, man-made fibres, rubber products other than tyres, plastic and textile products. Twelve industries were identified where foreign controlled enterprises had marginal share (less than 10 per cent). These were cotton textiles, breweries and distilleries, textile machinery, steel forgings, foundries, cement, ceramics and structural clay products, paper and paper products, wood products and glass containers. Foreign shares during this period also increased in motor vehicles, automotive components, transport equipment other than vehicles, dry batteries, toiletries and other chemical lamps, rubber products (other than tyres and tubes) and paper and paper products (Table 4.3).

Table 4.3 *Percentage share in sales of foreign controlled enterprises in Indian manufacturing in 1975 and 1980 (Medium and large non-Government public limited companies)*

Industry	FCE'share in Sales (%) 1975	1980
Grain and pulses mills	–	–
Edible oil mills	15.41	18.11
Sugar mills	–	–
Other processed foods	82.84	80.52
Cigarettes	85.14	78.23
Tobacco products, n.e.s.	–	–
Cotton textiles	6.78	5.73
Jute textiles	–	–
Silk and Rayon textiles	–	–
Woollen textiles	–	–
Other textile products	13.68	19.23
Breweries and distilleries	3.96	3.04
Leather and leather products	98.21	97.94
Miscellaneous	0.39	0.33
Iron and Steel mills	–	–
Aluminium manufacture	90.96	89.86
Other non-ferrous metals	45.46	36.13
Motor vehicles	16.96	19.45
Automobile components	65.99	66.07
Other transport equipment	43.95	52.21
Electric cables	36.45	32.01
Dry batteries	83.11	89.32
Electric lamps	62.05	63.57
Electrical machinery and equipment, n.e.s.	59.03	53.30
Machine tools	38.56	35.08
Textile machinery	9.52	7.26
Non-electrical machinery n.e.s.	44.80	45.31
Steel tubes and pipes	51.89	51.16
Steel wire ropes	37.67	36.83
Steel forgings	6.04	5.05
Foundries and engineering workshops	8.52	7.54
Metal products, n.e.s.	74.27	69.64
Chemical fertilizers	46.80	37.46
Dyes and dyestuffs	30.32	30.57
Man-made fibres	18.60	17.83
Plastic raw materials	71.50	71.78
Basic industrial chemicals	55.45	53.85
Medicines and pharmaceuticals	72.84	71.07
Paints and varnishes	55.01	52.13
Toiletries and other chemicals	70.73	72.11
Safety matches	100.00	100.00
Cement	6.37	5.24

Industry	1975	1980
Asbestos and asbestos products	46.18	43.78
Ceramics and structural clay products	3.08	3.92
Tyres/tubes	69.40	60.13
Other rubber products	12.49	13.55
Paper	3.35	3.95
Products of paper and board	5.33	6.76
Wood products and furniture	3.15	3.14
Glass containers	19.18	8.08
Other glass products	52.34	50.78
Plastic products	24.31	18.01
Industrial and medical gases	66.92	63.13
Miscellaneous	26.99	32.30
Manufacturing	32.78	31.41

Source : Nagesh Kumar, 1990.

Foreign controlled enterprises also had high market share in the consumer goods sector including processed foods, cigarettes, toiletries and leather goods while their share in traditional industries, such as jute, cotton textiles, paper, cement and sugar was also discernible. This was the completing phase of a cycle that had set in during the fifties and the sixties.

During the early eighties, large number of foreign collaboration ventures (both technical and financial) were approved in sectors like industrial machinery and parts, electrical machinery and equipment, computer hardware and electronics, chemicals and pharmaceuticals as well as vehicles and ancillaries, precision instruments, paper products, sanitaryware, fibre boards, jewellery etc. Countries which got the maximum number of clearances were the USA, West Germany, UK, Japan, Switzerland, Italy and France in order of rank (Bhusan, 1983). The respective parent countries entered with specific background and support. While for Britain, it was primarily the old colonial ties, for West Germany and Japan it was new technological strength. USA, in contrast, entered with its diversified range of products and not essentially with a technological edge. The respective sectors of foreign operation are thus important indicators to assess the significance of foreign capital (Kumar, 1990). The sector through which foreign capital essentially operates is the organised private corporate sector to which the foreign controlled enterprises selected for the present analysis belong. They also speak of a considerable presence of MNCs in terms of number of units. They are also representative of the diversification phenomenon of the multinational corporations with a single corporation manufacturing various types of products, creating a divergent product-mix identity. For example Hindustan Lever, Procter and Gamble (I), Glaxo India. In the analysis, production units of a single corporation producing different items have been treated as separate plants.

Seven broad industry groups can be identified where MNC presence is discernible. The most dominating presence of the MNCs is in the consumer goods sector. Around 20 per cent of the total units of the MNCs in India in 1990 including branches, subsidiaries and joint ventures, are in this sector. Of this, again, consumer non-food alone accounts for 13 per cent of the total units. Almost all the parent countries that have their MNCs operating in India have units in this sector. The UK controls 53 per cent of the consumer goods sector units with almost an equal participation in consumer food sector and non-food sector. The large presence of subsidiaries of the British firms in tea plantations leads to this pattern. Special mention should be made about the Lawrie group having large scale international operation. Besides tea, British firms have also perceptible presence in other consumer food items, both in number and in control with Cadbury India, Harrison Malalayalam, Kissan Products, Glaxo India, etc as the major units. In the non-food consumer goods sector, Britain's presence is primarily seen in products like electrical items (fans, bulbs) rubber goods, leather goods, textile and textile related goods, paints and varnishes, records, cigarettes, automobiles etc. Important companies are Gramaphone India, Vazir Sultan, Godfrey Philips, J.L. Morrison, Standard Batteries, etc. The USA's presence in consumer goods sector is next in volume but much less (18 per cent) than that of the UK. But the American firms have more units in the consumer non-food sector, almost five times more, than in the consumer foods sector. Prominent non-food products include electrical goods, domestic appliances, electronic items, personal computers and softwares, rubber goods and cosmetics and toiletries. Ponds India, Colgate Palmolive, Procter and Gamble India, Johnson and Johnson and Pepsi are well-known companies in this group. Even though American firms are very few in the consumer goods sector, they are the giants of the international corporate sector. The next country in this sector in the order of importance is Japan (8 per cent). All its units are in the non-food sector. Internationally well-known firms like Matsushita Electric, Honda Motors or Suzuki Motors have joint ventures in this sector. Sweden has got a discernible presence (8 per cent) in the consumer goods sector, primarily in non-food items such as electronics, reprographic machines etc. Switzerland and Italy account for 3 per cent share in this sector primarily in cosmetics, textile goods and leather products. West German and Dutch firms have equal presence in the consumer goods sector (2 per cent) specialising in electrical items, phonographic equipment, films, rubber goods and textiles. Kodak and Philips are well-known Dutch firms in this group. Although the Bahamas has a nominal presence in terms of number of units (1.5 per cent), it has a giant corporation in this sector—Nestlé India. Similarly, Unilever group (Holland) has got only one subsidiary in this sector, the Hindustan Lever, which is the largest MNC-controlled enterprise in India with a market share of more than 40 per cent. In consumer goods sector, although Switzerland's share in terms of number of units is minimal (3 per cent), in terms of sales and profit Bata India needs mention.

Multinational presence is discernibly high (10–12 per cent) in chemicals and engineering sectors. In chemicals again, the British presence is phenomenal, although American presence is not small with respect to the volume. With respect to profit and sales, there is not much difference and American firms like Union Carbide are among the highest earners of profit. About 33 per cent of the units in chemicals are British. Some of these are old and well-known firms such as ICI, Nocil, Alkali Chemicals. American firms account for 23 per cent of the units with Union Carbide manufacturing chemicals as the primary product and also many other items like electronic items, computer software, metal products, plastic items and marine products. West German firms account for 14 per cent and have some well-known MNCs among them such as Hoechst, Boehringer Knoll, Bayer etc. Switzerland and Italy have almost equal share in chemicals—8 per cent and 6 per cent respectively, (Indian Oxygen is an example from Switzerland) whereas Japan and Sweden have identical share of 4 per cent each. Engineering is the other sector that experiences a formidable presence of MNCs, dominated by British firms. Along with many medium ranking firms, giant organisations such as Simon Carves and Guest Keen Williams operate in this sector. Presence of American and West German firms in engineering sector is also significant (21 per cent and 20 per cent respectively) with a few giant firms, such as Kaiser Corporation (Hindustan Aluminium) Gould Incorporated (Bimetal Bearing), Dana Corporation, Otis Elevator from the USA and FAG Kergel Fischer, Robert Bosch, Reing Dichtungs from West Germany. Beside these three countries, Sweden follows with 7 per cent share. Next comes the machinery items where the multinationals' presence is moderately high (8-10 per cent). Britain has the largest share of units (37 per cent) with some old companies operating such as, Duphar Interfarm, Tractors India, Greston and Grover, Holman Climax, Mather and Platt, Warren Tea etc. West German firms have the next highest presence in machinery after the British and some of them are very big ones, e.g., Goetze AE, Alfred Schulte, Volkmann GmbH, Reiners Verwaltungs, Gedore Werkzeng Fabrik, etc. American firms share 16 per cent of the total machinery units. Mentionable among them are Chrysler Corporation, Caterpillar Inc. etc. Besides these three, Switzerland has a control over 9 per cent of machinery units.

Presence of multinational corporations is moderate (6-8 per cent) in electrical and pharmaceuticals sectors in terms of number of units. But in terms of profit earned and foreign exchange repatriated, these two are very significant sectors. In the electrical sector, Britain's share is 29 per cent, with General Electric, English Electric Corporation and Blackwood Hodge as the important ones. With 21 per cent share in the electrical units, the USA has Chicago Pneumatics Vicers systems, Champion Spark Plug as major companies. Japan's presence is also quite significant in this sector, more than that of West Germany. Nearly 15 per cent of the total MNC controlled electrical units are Japanese controlled by giant firms like Matsushita Electric, Nippon Denro, Sumitomo Corporation, Hitachi Limited, Toshiba Corporation and Yokogawa Electric. Besides consumer goods, electrical equipment is another sector (in which again many Japanese items are consumer oriented) where inroad of Japanese corporations has been significant since the eighties. West Germany accounts for 13 per cent of the electrical units with some well-known multinationals operating such as W. Gunther, Algomeine electricals and, especially, Siemens which has electrical equipment as one of its products. In the pharmaceutical sector, although Britain has the largest share of the units (30 per cent), in terms of sales and profit, West German and American presence is equally significant. American and West German firms account for 29 per cent and 15 per cent of the foreign controlled pharmaceutical units in the country. Among British corporations, significant are Glaxo India, Rhone Poulenc (May and Baker), Organon etc. American and West German giants in this sector are Pfizer, Procter and Gamble, Parke Davis, Abbott Lab. and Hoechst, Bayer BASF, E. Merck, German Remedies etc.

Swiss firms also account for 10 per cent of the pharmaceutical units owned or controlled by MNCs. Important firms are Hindustan Ciba-Geigy, Roche Pharma, Sandoz India.

The next group with low-medium presence of multinational corporations (6 per cent) consists of automobile and petrochemicals sectors. In automobile, British share is again the highest (33 percent) followed by Japan (25 per cent). The well-known corporations controlled by the UK are Ashok Leyland, Rane Brake, etc. There are some in the medium ranking group. But in case of Japan, almost all are international automobile giants like Honda Motors, Suzuki Motors, Yamaha Motors, Toyota Motors, Nissan Motors, etc. In automobile, the presence of the USA and West Germany are 19 per cent and 14 per cent respectively.

In the remaining sectors, the presence of multinational corporations in terms of number of units is low to very low. In rubber, metal products, textile, electronics and iron and steel, the percentage of units owned or controlled by MNCs is quite low (between 2 and 4 per cent). But some of these sectors like electronics, rubber and textile are highly profit-generating sector of the Indian industry. In rubber, the UK and the USA together share 87 per cent of the total units. Goodyear Tyre, Firestone Tyre are the significant names. In textile again, British-owned or controlled companies account for 39 per cent. American firms are not significant in this sector. Instead, West German and Swiss firms account for 17 per cent of the units respectively. Sreeram Needle Bearings, Sussen Textile Bearings having joint venture with West Germany and Modi Carpet and Nirlon Fibres having tie-up with Switzerland are important. In metal products, Britain controls 41 per cent units while Switzerland, Sweden and Italy control 12 per cent each. Presence of the American and West German firms in this sector is almost nil. In iron and steel, British and West German presence is dominant. Many British firms have been operating in this sector since pre-Independence days, having close association with mining operations. For example British Steel Piling and Ennore Foundries. West German association with iron and steel and machineries sectors of India is well known. Nearly 18 per cent of the units have German origin. In Tata Engineering and Locomotive Corporation of Jamshedpur, Daimler Benz of West Germany has 12 per cent equity participation. Similarly, in Holtech Engineering of Ahmedabad, Deutsche Babcock has 31 per cent equity share. Japanese interest in iron and steel also needs mentioning. These firms are small in terms of number of units (9 per cent), but significant in terms of operation. In Marmagao the main iron ore operation is done by Japanese firms. In electronics sector American presence is discernible (35 per cent) enjoying ownership of the only branch in India—the Apple Industries Limited. Besides, Digital Equipments, Modi Xerox are important American joint ventures. Nearly 25 per cent of the electronic units are owned or controlled by British firms while Swedish corporations account for 12 per cent.

Presence of multinational corporations is very low (less than 2 per cent) in terms of number of units in non-metal products, agricultural

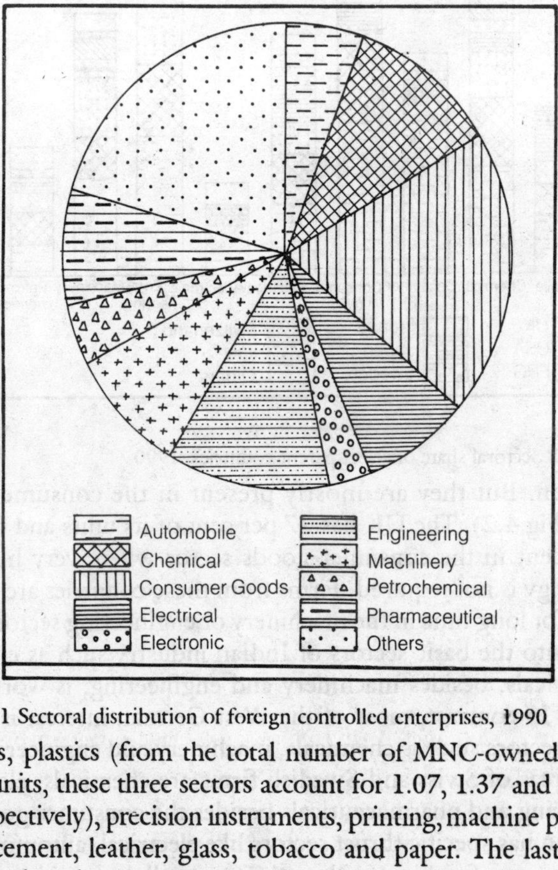

Fig. 4.1 Sectoral distribution of foreign controlled enterprises, 1990

products, plastics (from the total number of MNC-owned or controlled units, these three sectors account for 1.07, 1.37 and 1.68 per cent respectively), precision instruments, printing, machine products, wood, cement, leather, glass, tobacco and paper. The last six sectors have less than one per cent share in each (Fig 4.1).

The UK and the USA are found to have units in almost all the major and minor industrial sectors in India as branches, subsidiaries or joint ventures with both majority and minority equity par-

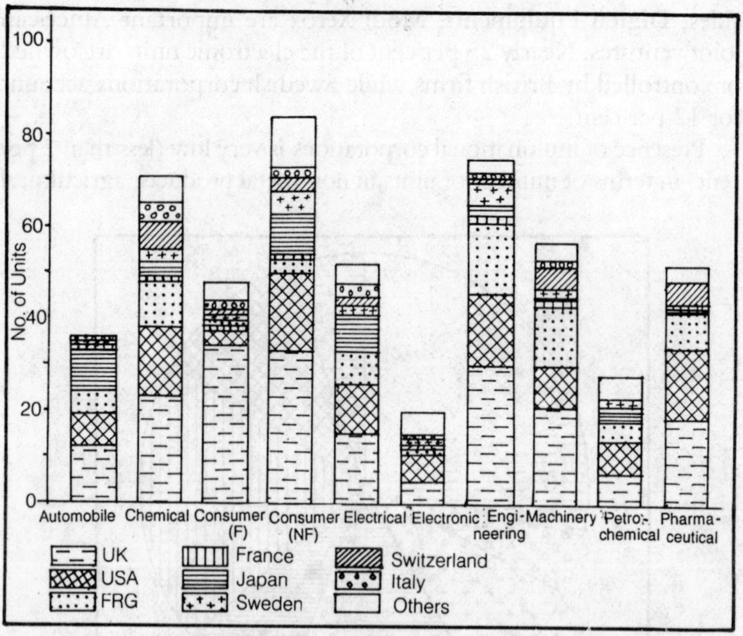

Fig. 4.2 Sectoral share of select parent countries, 1990

ticipation. But they are mostly present in the consumer goods sector (Fig 4.2). The UK has 27 per cent of its units and the USA 17 per cent in the consumer goods sector where very high level technology is not required. Firms from these countries are also operating for long time in the machinery or engineering sectors. Their inroad into the basic sectors of Indian industry such as chemicals or electricals, besides machinery and engineering, is worth mentioning. In contrast, most of the West German interest is only in the key sectors such as chemicals, machinery and engineering. The thrust areas of Swiss and Swedish firms are chemicals, electricals, engineering and pharmaceuticals besides the consumer goods sector. Japan has specific thrust sectors like electrical, automobile and consumer non-food items, though Japan collaborates in engineering, machinery, iron and steel or petrochemicals in a small way (Fig. 4.3.).

The range of diversification of products of these multinational corporations is another aspect that needs special mention. The

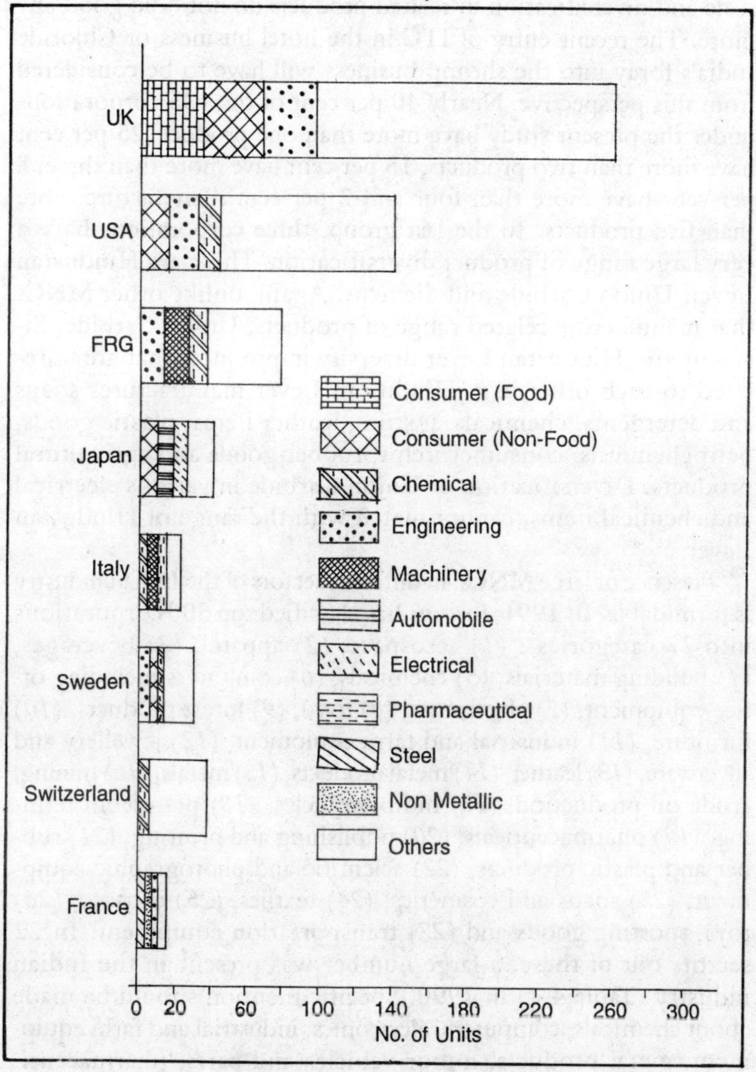

Fig. 4.3 Thrust areas of investment of select parent countries, 1990

moment they have found an area that could be more rewarding, MNCs have directed their investment there, often with considerable support from the Indian government. For this, the large MNCs have not remained confined to one industry (Goyal, 1980). Hence, the traditional rules of industrial geography regarding economy of scale and diversification in related products do not hold good any more. The recent entry of ITC in the hotel business or Chloride India's foray into the shrimp business will have to be considered from this perspective. Nearly 40 per cent of the 435 corporations under the present study have more than one product, 25 per cent have more than two products, 15 per cent have more than three, 8 per cent have more than four and 2 per cent manufacture more than five products. In the last group, three corporations have a very large range of product diversification. These are Hindustan Lever, Union Carbide and Siemens. Again, unlike other MNCs that manufacture related range of products, Union Carbide, Siemens and Hindustan Lever diversify in products that are unrelated to each other, e.g. Hindustan Lever manufactures soaps and detergents, chemicals, textiles, leather items, plastic goods, petrochemicals, consumer items, rubber goods and agricultural products. Diversification of Union Carbide in various electrical and chemical items, cannot match with the range of Hindustan Lever.

Presence of large MNCs, in different sectors of the Indian industry is formidable. In 1991, *Fortune* has classified top 500 corporations into 27 categories : (*1*) aerospace, (*2*) apparel, (*3*) beverages, (*4*) building materials, (*5*) chemicals, (*6*) computers including office equipment, (*7*) electronics, (*8*) food, (*9*) forest products, (*10*) furniture, (*11*) industrial and farm equipment, (*12*) jewellery and silverware, (*13*) leather, (*14*) metal products, (*15*) metals, (*16*) mining, crude oil production, (*17*) motor vehicles, (*18*) petroleum refining, (*19*) pharmaceuticals, (*20*) publishing and printing, (*21*) rubber and plastic products, (*22*) scientific and photographic equipment, (*23*) soaps and cosmetics, (*24*) textiles, (*25*) tobacco, (*26*) toys, sporting goods and (*27*) transportation equipment. In 22 sectors out of these, a large number was present in the Indian industry (Table 4.4) in 1990. Specific mention should be made about chemicals, computers, electronics, industrial and farm equipment, metal products, motor vehicles and parts, pharmaceuticals, scientific and photographic equipment, soaps and cosmetics and finally transportation equipment. On an average 40 per cent of the world's biggest corporations have entered the above industrial sectors in India.

Table 4.4 *Presence of the largest MNCs in different sectors in Indian Industry (1990)*

	Sectors	Total number of the biggest corporations in sectors	No. of corporations operating in India
1	Apparel	02	01
2	Beverage	16	02
3	Building material	18	01
4	Chemicals	43	21
5	Computers	15	06
6	Electronics	45	17
7	Food	46	05
8	Forest products	26	01
9	Industrial & farm equipment	28	10
10	Metal product	18	07
11	Metals	41	04
12	Mining	14	01
13	Motor vehicles and parts	40	18
14	Petroleum Refining	54	06
15	Pharmaceuticals	19	11
16	Publishing/printing	13	03
17	Rubber & plastic products	10	01
18	Scientific & photographic equipments	07	04
19	Soaps, cosmetics	08	03
20	Tobacco	07	02
21	Toys, sporting goods	01	01
22	Transportation equipment	03	01

Source : *Fortune*, No.15, 1991, pp 92-105.

4.2 Spatial Organisation and Levels of Activities :

The locational pattern of multinational corporations exhibits a relentless drive to expand, to develop forces of production and to rearrange the social structure of accumulation. Regardless of the initial distribution of factor supplies, the MNCs attempt to alter the basis of industrial space-economy in various directions. Each crisis is overcome by producing a new breed of corporation in terms of scale or organisation or range and degree of diversification of products. Old products, obsolete processes or uncompetitive plants disappear with their entire lot of labour and regional liabilities.

Production organisation and distributional pattern of industries and their reorganisation thus can be seen as structuring of industrial space (Massey and Megan, 1978). It varies by industry, depending on the respective conditions of individual types, but simultaneously also reflects an aggregate dynamics. Massey and Megan indicate that industrywide and worldwide dynamics are antecedent of factor-supply differentials operating in various regions that may finally lead to locational changes. However, firms do not locate simply due to factor-supply conditions, they require both cause and capability for orienting a spatial organisation and producing a new set of factor-supply conditions (Estall and Buchanan, 1961). Orientation and reorientation of locational pattern of industries may also occur with or without restructuring. Owing to everpresent drive for competitive advantage, restructuring in such case becomes redundant (Walker and Storper, 1981).

Traditional studies of industrial distribution and geographical concentration of industries have focused on specific factors for specific industries or groups of industries. Wheat (1973) stresses on the pull of markets and climate. Fuchs (1962) stresses on labour differentials and natural resources, whereas North (1955) brings out the importance of only natural resources. Perloff *et al.* (1960) argue on behalf of the economies of scale and agglomeration effects while Hamer (1973) directs our attention towards the advantages of reduced land cost enjoyed in smaller urban centres. Regarding these traditional factors, it has been repeatedly argued that corporate locations do not follow rules of traditional practices. For example, natural resources are no longer major factors, due to efficient processing, availability of substitutes and expansion of assembly-type production system. Similarly, the market factor loses its importance owing to intraindustry and inter-industry, inter-plant linkages and transactions. Market causality also gets undermined with the creation of markets by collective actions of capitalists. Nonetheless, agglomeration theory and economies of scale make a case for industrial concentration in larger urban centres. Shared use of infrastructure, immigration of labour, access to innovation and information add strength to this argument. However, with improvement in transport and communication, the case of agglomeration does not hold its former position at least for large corporations. Walker and Storper (1981) strongly argue that in case of multinational corporate locations, rule of profits, dynamics of accumulation and availability of cheap labour (labour factor) play crucial roles.

Locational theories of foreign direct investment primarily highlight three basic types of situations : (*i*) ownership-specific advantages, (*ii*) locational advantages and (*iii*) the eclectic hypothesis. In the first case, multinational corporations establish subsidiaries in a foreign country due to combined advantages of technology, product differentiation and entrepreneurial and managerial capacity (Hymer, 1976; Kindleberger, 1969). Locational advantages highlight the differential existing between the parent and the host country in terms of economic and political environments, price structure, productivity of inputs and large market. Relief in tariff and tax regulations offered by host governments acts as investment incentives. The eclectic hypothesis formulated mainly by Dunning (1981) attempts a synthesis of the above two and argues that MNCs can internalise both ownership and location-specific advantages through investing abroad. Knickerbocker's (1973) theory of oligopolistic reaction argues that larger firms in the process of competing with each other would tend to create a cluster of similar production items, while Vernon's (1966) product cycle theory highlights the decision of a firm to relocate its production plant in a foreign country at a specific sequence of product development.

The spatial organisation of the MNCs can be seen as a process of centralising and perfecting the process of capital accumulation following the national specificity and regional specialisations. To analyse the given spatial pattern, a useful starting point is Chandler and Redlich's (1961) scheme of corporate structure discussed in Chapter 2. Level III is the lowest level which is concerned with the day to day operation of the enterprises, production and manufacturing, etc. Level II is the corporate headquarters in the host country that is responsible for the entire operation in the host country. In many corporations, Level II operations are considerably autonomous and allowed to enjoy sufficient decision-making power. MNCs depend on these Level II managers to a large extent in their attempt to integrate with host countries. Level I is the top management, the area of goal determination and planning. This level sets the framework according to which the lower levels operate. Geographically, it is completely separate from the other three levels and invariably located in the parent country from where it plans strategy rather than tactics (Hymer, 1971).

Applying this scheme, the highest offices of the multinational corporations with Level I activity would be found located in large cities of the parent countries. The largest cities in the host countries would be entrusted with Level II activities. Level III activities would be seen to be geographically more mobile, at times, located at interior centres or small towns or big village settlements of the host countries. With facilities of spatial expansion and cheap labour, the location decisions about Level III would still vary with differentials in infrastructure offered by respective regional governments of host countries. Since business will be concentrated in core cities, geographic specialisation would come to reflect the hierarchy of corporate decision-making and the occupational distribution of labour would depend on its functional placement in the international hierarchical economic system (Banerjee-Guha, 1990). The structure of income and consumption would also tend to parallel the structure of status and authority (Hymer, 1971) that finally would create a sharp contrast between the growth rates of core and peripheral cities of host countries, leading to uneven spatial development.

The division of operation of the MNCs is thus not merely functional or occupational but geographical. The occupational aspect gets expressed in the decentralisation of divisions, each concerned with one product line and tied up with respective head offices. In some cases, even one unit of a Level III plant may have more than one product line and tied up with single Level III and Level II offices. The entire network of operation is held together by a highly efficient locational dynamics. By centralising control on the already distorted and hierarchically organised economic space of the Third World host countries, the MNCs effectively strengthen the core-periphery hiatus, disparity in spatial development and add to the primacy of urban systems (Banerjee-Guha, 1990).

It must be mentioned that the spatial distribution of industrial firms in the organised sector in India is not even (Table 4.5). To understand the actual degree of unevenness, a disaggregation of the national space into regional space is necessary. In the early sixties, western and southern regions together shared 61 per cent of the total industries of the country which rose to 62 per cent in the early seventies. In contrast, northern and eastern regions accounted for 15 per cent and 24 per cent in early sixties which became 18 per cent and 20 per cent respectively in the early seventies. Within the regions in 1973 Maharashtra cornered 45 per cent share of the western region and 14 per cent of the total Indian industries. Gujarat shared 9 per cent of the total industries, Andhra 12 per cent, Karnataka 5 per cent, Tamil Nadu 8 per cent, West Bengal 7 per cent and Bihar 9 per cent. Within the eastern region, West Bengal and Bihar accounted for 80 per cent of the regional industries while Orissa and

Table 4.5 *Distribution of industrial firms in organised sector*
% share of States

	1961	1973	1986
States : SOUTHERN REGION	30.71	31.01	33.38
Andhra Pradesh	09.95	12.13	09.55
Tamil Nadu	11.23	08.37	08.43
Karnataka	04.60	05.43	08.33
Kerala	04.93	04.62	06.49
Pondichery	0.00	0.46	0.58
WESTERN REGION	30.00	31.10	33.15
Maharashtra	16.58	14.15	13.06
Gujarat	07.67	09.01	09.08
Rajasthan	01.83	02.95	06.52
Madhya Pradesh	03.89	04.84	04.35
Goa	0.00	0.15	0.14
NORTHERN REGION	14.87	17.90	19.12
Delhi	02.16	02.54	03.30
Uttar Pradesh	05.66	05.84	04.50
Punjab	07.00	06.51	06.61
Haryana	0.00	02.20	03.20
Chandigarh	–	0.20	0.25
Himachal Pradesh	0.05	0.31	0.75
Jammu & Kashmir	–	0.30	0.51
EASTERN REGION	24.40	19.96	14.28
West Bengal	08.65	07.44	05.57
Bihar	12.09	09.17	05.96
Orissa	0.99	01.26	0.73
Assam	2.50	01.84	1.26
Meghalaya	0.00	0.02	0.04
Manipur	0.07	0.15	0.11
Mizoram	0.00	0.00	0.14
Nagaland	0.00	0.00	0.00
Tripura	0.10	0.08	0.47
UNION TERRITORIES	0.02	0.03	0.07
Dadra & Nagar Haveli	0.00	0.00	0.03
Diu & Daman	0.00	0.00	0.02
Lakshadweep	0.00	0.00	0.00
Andaman & Nicobar	0.02	0.03	0.02

Source : CMIE, Bombay

the entire north-east had only 20 per cent. The eighties saw a strengthening of the previous pattern. Share of both southern and western regions increased with 33 per cent share to each. Maharashtra now accounted for 39 per cent of the total regional industries, less than 6 per cent from that of 1973, while in the southern region, the share of Karnataka increased considerably. There was even a 3 per cent rise from its share in nation's total. Percentage share of the northern region rose from 17.9 per cent in 1973 to 19.12 per cent in 1986. The only region which experienced a decline was the eastern region which now had a reduction of 6 per cent from the level of its national share of 1973. West Bengal and Bihar continued to corner 80 per cent of the eastern region's industries (Fig. 4.4).

It needs to be noted here that the economic history of eastern

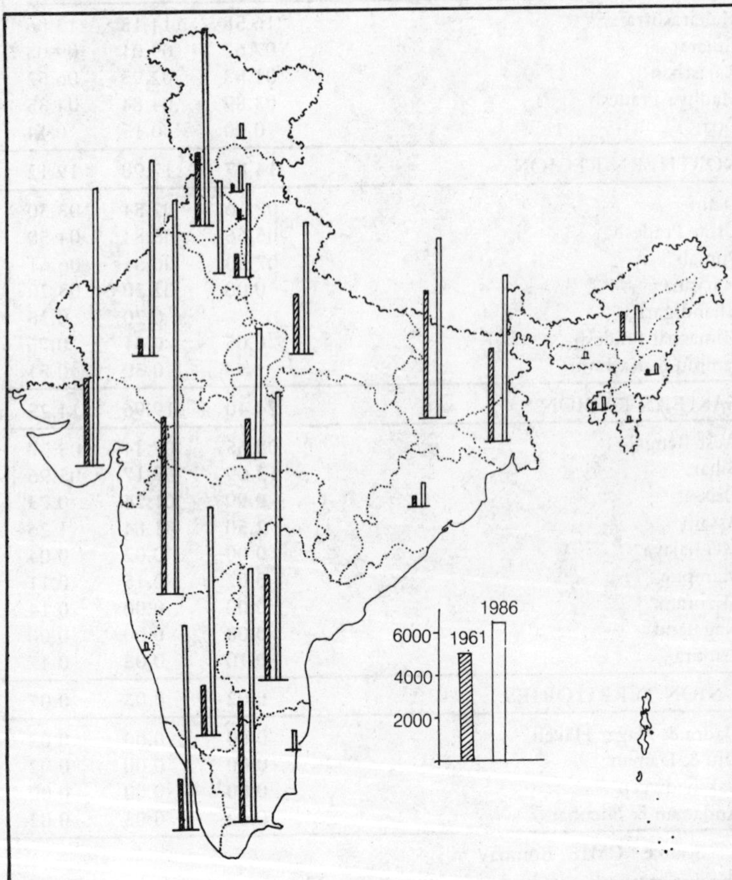

Fig. 4.4 Statewise distribution of registered factories in India

India had a different path since the days of the British. Conquered first among the regions by the East India Company, this region was very fertile, had suitable physiographical and climatic environment for tea and indigo plantations and also had a very rich deposits of iron ore and coal. In contrast, the western region was almost inaccessible till the coming of the railways in the mid-nineteenth century, had no possibility of raising tea or other plantations and also was the region where the British were resisted the longest, by the Marathas. To defeat the latter, the British needed the Parsis as collaborators and at times financiers too. Further, indigenous traders of the west also took advantage of the rising opium trade between India and China since the late eighteenth century. In the absence of any British monopoly in the region, they monopolised in the trade with opium grown in Malwa plateau and other locations of western and central India. It became a major source of capital accumulation for them that helped in increasing indigenous investment in the region (Munsi, 1993) in various sectors including real estates in Bombay. Thus competition faced by indigenous traders from the British in entering industry was less in the west than it was in the east (Bagchi, 1972) where by the mid-nineteenth century Bengali indigenous traders with intentions to enter industry were almost eliminated by the British. A number of established Bengali firms being defrauded by British partners retreated from trade and commerce (Nafziger, 1978). However, a large section of the Bengali urban professional class subscribed to western values and became an integral part of the western culture. Marwaris, the other trading community operating in eastern India who originally hailed from Rajasthan were mercantile in spirit (Banerjee and Ghosh, 1988) (they did not establish any major industry before World War I), protectionist in attitude towards foreign capital (Bagchi, 1972) and alienated from the population of eastern region. While they believed in horizontal expansion, Parsi and Gujarathi capitalists believed in vertical growth which benefited the western region through continuous accumulation of capital. Growth of an industrial bourgeoisie, however collaborative they were with the British, was therefore, evident in the west who could articulate the aspirations of the region, being also organically integrated with it. The basis thus was laid in the west for the rise of a territorially-based alliance between various factions of capital (Harvey, 1982). The nature of manufacturing industries thus conformed a regional pattern. Eastern region only had the plantations while market-oriented food and other consumer goods industries were located in the west. With planned development in the post-Independence era, the western region with some prior industrial growth and a more assertive regional bourgeoisie was able to draw further investments, both public and private, and contributed towards concentrated capital accumulation. The Marwari capitalists who replaced the British in the eastern region could not be the necessary interlocuters of regional development. In national planning years, while population pressure due to large scale refugee influx, shrinking of employment, obsolescence of industrial product mix along with lack of infrastructural facilities worked towards an industrial decline of the eastern region, in the west various factions of capital and the local state worked towards the accumulation of capital and social reproduction of labour, creating a rising effective demand for wage goods in local markets. Contrasting to this investment-conducive environment of the western region was also the distinct left-oriented political awareness of the east. The resultant flight of capital and manufacturing from the eastern to western and southern regions since the late sixties is analogous with the declining status of employment in those states of the US which showed a greater incidence of class struggle (Peet, 1983).

In West Bengal, since 1966-67 the share of the primary sector to the state domestic product has increased while that of the secondary sector has declined. In contrast, the share of primary sector in Gujarat, which was initially the same as that in West Bengal, slowly lost weight in the state's economy and the secondary sector and sector comprising transport, communication and trade gathered momentum since sixties. Overwhelming dominance of primary sector remained almost undisturbed in the eastern states in general despite a wave of nationwide planning for industrialisation (Banerjee and Ghosh, 1988). Also, the licensing authority discouraged investment in the eastern region and approved investments constituting only a small part of the investments actually applied for (Table 4.6). Bangalore, Trivandrum, Coimbatore, Hyderabad emerged as alternate locations along with Madras in the south. Since the sixties, in the eastern region, the growth rate in high voltage power consumption also came down compared to the western and southern states. With a trend in industrial restructuring—featuring an increase in demand for intermediate, producer and capital goods—the locational dynamics of industries in the country further underwent a change. Given a limited home market, a cluster of high potential industries for a considerable period of time attracted future investments. During the sixties and seventies, big industrial houses dominated by Marwaris and subsidiaries of MNCs did not invest in industries such as jute, cotton textile, tea manufacturing, chemicals and electrical engineering in the eastern region. The distribution of funds under control subsidy schemes, initiated to help balanced regional development was also lopsided, with heavy investments (45 per cent) going in the four developed states of Maharashtra, Gujarat, Tamil Nadu and Karnataka and very little in

Table 4.6 *Total licencees applied and approved for product-groups and in selected states during 1959-66*

State / Industry	Assam	Bihar	Orissa	West Bengal	Maharashtra	Gujarat	Tamil Nadu
Beverage industries							
Applied	–	7	–	–	26	4	8
Approved	–	4	–	–	14	2	3
Manufacture of rubber products							
Applied	2	–	2	68	69	10	21
Approved	0	–	0	36	41	7	15
Manufacture of chemicals and chemical products							
Applied	22	43	20	284	1033	290	139
Approved	12	11	9	127	525	125	72
Manufacture of machinery (except electrical machinery)							
Applied	3	38	9	233	428	99	111
Approved	3	17	8	153	279	60	78
Manufacture of electrical machinery, apparatus, etc.							
Applied	–	14	7	204	300	60	66
Approved	–	7	3	113	196	31	46
Manufacture of transport equipment							
Applied	94	11	5	127	90	34	41
Approved	2	10	4	61	45	12	21

Source : Compiled from the Industrial Planning and Licensing Policy, Vol. 2, part 3, statement IX, Planning Commission, GOI, 1967. As cited in Banerjee and Ghosh, 1988.

Note :The products are grouped according to the ASI classification.

the officially-declared backward states of Assam, Bihar, Orissa and Jammu and Kashmir. Only Andhra Pradesh and Rajasthan received a sizeable share among the backward states (Banerjee and Ghosh, 1988). Cornering of funds by powerful lobbies from the west and the south reflects the hidden traits of regionalism that underlies any territorially based alliance between various factions of capital (Harvey, 1982). This trait actually becomes an essential part of such alliances in order to defend class interests and offset class antagonisms. However, in many cases, the above investments or even concessions finance that went to western and southern zones actually went to areas close to existing industrial centres, belying the purpose of dispersal.

With the above political-economic backdrop, we will analyse the spatial pattern of Level II and Level III activities of multinational corporations in India in 1990. The analysis includes all 435 MNCs. No distinction has been made on the basis of size.

All 435 corporations have their Level II units in India. The western region distinctly emerges as the concentration centre. Nearly 47.36 per cent of the total MNC Level II offices, i.e., 206 out of 435 are located in the west. About 22.53 per cent of the Level II offices are located in the eastern region which are distinctly dominated by British corporations (Table 4.7). A large number of plantation offices from Assam and the North Bengal are included in this group. Southern and northern regions account for almost equal share of 15.63 per cent and 14.48 per cent respectively of the Level II offices of the MNCs (Fig. 4.5) in India.

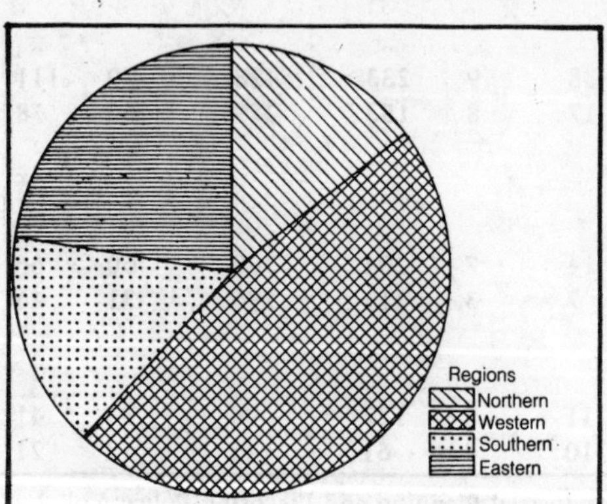

Fig. 4.5 Regional distribution of Level II offices of MNCs in India

Mention has been made that Hindustan Lever and Britannia have been treated as two separate entities because of the near equal equity holding of more than one parent country. Hindustan Lever has its Level II office in the western region while Britannia in the southern region. Besides these two, 18 countries out of 24 show preference for western region. Although British Level II offices have a larger share in the east (40.37 per cent) for reasons explained earlier, the western region accounts for a similar share (36.02 per cent). If the tea gardens are taken out, western region stands out as the preferred region of the British too. Countries that have exceptionally large percentage of their Level II offices in the western region are the USA (56 per cent), West Germany (60 per cent), Switzerland (52 per cent), Sweden (60 per cent), Italy (50 per cent), France (63 per cent), Canada (50 per cent), Belgium (66.66 per cent) and Japan (37.04 per cent). Corporations from Austria, Denmark, Hungary, Mexico and Turkey (one from each) have their Level II offices in the western region. Northern region is preferred by again Bahama Islands (Nestlé, 50 per cent), Bulgaria (100 per cent) and Panama (100 per cent). Japan has nearly equal number of Level II offices in

Table 4.7 *Regional locations of levels of activities*

Level II

Country	Total	North	West	South	East
Australia	3	1	1	1	0
Austria	1	0	1	0	0
Bahama Islands	2	1	1	0	0
Belgium	3	1	2	0	0
Brazil	2	0	1	0	1
Bulgaria	1	1	0	0	0
Canada	2	0	1	0	1
Denmark	1	0	1	0	0
Finland	1	0	0	0	1
France	8	1	5	0	2
Gulf	1	1	0	0	0
Holland	5	1	1	2	1
Hungary	1	0	1	0	0
Italy	16	4	9	3	0
Japan	27	9	10	6	2
Mexico	1	0	1	0	0
Panama	1	1	0	0	0
Singapore	1	1	0	0	0
Sweden	16	1	10	4	1
Switzerland	25	2	13	6	4
Turkey	1	0	1	0	0
UK	161	8	58	30	65
USA	101	21	58	11	11
W. Germany	50	9	30	4	7
UK/Holland	+3	0	1	0	2
UK/USA/Singapore/France	1	0	0	1	0
Total	435	63	206	68	98

northern and western regions. The percentage share of the northern region is 33.33 per cent. Dutch MNCs show preference for southern region with 50 per cent of their Level II offices located there while the eastern region is preferred by Canada (50 per cent), Finland (100 per cent) and the UK (39.62 per cent). The locational behaviour of the British corporations in selecting eastern and western regions as near equal choices is similar to that of the Japanese corporations' preference for west and north. The only difference is that all the Japanese corporations are post seventy entrants and, therefore, are guided by the contemporary locational dynamics while the UK corporations' concentration pattern in the east is largely a vestige of the colonial past when British direct investment was directed to plantations and extraction activities in a big way. It is only the Dutch corporations that also locate 50 per cent of their Level II offices in the southern region.

From the regions' point of view, in the western region the major countries are Britain and the USA (28 per cent each) followed by West Germany (15 per cent).

Japan, Italy and Sweden share 14 per cent of the total Level II offices each with Swtizerland and France having a significant presence. USA dominates in the northern region with a control over 33 per cent of the total Level II offices. West Germany and Japan control 14 per cent while Britain accounts for 13 per cent. In south, the most dominating presence is of Britain's having 44 per cent of the Level II offices followed by the USA (16.18 per cent). Switzerland and Japan are the countries next in importance with 9 per cent of the offices. In the eastern region, British-controlled Level II offices are more in number (68 per cent). USA-controlled ones, though next in the rank, are few (11-22 per cent). Besides West Germany (7 per cent) and Switzerland (4 per cent) no other country has a notable presence in the eastern region with their Level II offices (Fig 4.6)

The overall spatial distribution pattern of the Level II activities of the MNCs having considerable concentration in the western region of India indicates the interplay of a number of factors towards capital accumulation (Fig. 4.7). Adding to this are the industrial policies of the respective regional governments that promote local interest and act towards warding off place-specific devaluation. The pattern is analogous with the findings of corporate behaviour researches in Human Geography on headquarters' location of large industrial organisations in home and abroad. For example, Westway (1974) and Evans (1973) examined the concentration pattern of large British companies while Pred (1974) elaborated on the extreme

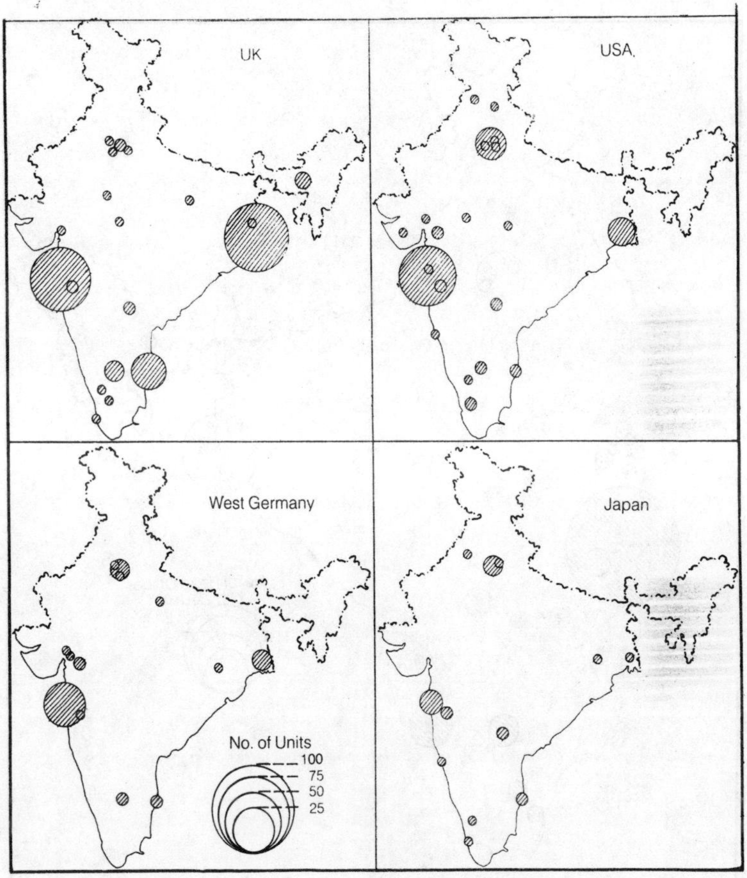

Fig. 4.6 Spatial distribution of MNC head offices of select countries, 1990

concentration pattern of large American corporations in the north-eastern seaboard area. In a study of spatial distribution of the American manufacturing activity in Britain, Dicken and Lloyd (1976) identified extreme concentration in areas of quick return irrespective of the need for balanced growth. Employment in foreign-controlled manufacturing companies in Britain was uneven and concentrated in the south-east and north-west even in the sixties. In the United States, argued Ohullachain (1985), foreign investments since the eighties started favouring sunbelt and Pacific locations compared to the earlier concentration areas of the industrial heartland of the north-east. Large steel mills, such as Bethleheim Steel, closed down establishments in indus-

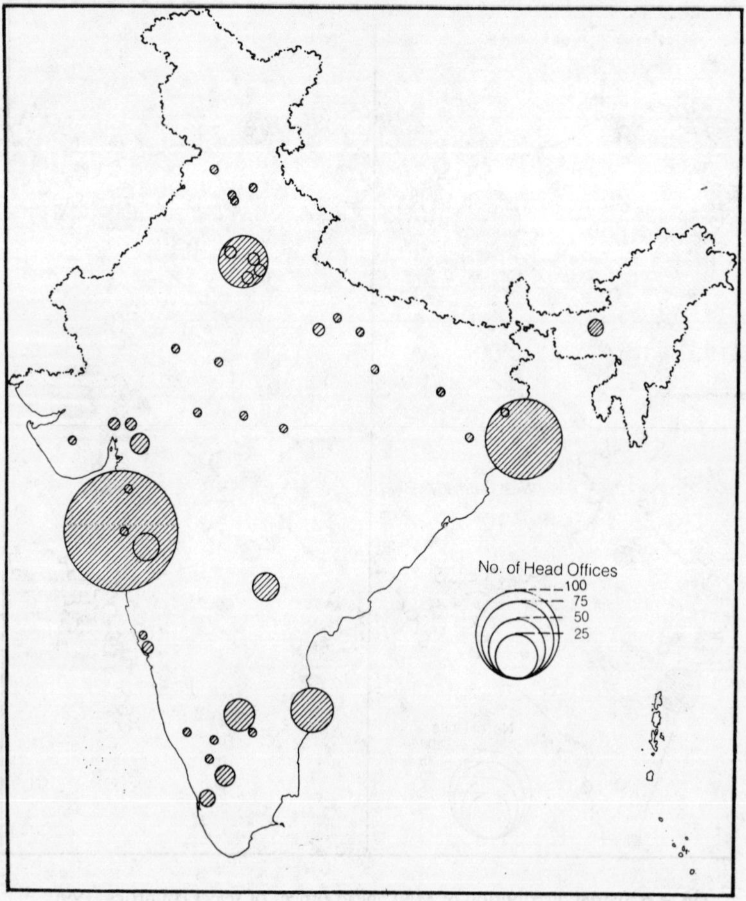

Fig. 4.7 Spatial distribution of head office locations of MNCs in India

trial headquarters like Pittsburg or Pennsylvania and moved out. It is the wage-rate differentials in these cases which determined the direction and destination of capital flows than the extant pattern of labour skills. On the other hand, laws and rules also acted as factors influencing Japanese firms to invest more in the west coast where regional governments acted as allies (Chang, 1989). In Australia, Taylor and Thrift (1980) found a high degree of spatial concentration of foreign corporations, even higher than that in Europe or the USA. They held the foreign-led corporate sector responsible for the intensified disparity between the core and the peripheral companies in Australia. In the Third

Table 4.8 *Regional locations of levels of activities*

Level III

Country	Total	North	West	South	East
Australia	5	1	2	2	–
Austria	2	–	2	–	–
Bahama Islands	9	4	1	4	–
Belgium	2	–	2	–	–
Brazil	1	–	1	–	–
Bulgaria	1	1	–	–	–
Canada	11	1	4	4	2
Denmark	1	–	1	–	–
Finland	2	–	–	1	1
France	10	1	6	1	2
Gulf	6	2	2	2	–
Holland	5	–	2	1	2
Hungary	–	–	–	–	–
Italy	14	2	11	1	–
Japan	36	11	12	9	4
Mexico	–	–	–	–	–
Panama	–	–	–	–	–
Singapore	–	–	–	–	–
Sweden	37	3	22	8	4
Switzerland	51	9	21	12	9
Turkey	1	–	1	–	–
UK	368	33	119	113	103
USA	166	36	74	40	16
W. Germany	78	6	51	10	11
UK/Holland	44	10	11	15	8
UK/USA/Singapore/France	6	1	3	1	1
Total	856	121	348	224	163

World, naturally MNCs contributed in large measure towards industrial concentration and regional disparity. In Brazil their favoured region is the south-east. Even generous fiscal incentives of other regions cannot pull them out from these favoured locations (Cunningham, 1981). Similarly in Bendel state of Nigeria, Abumare (1978) notices acute concentration of multinational firms in large port locations contrary to the State Government's industrial location policy.

Location decisions at the plant level or Level III activities involve a variety of factors like access to markets and supplies, labour, quality of life, taxes and financing, transportation and the site itself (Schmenner, 1982) that ensures accumulation of capital. Japanese investors in the United States besides the above, even considered the life style needs of Japanese expatriates as deciding locational factors. For example, the Kentucky State in the United States lured

Toyota to open an assembly plant in Georgetown by providing $ 112 million for new roads, employee training programmes, grants and low cost loans and above all 500 acres of free land (Tolchin and Tolchin, 1988) for residential purposes. In India Hindustan Lever was granted liberal loans to set up plants in Maharashtra under medium and small industries heads (Goyal, 1979). In Maharashtra and Karnataka lands have been given at a nominal price to the MNCs to set up industrial plants and related residential complexes. In the port of Kandla, in order to retain the interest of an American corporation, the Gujarat government has given clearance to the corporation to set up independent transhipment facilities.

With such factors in operation, no wonder 41 per cent of the total MNC plants are located in the western region. The second best location is the southern region, although with much less (26.17 per cent) proportion of plants. Eastern region accounts for 19 per cent plants inclusive of tea gardens while the northern region accounts for 14 per cent (Fig. 4.8). It is obvious that without the tea plantations, the eastern region will rank the last (Table 4.8).

Among the major parent countries, West Germany, Sweden and Italy prefer western region the most and locate 65, 66 and 79 per cent of their plants there. No other region has been so distinctly preferred by other countries. UK, USA, Switzerland, Japan and Holland also show a locational bias towards the western region with 32, 45, 40, 33 and 40 per cent of their plants in this region. But their plants are found in other regions too in large number. For example, Britain shows equal preference towards the southern region with 31 per cent of its plants located there. For that matter even northern region gets preference from the USA (22 per cent of its plants are located in the north) and Japan (31 per cent of its plants are located in the north). It is only the eastern region that does not receive any preference from any MNC parent country with respect to location of plants excepting some minor interest from Holland and the UK. These two countries have set up 40 per cent and 28 per cent of their plants there. There are some plants of a few countries located in the east, for example, 14.11 per cent of the West German plants and 10 per cent of the USA plants. Analogy can be drawn with Peet's (1983) analysis, mentioned earlier on the changing geography of manufacturing employment in the USA indicating employment loss in high class struggle states and gain in low class struggle ones.

From the regions point of view, presence of the UK is the most significant in the western region with 34 per cent of the total plants being British controlled followed by the USA (21 per cent) and West Germany (15 per cent). In the northern region, dominating presence is of the USA (39 per cent) and Italy (23 per cent). In the south, British controlled plants are 50 per cent of the total followed by the USA (18 per cent). In the eastern region, only British plants are found to have a significant presence controlling 63 per cent of the total. No other country has a significant presence in the region (Fig. 4.9).

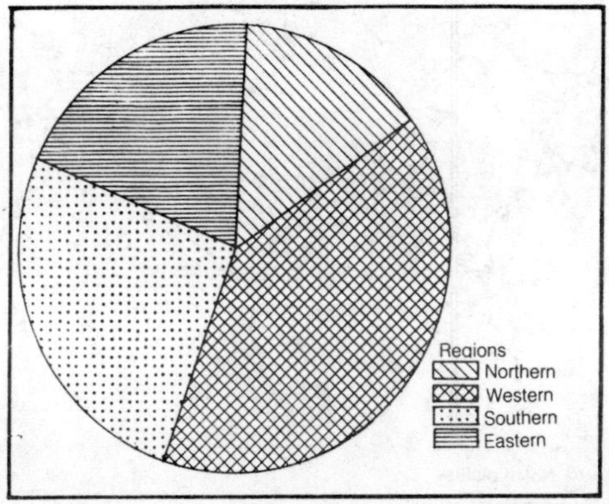

Fig. 4.8 Regional distribution of Level III offices of MNCs in India

Locational arrangement of the various level of activities of multinational corporations is a dynamic phenomenon. Both ownership specific advantages and locational advantages (Dunning, 1977; Dunning and Norman, 1979) are constantly changing. Given the continental scale of the country and the overriding prevalence of economies of scale, industrial firms in general have an uneven distribution in India. It functions as a premise for the multinational corporations for their benefits and contribute towards further industrial concentration. Locational dynamics of MNCs thus unfolds a process of accumulation rather than a static allocation of activities to their best locations. Concentration of Level III activities in the western region reflects its valorised status vis-a-vis capital and labour factors.

This phenomenal geographical concentration also suggests the significance of labour factor heterogeneity in location decision. In the early eighties, Storper and Walker (1981) worked on the het-

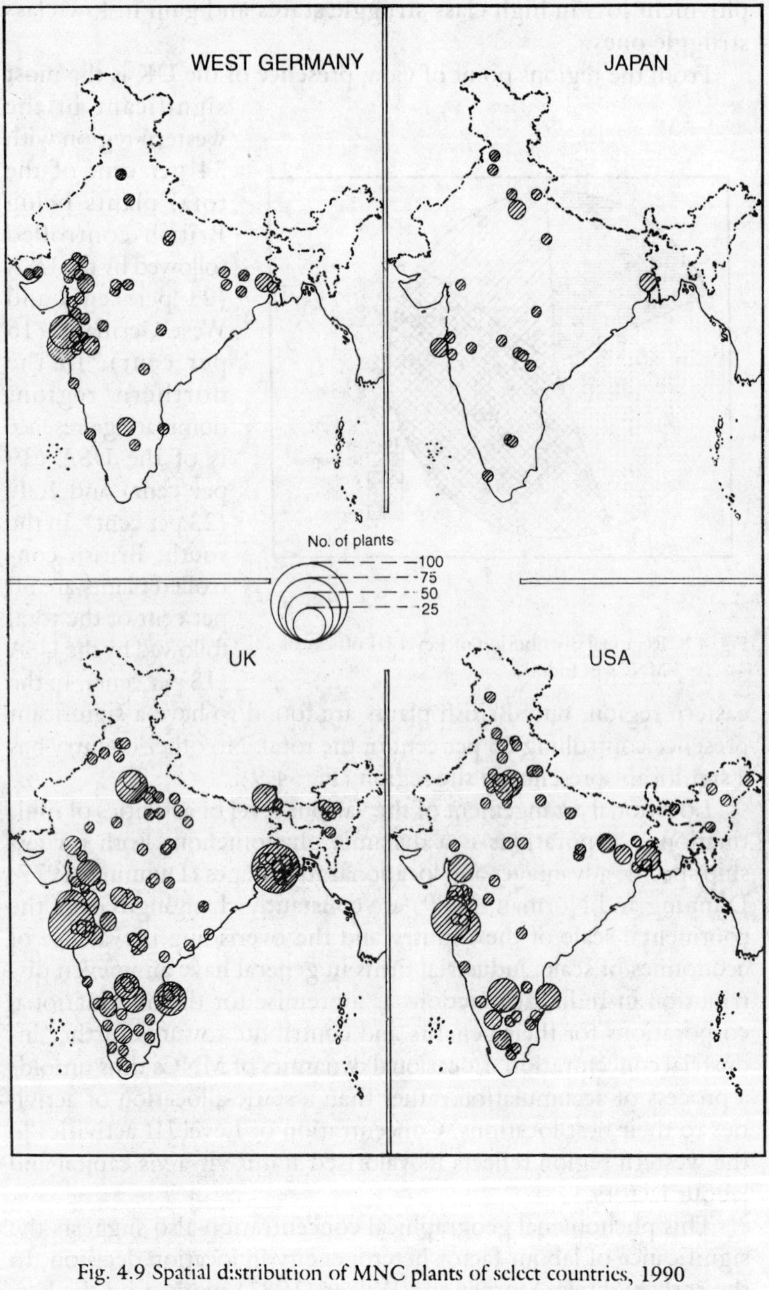

Fig. 4.9 Spatial distribution of MNC plants of select countries, 1990

erogeneity of labour and distinguished several dimensions of variability in them. These are (*i*) conditions of purchase including wage level, work rules, etc.; (*ii*) performance capacity including technical skill, discipline as it affects job performance and creativity; (*iii*) labour control and actual performance or the use of supervision or monitoring to counter workers' resistance, and (*iv*) reproduction of generation of identifiable work characteristics than can persist over a time period. Considering labour as a factor of location and spatial shift of the foreign corporate sector in India, it can be stated that the complex network of heterogeneity of labour has overridden the singular factor of labour-skill and resource. Due to this, eastern region has not been favoured by the foreign corporations even in selective sectors like iron and steel or engineering that have a long tradition of growth in this region due to the proximity of resource and a traditional skill of workers. The political economy of labour (Malecki, 1985) focussing on the latter's heterogeneity brings out some related facts about locational decision of firms with wide ranging operations. Natural resources for these firms do not figure as a major factor owing to more efficient processing opportunities, available substitutes, expansion of assembly type production and availability of material inputs in the form of produced commodities. These plants are footloose in these aspects and enjoy a locational freedom to select primarily on the basis of interindustry linkages and labour heterogeneity. In addition, as foreign firms essentially rank potentials of communication and information diffusion as important additive factors of location, their metropolitan bias is distinct. Also the political situation of the respective states, tariff and non-tariff barriers, tax rates and special investment incentives (Chang, 1989) have worked their ways to help MNCs to locate in western Maharashtra, southern Gujarat and subsequently in southern Karnataka and different areas of Tamil Nadu as well as in and around the National Capital Region. The most favoured region has, however, been the western region since 1971. During the eighties, relative positional changes have occurred, with Bangalore in the southern region evolving as a strong contender, but the ranking of western region with Bombay as the concentration area has continued even in the mid-eighties (Fig 4.10). By far Bombay-Ahmedabad and Bombay-Poona region making an elongated belt in the western coast of Maharashtra and Gujarat are identified as the most preferred investment location for foreign capital for almost all the parent countries with which a parallel can be drawn with the New York Metropolitan area. During the late seventies, the latter was the preferred investment area of the foreign firms in the United States (Bagchi-Sen and Weeler, 1989). Later, in the early eighties, Miami area accounted for greater number of foreign transactions but the former remained the most important location in terms of dollar value of investment. In case of India also, in the eighties a few locations of the southern regions proved to be more attractive for foreign collaborations than even Bombay due to tariff and investment benefits from respective state governments. But the value of investment in foreign controlled sector in terms of rupee remained much higher in the west in and around Bombay. However, dispersal to the south and also to the north became a dominant locational characteristic of this period, especially of the collaborations with West Germany and Japan and partly with France. Excepting in some few cases like Nellore in Andhra or Kurnool in Karnataka, foreign controlled firms did not get located in any minor urban settlements and always have shown extreme bias towards larger cities. In case of the above two exceptions also their proximity to Madras and Bangalore cannot be ruled out as a probable cause. Corporate hierarchy and urban hierarchy, therefore, go hand in hand (Goddard, 1977) and make location an active moment in the overall circulation and accumulation process of capital restructuring space economies and creating 'spatial fix' (Harvey, 1982). Further, the acute concentration of MNCs in Bombay region, independent of any specific industry type especially in the case of the US firms, can be explained by the capital accumulation process (Brown and Burrows, 1977) in more developed regions and the consequent backwash (Murdal, 1957). The capital-intensive technology reduces demand for labour in the developed area on the one hand, but at the same time labour immigration from less developed regions offsets the increasing wage rate, unionisation of labour and thereby the rising labour cost (Banerjee and Ghosh, 1988). The cheap labour reserve hailing from the less developed regions reduces the need to remove plants to these regions on the one hand and increases flexibility of production restructuring by using non-Fordist methods. Essentially, therefore, it becomes a factor for new capital accumulation at the centre while higher rate of return due to advanced technology attracts further centralisation of capital drawing even from interior, less developed areas in the form of savings. In case of Bombay the above mechanisms of 'cumulative causation' have tended to accentuate economic inequalities between western and other regions in general, and within western region, in particular. It also has given rise to a specific territoriality of 'human resource complex' adjusted to capital's requirements (Harvey, 1982). Competitive policy of the regional governments, especially of Maharashtra, to attract foreign capital and promote industrial development belying the goal of balanced development has acted as an additive factor. In June, 1993 Maharasthra Industrial Development Corporation areas have got exempted from the control and permission of Maharashtra Regional and Town Planning Act for buying less than 10 hectares of land for industrial development. Also within a broadly designated industrial zone no permission from the local authority would be henceforth required to change land use from agricultural to industrial (Swamy, 1993).

Penetration of foreign capital into the core sectors of Indian industry and their acute concentration primarily in the western region followed by south and north reveal the basics of the spatial policy of foreign corporate sector. By concentrating organised investment in a small part of the country which is comparatively developed than interior and backward areas, it essentially reiterates the general spatial trend of capital towards accumulation and centralisation. The geographical heartland of the country in this process has become poorer and economically peripheral while the economic heartland got shifted to the geographical periphery in coastal regions—a trend set during the colonial times.The above pattern also brings out the metropolitan bias in the spatial policy of multinational corporations with subsequent distortions in the settlement system aggravating primacy.

4.3. Corporate Hierarchy and Settlement Hierarchy :

Spatial perspectives on industrial organisations developed during the seventies (Hamilton, 1974; Collins and Walker, 1975) even though drew heavily on the literature in organisation theory, business administration and industrial economics, these were pioneer studies indicating the relationship between settlement hierarchy and corporate hierarchy. Latter they opened up a whole range of questions and issues on regional development policies and implications focusing on the alliance between corporate and settlement hierarchy. Notwithstanding the danger of oversimplifying a complex relationship between urban and corporate hierarchy into an isomor-

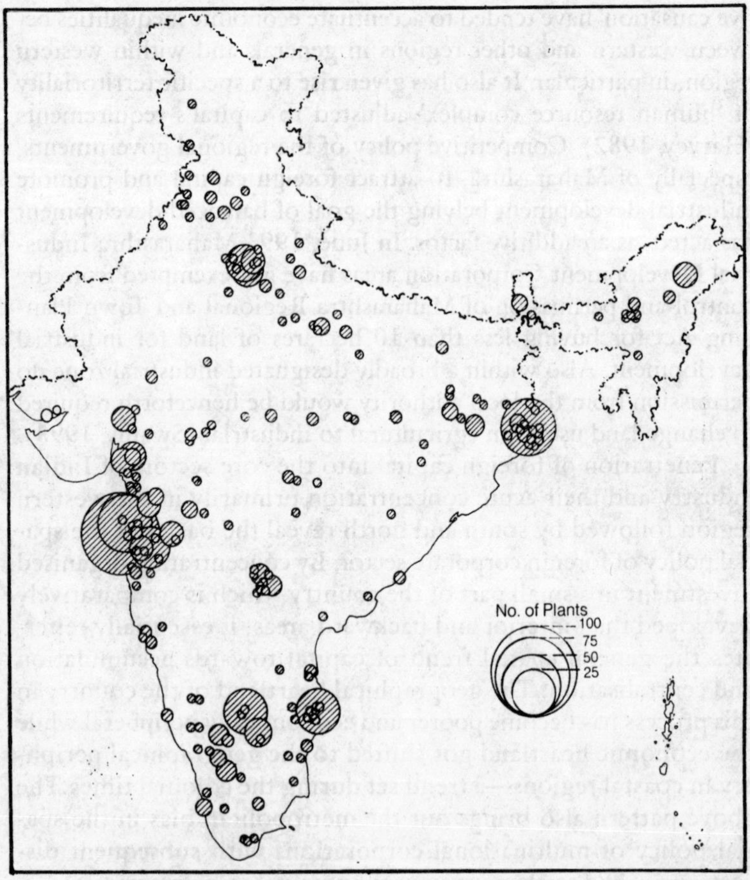

Fig. 4.10 Spatial distribution of MNC plants in India

phic one it can be argued that the processes of corporate growth and change operate through a system of city-focusing labour/market areas. Goddard (1977) offers a wider implication suggesting that the relevant scales for the analysis of the processes and problems of spatial economic development are the city system, corporate system, the local labour market and the nation and not the conventional division of the national territory into homogeneous regions.

The division of multinational corporations' functions between units and settlements is influenced by a large range of factors both external and internal to the corporations. Simplifying it, at one extreme, headquarters will require access to an information rich environment and tend to be located in major metropolitan centres while production activities will be widely dispersed amongst smaller places, especially in the periphery of the national territory (Goddard, 1975). But the complexity of the problem suggests that the organisational strategy decision influenced by such factors do also alter the arrangement of geographical centralisation or decentralisation of economic/industrial activities and growth of a settlement system in a specific manner (Chandler, 1962). Chapman (1979) notices that even in the present age of electronic communications, role of cities as 'the switching points' for the exchange of information has increased in importance. He associates this feature with the sharp rise of quaternary workers in all large urban centres of the world. The resultant dominance regarding innovation and information that the large urban centres enjoy, he feels, will be on the increase and even government policies of job dispersal may be thwarted in the face of this trend as it happened in the Netherlands (Dietvorst and Wever, 1977). These constraints in achieving diffusion also suggest that spatial variations in access to information continue to exercise an important influence upon patterns of economic development (Tornqvist, 1970).

For a long time, supporting evidence on the relationship between corporate structure and urban hierarchy was limited and tangential (Goddard, 1977). The few direct studies undertaken during the late seventies concentrate on the division of corporate functions between cities and more specifically on longitudinal geographical patterns of the intercorporate linkage and their impact on the urban systems. Studies on urban employment trends have tended to focus on industrial structure of employment and thereby concentrated more on the identity of a region in terms of its products than on the range of functions of various industries and its relation to specific regions. Westaway (1974) and Tronqvist (1970) are among a few who have worked on the functional industrial hierarchy having larger cities as cores with excess managerial and professional occupations and smaller urban centres as periphery having production occupations. Later, studies on the spatial distribution of headquarters of large corporations have shown pronounced concentration of headquarters in larger metropolitan centres with variations in the degree of concentration from country to country (Taylor and Thrift, 1980). Even if production operations have shifted in many developed countries to smaller urban centres, larger corporate activities that include producer services, such as, administration, developmental and financial functions, legal services advertising etc. have renewed the tendency towards centralisation. Since the seventies these complex corporate activities have been found responsible for making world cities (Cohen, 1981; Soja, Morales and Wolff, 1983; Thrift, 1986 Sassen, 1990). Many industries which would otherwise have shifted out to avoid the rising cost in metropolitan cities decided to continue their operation from the latter in order to use the benefits of scale economy in various ways. Studies on locational dynamics of large firms in the United States had indicated extreme concentration of headquarter functions in the New York metropolitan area and other major centres of the 'manufacturing belt' since the sixties (Ullman 1958; Goodwin 1965). The subsequent shift to the sunbelt cities or middle-sized metropolitan complexes in the north-east did not however, remove the importance of metropolitan dominance (Semple, 1975). The above shift, argued by Stephens and Holly (1981), was associated with regional changes in the rank-size rule of metropolitan areas, and therefore, directly drew upon the concentration and migration pattern of population rather than the actual relocation of corporate headquarters. Cohen (1979) reveals that the relocation of headquarters outside New York did not affect the closeness of their ties with the financial services of the latter, suggesting that control and locations are not necessarily synonymous. Studies on Britain (Johnston, 1968), in contrast showed that since the seventies the corporate control became more concentrated. Goddard (1977) corroborates it and draws a parallel between the centralised urban systems of Britain and Sweden. He finds the centre of corporate control in the national capitals of the countries. Interestingly when Goddard and Morris (1976) find evidence of both relative and absolutely increasing centralisation in the south-east of Britain of fast-growing indigenous companies following a decentralisation from Greater London, Westaway (1974) finds evidence of centralisation in Greater London area of primarily the foreign subsidiary headquarters indicating a push of the indigenous firms from the highly priced city area. In the USA, concentration pattern of the New York Metropolitan area later in the eighties shifts to Miami Urban Complex (Taylor and Thrift, 1980). In Australia and New Zealand, Johnston and Rimmer (1967) identify the dominance of four main corporate centres with varying degrees of specialisation. Le Meron (1977) finds the same trend operating with more intensity in the mid-seventies in the Auckland area. Larger the corporations more is the concentration in capital cities with inter-city variations depending upon their control of the internal political-economic situation. Taylor and Thrift (1980) also notice inter-metropolitan adjustments in the share of concentration between Melbourne and Sydney but with continuing metropolitan dominance. Increased metropolitan concentration of corporate headquarters, according to them, is due to the foreign ownership of industrial firms and the related oligopolistic structure. Commenting on the external control of local industry and the related impact on the settlement hierarchy, Pred (1973) suggests that control relationships do not necessarily exist in a regularly hierarchial framework. Major corporations are at times located in cities below the top tier in the urban hierarchy from which control of manufacturing plants is larger and more efficient. Further, relative higher cost in developed areas also does not act as a factor for dispersal as the fast growing service sector tends to be centrifugal and frustrates any potential move for dispersal.

Due to the lack of suitable employment data, though most of the above studies use location data of industries, they do throw considerable light on the linkages between corporate and urban hierarchy in general and also between foreign corporation locations and urban system, in particular. For the latter, despite large scale diversity of parent and host country characteristics, motives, strategies and status of individual firms in the international market, an overall metropolitan dominance in the location of foreign corporate headquarters and a close relation between settlement and corporate hierarchy have been repeatedly seen, in both developed and less developed countries. Only, in case of the latter it attains a special significance. In most of these countries, including the large ones with long history of urban growth primacy is strengthened in the regional settlement systems indicating dissociation of large urban centres from their less developed hinterland and a perpetuation of internal dependency. Colonial cities later turned national and regional capitals in South Asia, including India, Latin America and Africa (Gilbert, 1974). Being primarily centres of concentration and centralisation, these large cities rarely contribute towards regional development and diffusion. The extreme urban bias in planning of these countries is again reflected in the concentration of sophisticated infrastructure and related facilities in large urban centres adding further towards centripetalism. Multinational corporations make use of this distorted settlement system and attempt to thwart any proper move of dispersal taken by host countries *pari passu* praising the Anglo-Saxon concept of diffusion and growth.

In the present analysis on multinational corporate hierarchy and urban hierarchy, the settlements of each region in India have been classified into ten groups from S_1 to S_{10} (Table 4.9) on the basis of population size. Location of headquarters and plants have been examined separately.

Table 4.9 *Settlement status and population base*

Settlement status	Population base
S_1	10 million and above
S_2	5 – 10 million
S_3	1 – 5 million
S_4	5 lakh to 1 million
S_5	1 lakh to 5 lakh
S_6	50,000 to 1 lakh
S_7	20,000 to 50,000
S_8	10,000 to 20,000
S_9	5,000 to 10,000
S_{10}	less than 5,000

The locational pattern of multinational headquarters (termed as Level II activities in this analysis) in India in 1990 clearly shows a metropolitan bias. Nearly 90 per cent of the total 435 Level II offices are located in metropolises. Even the share of cities with population less than 1 million is small. In other words, 98 per cent of MNC head offices are located in Class I and above cities (Fig. 4.11). About 76 per cent Level II activities are located in the four largest cities of Delhi, Bombay, Madras and Calcutta. Bombay has the maximum number (39 per cent of the total), Calcutta has 20.23 per cent—both having S_1 status, Delhi 9.89 per cent and Madras 6.67 per cent—both having S_2 status. Nearly 14 per cent of the Level II activities are located in cities of S_3 category such as Bangalore, Pune, Hyderabad etc. (Table 4.10).

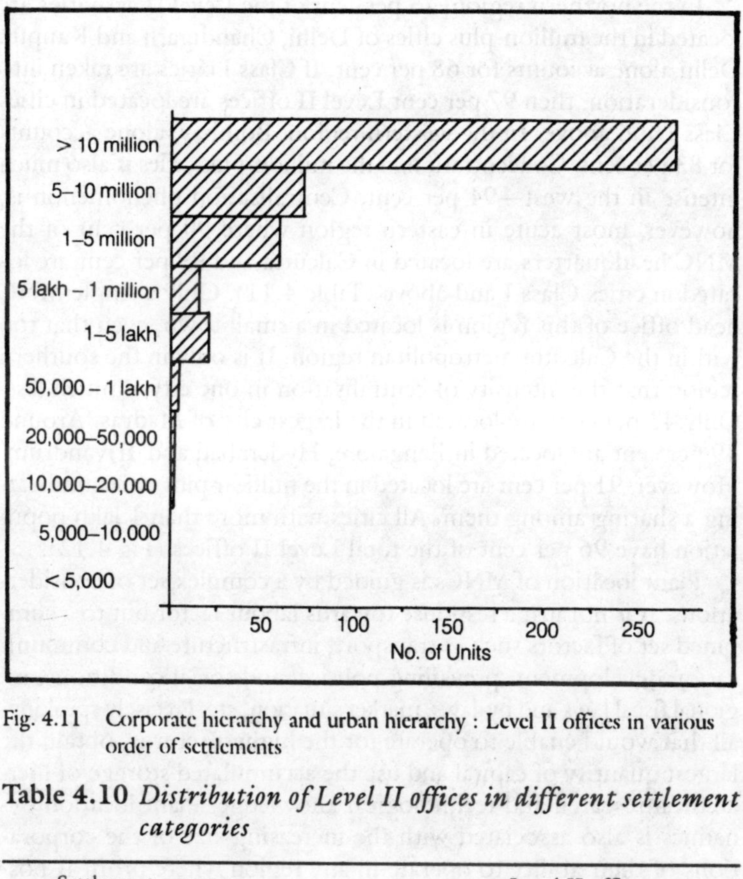

Fig. 4.11 Corporate hierarchy and urban hierarchy : Level II offices in various order of settlements

Table 4.10 *Distribution of Level II offices in different settlement categories*

Settlement category	Population	Level II offices Nos.	Per cent
S_1	(10 million and above)	259	59.54
S_2	(5-10 million)	72	16.55
S_3	(1-5 million)	59	13.56
S_4	(5 lakh-1 million)	15	3.45
S_5	(1-5 lakh)	21	4.83
S_6	(50,000-1 lakh)	5	1.14
S_7	(20,000-50,000)	2	0.46
S_8	(10,000-20,000)	2	0.46
S_9	(5,000-10,000)	0	–
S_{10}	(Less than 5,000)	0	–

Source : Computed from data of Company Annual Reports.

In the northern region, 75 per cent of the Level II activities are located in the million-plus cities of Delhi, Chandigarh and Kanpur. Delhi alone accounts for 68 per cent. If Class I cities are taken into consideration, then 97 per cent Level II offices are located in cities Class I and above. In the western region, Bombay alone accounts for 83 per cent. Concentration in the million-plus cities is also much intense in the west—94 per cent. Centralisation phenomenon is, however, most acute in eastern region where 90 per cent of the MNC headquarters are located in Calcutta and 99 per cent are located in cities Class I and above (Table 4.11). Only a single MNC head office of this region is located in a small town, even that too within the Calcutta metropolitan region. It is only in the southern region that the intensity of centralisation in one city is much less. Only 42 per cent are located in the largest city of Madras. Around 49 per cent are located in Bangalore, Hyderabad and Trivandrum. However, 91 per cent are located in the million-plus cities, indicating a sharing among them. All cities with more than 1 lakh population have 96 per cent of the total Level II offices (Fig 4.12).

Plant location of MNCs is guided by a complex set of considerations. It is not just a response towards labour factor but to a combined set of factors such as transport, infrastructure and communication development, prevailing political and social conditions, regional fiscal laws and by-laws, market situation, etc. Precisely speaking, all that would enable to operate for the highest returns, obtain the largest quantity of capital and use the accumulated storage of hierarchical research and technological knowledge. Plant location dynamics is also associated with the increasing size of the corporations of their ability to operate in any region where profit is possible. This flexibility offers them the advantage of selecting the best possible plant locations in any single country given the country's internal possibilities. Depending on the scale of operation and diversity of products, MNCs in addition make use of unorganised units and labour. Even in the United States, foreign corporations are found to produce increasingly through small and medium-sized firms (Bagchi-Sen and Wheeler, 1989). In Thailand large companies are permitted by local law to develop ancillaries which can operate even within their factory premises with a possibility of functioning in two qualitatively different divisions within a single name. The unregistered small entity uncovered by labour laws recruit and pay workers according to its own rules and service conditions and simultaneously pose to be constant threat to the organised work-

Table 4.11 *Intra-regional distribution of Level II offices in different settlement categories*

Settlement Category		No. of Level II offices							
		Northern region		Western region		Southern region		Eastern region	
	Population	No.	%	No.	%	No.	%	No.	%
S_1	(10 million >)	–		171	(83%)			83	(89.80%)
S_2	(5-10 million)	43	(68.25)	–	–	29	(42.65)	–	–
S_3	(1-5 million)	4	(6.34)	22	(10.68)	33	(48.53)	–	–
S_4	(5 lakh-1 million)	5	(7.94)	6	(2.92)	3	(4.41)	1	(1.02)
S_5	(1-5 lakh)	9	(14.29)	4	(1.94)	–	–	8	(8.16)
S_6	(50,000-1 lakh)	1	(1.59)	2	(0.97)	1	(1.47)	1	(1.02)
S_7	(20,000-50,000)	1	(1.59)	–	–	1	(1.47)	–	–
S_8	(10,000-20,000)	–	–	1	(0.49)	1	(1.47)	–	–
S_9	(5,000-10,000)	–	–	–	–	–	–	–	–
S_{10}	(Less than 5,000)	–	–	–	–	–	–	–	–
		63		206		68		93	

Source : Computed from data of Company Annual Reports Figures

ers. Multinational corporations in India have been exploiting the service of the unorganised sector since long. Bata India uses the service of a large contingent of contract labourer located in and around Batanagar-Nungi area who sit at home and manufacture shoe-lace, socks and shoe horns for this giant Swiss multinational firm without adding much to production and reproduction cost. Bata India also buys items from numerous small producers scattered all over the country especially from Faridabad near Delhi and sell these under their brand name. In the same way, Hindustan Lever's contract labour size increases every month and with that the corporation's spatially spread in the country. In 1990, it had about 32 sub-contracting firms producing solely for the corporation.

The spatial distribution of 435 plants shows that nearly 70 per cent are located in settlements with population above one lakh. The lower order settlements accounting for 30 per cent of the plant locations are mostly (80 per cent) located in the metropolitan regions of large cities or near them. Besides plantations and tea gardens, very few plants are located in the interior areas of the country (not even 10 per cent). Less than one per cent plants have gone in the backward or industrially deprived areas. The situation is similar to the location of 'rural banks' in India in semi-rural areas, industrial township and even in metropolitan areas, making them not quite rural (Datta, 1977).

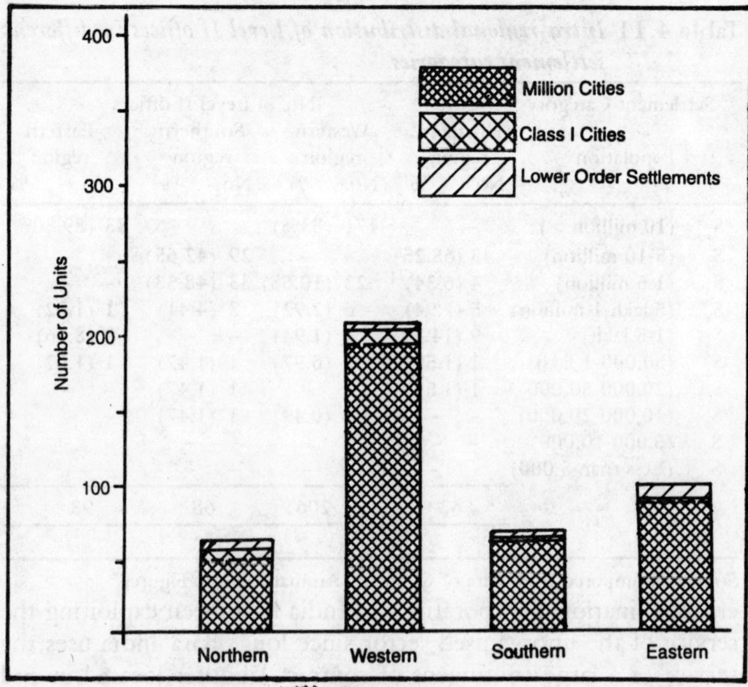

Fig. 4.12 Intra-regional distribution of Level II offices : Dominance of hierarchy

More than one-fourth of the multinational corporation plants are located in the largest four cities of India (Fig 4.13) of which Bombay alone accounts for 12.50 per cent. Calcutta, due to an early start, still offers location to 6 per cent of the plants and Madras to 5 per cent. Delhi being the national capital, does not offer a very conducive location and only 1.4 per cent of the MNC plants in India are located there.

Nearly 50 per cent of the plants are located in cities with population of one million and above (Table 4.12).

Table 4.12 ***Distribution of Level IV activities in different settlement categories***

Settlement Category Population		Level III Activity Units No.	Per cent
S_1	(more than 10 million)	162	18.93
S_2	(5-10 million)	51	5.96
S_3	(1-5 million)	142	16.59
S_4	(5 lakh-1 million)	125	14.60

Settlement Category	Population	Level III Activity Units No.	Per cent
S_5	(1-5 lakh)	112	13.08
S_6	(50,000-1 lakh)	71	8.29
S_7	(20,000-50,000)	58	6.78
S_8	(10,000-20,000)	52	6.07
S_9	(5,000-10,000)	21	2.45
S_{10}	(Less than 5,000)	62	7.25
		856	100.00

Source : Computed from primary data.

In the northern region, 77 per cent of the total regional plants are located in cities with population of one lakh and above. The

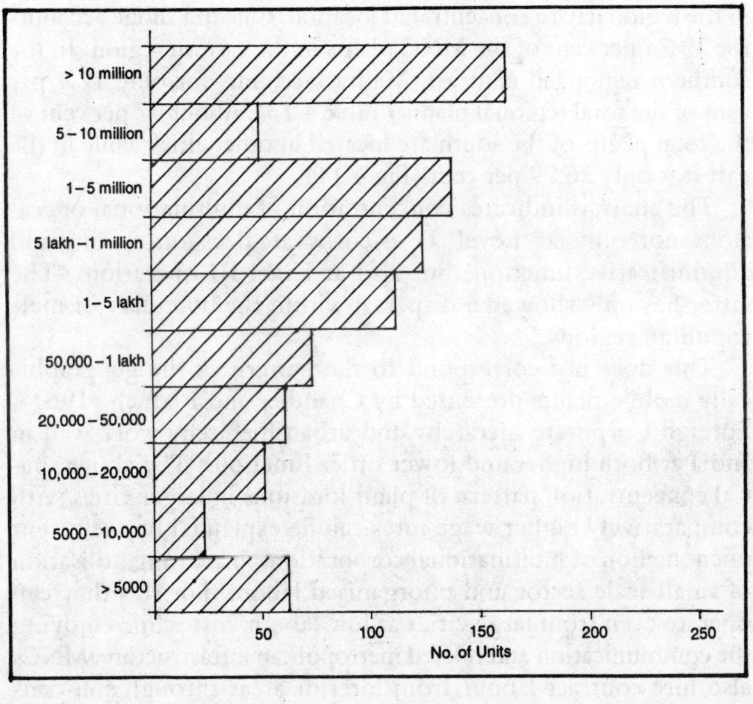

Fig. 4.13 Distribution of MNC plants in India in various order of settlements

largest number of plants is located in urban settlements with population between five lakh and one million (36 per cent). In the western region, Bombay alone has the largest number of plants than any other category of settlements (31 per cent) although the total plant coverage by cities is the same as that in the north. About 73 per cent of the plants in the western region are located in Class I cities and above. Almost all the plant locations in lower-order settlements are in the inner or outer periphery of the metropolitan areas. In slight contrast, a little less proportion of plants are located in Class I cities in the southern and eastern regions 64.73 and 60.73 per cent respectively. This means nearly 40 per cent of the plants in the eastern region and 35 per cent of the plants in the southern region are located in settlements with less than 1 lakh population base. However, in the eastern region, it is due to the location of a large number of plantations in the north-east and northern West Bengal that a large number of plants (43) is found to be located in S_{10} category of settlements. Besides plantations,the other MNC plants in the region have a concentrated location. Calcutta alone accounts for 33.74 per cent of the MNC plants in the eastern region. In the southern region, in contrast, Madras accounts for only 17.4 per cent of the total regional plants (Table 4.13). About 47 per cent of the total plants of the south are located in other cities while in the east it is only 26.99 per cent (Fig 4.14).

The analysis indicates concentration of multinational operations not only at Level II in corporate decision-making and administrative functions but also at Level III operations. The latter has only showed a dispersal within the boundary of metropolitan regions.

This does not correspond to the pattern of the geographically mobile plants presented by Chandler and Redlich (1961). Foreign Corporate hierarchy and urban hierarchy work well in India at both higher and lower order functions. The above spatial concentration pattern of plant locations in larger cities with comparatively higher wage rates can be explained by the recent phenomenon of multinational corporations' increasing utilisation of small-scale sector and unorganised labour. For this they can operate even from large cities at low labour cost while enjoying the communication and related metropolitan infrastructure. MNCs also hire contract labour from interior areas through sub-contracting firms which does not add employment to the organised sector or contribute towards organised plant. Procter and Gamble,

Hindustan Lever, Cadbury India or Bata India and their sub-contracting firms are good examples. Procter and Gamble's new toiletry items from its new branch Procter and Gamble Home Products (PGHP) are not made in any PGHP factory (it does not have any in India) but by the sub-contracting labour or other

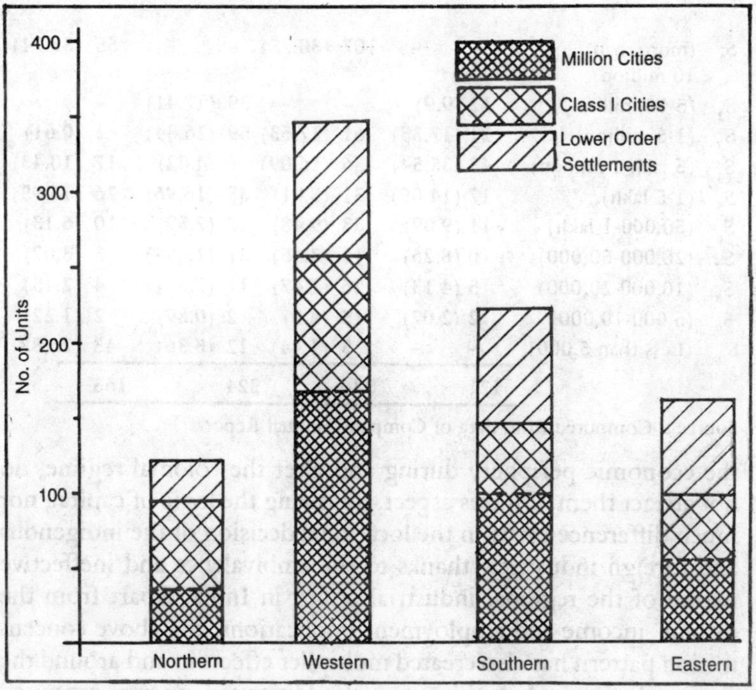

Fig. 4.14 Intra-regional distribution of MNC plants

units of Procter and Gamble. This calls for in-depth analysis of the labour control strategies of MNCs in host countries (Jenkins, 1987) and the related impact on labour processes.

The implications of the locational preferences of the MNCs in India are significant for regional and national economic development. At the aggregate regional level, MNCs have clearly contributed to industrial concentration in metropolitan areas to a large measure. The geographical heartland of the country constituting Madhya Pradesh, Bihar, eastern Maharashtra, western Andhra and northern Karnataka, eastern Rajasthan and Orissa that had remained

Table 4.13 *Intra-regional distribution of MNC plants in various settlement categories*

Settlement Category		No. of MNC Plants							
	Population	Northern region		Western region		Southern region		Eastern region	
		No.	%	No.	%	No.	%	No.	%
S_1	(more than 10 million)	–	–	107	(30.75)	–	–	55	(33.74)
S_2	(5-10 million)	12	(9.9)	–	–	39	(17.41)	–	–
S_3	(1-5 million)	21	(17.35)	61	(17.53)	59	(26.34)	1	(0.61)
S_4	(5 lakh-1 million)	43	(35.54)	56	(16.09)	9	(4.02)	17	(10.43)
S_5	(1-5 lakh)	17	(14.05)	31	(8.91)	38	(16.96)	26	(15.95)
S_6	(50,000-1 lakh)	11	(9.09)	33	(9.48)	17	(7.59)	10	(6.13)
S_7	(20,000-50,000)	10	(8.26)	12	(3.45)	31	(13.84)	5	(3.07)
S_8	(10,000-20,000)	5	(4.13)	26	(7.47)	17	(7.59)	4	(2.45)
S_9	(5,000-10,000)	2	(2.07)	15	(4.3)	2	(0.89)	2	(1.22)
S_{10}	(Less than 5,000)	–	–	5	(1.44)	12	(5.36)	43	(26.88)
		121		346		224		163	

Source : Computed from data of Company Annual Reports.

the economic periphery during and after the colonial regime, do not attract them. On this aspect, following the logic of capital, not much difference exists in the locational decision of the indigenous and foreign industries, thanks to the ambivalence and ineffective nature of the regional industrial policy in India. Apart from the instant income and employment implications, the above concentration pattern has also created multiplier effects in and around the metropolitan areas but with not much addition to long term organised employment and hence to rise in per capita income and regional development. Sub-contracting of labour is neither associated with integration of skill nor does with spatial growth. It is also worth emphasising that the structural concentration of foreign corporate plants is a coronary to this reflecting the political economy of MNCs. In Brazil out of some 103 MNC plants, only 14 are found to be located outside the states of Sao Paulo and Rio de Janeiro and more than one-third of all the plants are located in the municipality of Sao Paulo alone. The metropolitan area of Sao Paulo has more than 50 per cent of the total MNC plants (Cunningham, 1981). In South Africa, in the eighties, the greatest absolute concentration of MNC plants occurred in the national core area of Pretoria-

Witwaterstand-Vereeniging complex. Secondary cores were found in the metropolitan Cape Town, Durban and Port Elizabeth regions. Together, these four metropolitan areas accounted for more than 83 per cent of the foreign-controlled jobs (Rogerson, 1982). In India also, more than 90 per cent of the MNC plants in 1990 are located in the metropolitan cities and their immediate peripheries. The patterning of space economy in the above line is closely related to a compulsive pressure of the MNCs to break down spatial barriers and annihilate space by time (Harvey, 1985), having association with the development in communication and infrastructure, changes in social division of labour and technology and also the locational requirements of various functions of capital. Collectively and continuously these revolutionise space relations and the geographical landscapes of production, exchange and consumption.

All these raise a number of policy-related issues, focusing on regional development, regional disparity and the relevant regional tensions. In the existing state of affairs, such issues are especially crucial and call for in-depth analysis of MNC activities from various disciplines of social science.

5
Foreign Corporate Space and Consumer goods Sector

Prologue

Between 1976 and 1981, the Indian Industries in which foreign shares increased were mainly in the consumer goods sector like motor vehicles, automotive components, dry batteries, toiletries, electrical goods, rubber consumer goods, paper products, processed food etc. In spite of the argument that multinational corporations are invited for better technology or for earning foreign exchange, it has been repeatedly found that they have also entered quite a few sectors where not much high technology is required and where indigenous industrial operations can be developed. MNCs do not need to invest much in capital inputs for manufacturing these products and can keep their profit margin high. Besides export facility, they also get a large domestic market for such products especially in a country like India. Hindustan Lever, the biggest MNC in this sector, entered India in 1933 with a share capital of Rs. 28 lakh. In 60 years it amassed a share capital of Rs. 344 crores. Since 1982 it has repatriated Rs. 58 crores from India in the form of dividends alone. In 1987 in one year it repatriated Rs. 12 crores. Profitability rate of MNCs in consumer goods sector is very high (Table 5.1). This chapter attempts an analysis on the spatial dynamics of the consumer goods MNCS in India with two case studies of Procter and Gamble (India) and Hindustan Lever.

In total 129 MNCs operating in consumer goods other than

Table 5.1 *Profitability of the branches and subsidiaries of the multinational corporation engaged in consumer goods industries : 1973-74*

(Rs. crores)

Industry	No of units	Assets	Turnover	Profit before tax (P.B.T.)	P.B.T. as % of assets	P.B.T. as % of turnover
Tea processing & manufacturing	2	50.69	154.14	7.42	14.6	4.8
Sugar	1	31.14	38.94	2.80	9.0	7.2
Aerated and mineral water and other beverages	1	5.55	5.05	2.67	48.1	52.9
Perfume, cosmetics and other toilet preparations	5	12.97	30.28	5.41	41.7	17.9
Bakeries and confectionary and other food industries	4	36.01	64.16	3.84	10.7	6.0
Canning and preservation of fruits and vegetables	1	1.26	2.31	0.06	4.8	2.6
Cigarette	2	85.51	305.52	10.19	11.9	3.3
Thread and thread ball making	1	12.92	8.99	2.67	20.7	29.7
Footwear	1	32.54	56.34	1.10	3.4	1.9
Paints and varnish and allied products	5	22.34	33.78	2.65	11.9	7.8
Matches	2	13.51	39.09	1.16	8.6	3.0
Total	25	304.44	738.60	39.97	13.1	5.4

Source : Ghose, 1977.

pharmaceuticals have been selected. This includes the corporations manufacturing consumer goods in addition to pharmaceuticals or drugs, such as Procter and Gamble of the USA. The data and information of 1990 are collected from the Bombay Stock Exchange Library, Office of the Company Affairs, Government of Maharashtra; Ministry of Industries, Government of India; Annual Year Books of respective companies, library of the Institute of Capital Market, UTI, New Bombay, library of Business India, Bombay, Institute of Studies in Industrial Development, New Delhi and CMIE, Bombay.

5.1. Parent Countries : Status and Product Mix

For the purpose of analysis,* the corporations in the consumer goods industry have been classified into three broad groups, namely (*i*) those producing food and related products, (*ii*) those producing consumer goods other than food and (*iii*) those producing both food and non-food products.

Out of the total 129, 35 are in the first group engaged in the production and manufacture of food and related products. They constitute 27.13 per cent of the total. In the second groups, there are 84 corporations manufacturing non-food consumer goods. They constitute 65.11 per cent. Ten corporations fall in the third group manufacturing both food and non-food consumer products. They constitute 7.76 per cent.

Individual consumer food products are identified as (*1*) tea, (*2*) coffee, (*3*) cocoa, (*4*) soft drinks, (*5*) chocolates, (*6*) malt, maize and rice flakes, (*7*) dairy and poultry products, (*8*) fruits and vegetable products, (*9*) bakery products, (*10*) spices, (*11*) cooking oil, (*12*) sea-food, and (*13*) other food products.

Products of non-food consumer goods MNCs are (*1*) cosmetics, (*2*) toiletries, (*3*) health and dental products, (*4*) woollen and cotton clothings, (*5*) fabrics, (*6*) cotton and synthetic threads, (*7*) silk materials and other textile products, (*8*) tobacco, cigars and cigarettes, (*9*) liquour and spirit, (*10*) coir products, (*11*) paper and paper products, (*12*) plastic products (*13*) optical frames and lenses, (*14*) records and cassettes, (*15*) photographic plates, (*16*) camera, (*17*) soaps and detergents, (*18*) leather goods, (*19*) rubber goods, (*20*) decorative laminates, (*21*) glazed tiles and ceramic products, (*22*) carpets and furnishings, (*23*) furniture, (*24*) starch, (*25*) asbestos, (*26*) matches, (*27*) calculators, (*28*) personal computers,

* Based on 1990 data

(*29*) fans, (*30*) bulbs, (*31*) batteries and torches, (*32*) refrigerators, (*33*) washing machines (*34*) air coolers (*35*) vacuum cleaners and dryers, (*36*) other domestic electrical appliances, (*37*) amplifiers, (*38*) radio, (*39*) television, (*40*) VCR and VCP (*41*) music systems, (*42*) electrical and electronic typewriters, (*43*) sewing machines, (*44*) blades and shaving system, (*45*) drawing equipment, (*46*) light vehicles, such as motor cycle, scooter, mopeds, bicycles and cars, (*47*) jeeps, (*48*) oil paints, (*49*) gum and printing ink.

The country that has the largest share of corporations in consumer goods sector is the UK. Out of 129, 62 (48.06 per cent) corporations are UK owned and/or UK controlled. This large share, however, is primarily due to the long presence of British capital in mainly tea and also in coffee plantations. Out of the total 62 UK controlled corporations, 25 manufacture food and related products of which 21 are tea corporations. Goodricke group, a wholly-owned subsidiary of the Lawrie group and the largest private sector tea manufacturer in the world is one such company (Fig. 5.1). Share of the USA comes next (18.60 per cent). Here 24 corporations are engaged in the production of consumer goods, of which 5 produce only food and related products, 18 produce non-food items and one (Pfizer) is in the production of food (animal products) and non-food items both. In the consumer goods sector the country with the next highest share is Japan. The number of Japanese corporations is 13 (10.08 per cent) and all are in non-food subsector. Switzerland is the only other country besides the UK and the USA which has corporations in both food and non-food sectors.

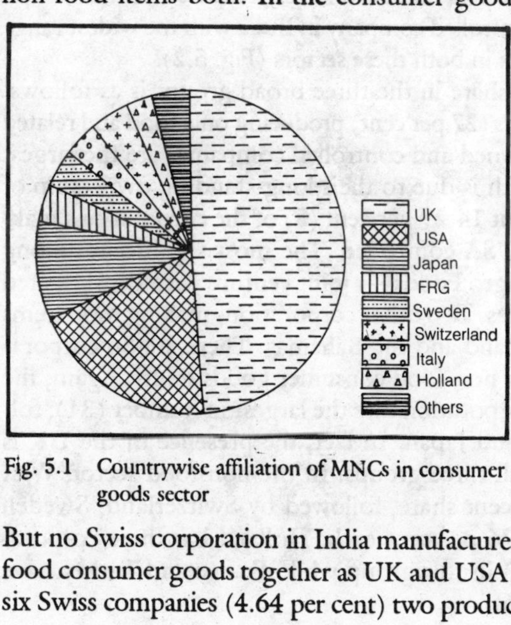

Fig. 5.1 Countrywise affiliation of MNCs in consumer goods sector

But no Swiss corporation in India manufactures both food and non-food consumer goods together as UK and USA have. Out of the total six Swiss companies (4.64 per cent) two produce only food products and four manufacture non-food consumer items. Germany and Sweden have the next share of companies—five each. While all the five corporations manufacture only non-food consumer items, one Swedish Company (Alfa Laval), out of five, produces both food (dairy products) and non-food (electronic goods and pharmaceuticals) products. The other four Swedish corporations manufacture non-food consumer goods. Italy has the next share (3.09 per cent). All the four companies, controlled by Italian MNCs, manufacture non-food consumer goods items. Holland has three corporations in the consumer goods sector producing only non-food items. Some of them are giant ones such as Philips. France, the Bahamas and Turkey have only one corporation each in the consumer goods sector. The Bahama-based corporation is the giant Nestlé, producing food (milk and related) products. The French and Turkish corporations are in the non-food sector. Two corporations have not been grouped under any single parent country because large proportion of their equity shares is held by more than one foreign country. They are Britannia (equity share owned by companies of UK, France and Singapore) and Hindustan Lever, Lipton and Brooke Bond of the Unilever Group with cross-country parentage of Holland and UK. The first two companies produce both food and non-food products simultaneously while the last two produce only food and related products. Hindustan Lever, it has been mentioned, is the largest foreign-controlled company in India with the widest range of diversified products in both these sectors (Fig. 5.2).

The countrywise share in the three broad groups is as follows. Of the 35 corporations (27 per cent) producing only food and related products, the UK owned and controlled companies are the largest in number (27) which is due to their long-standing ownership of tea plantations. About 14.29 per cent (5) of the corporations making food items are USA controlled. The most significant among these is the Punjab Agro Foods—a joint venture with Pepsi floated during the late eighties. Two other corporations making food items are based in Switzerland and the Bahamas. There are 84 corporations producing only non-food consumer goods items. Again, the British-controlled corporations are the largest in number (31), followed by the USA and Japan. In fact, the presence of the UK is consistently felt in all three groups. In the non-food sector, West Germany has 6 per cent share, followed by Switzerland, Sweden and Italy sharing 4.76 per cent each. Holland has three corporations (3.57 per cent) in this group while France and Turkey have one corporation each.

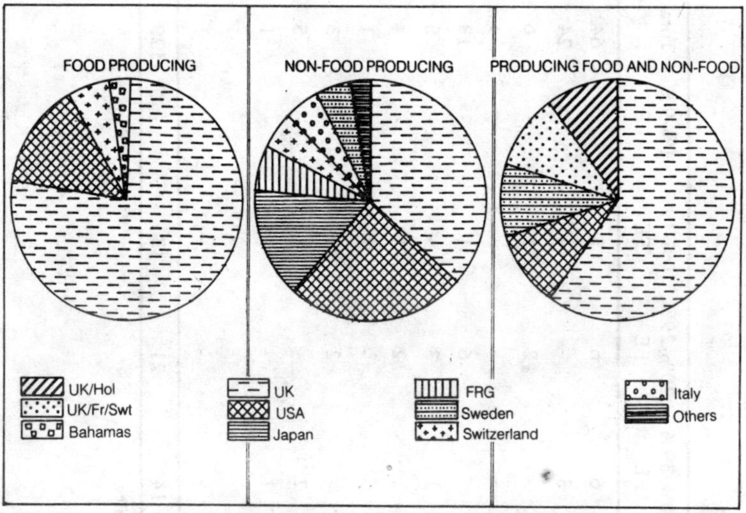

Fig. 5.2 Countrywise affiliation of MNCs in different consumer goods sectors

There are altogether ten foreign-controlled companies producing both food and non-food consumer goods in India. Out of these, again, Britain controls the largest number—6 corporations (60 per cent). The remaining four corporations are (*1*) Pfizer, controlled by USA, (*2*) Alfa Laval, controlled by Switzerland, (*3*) Britannia controlled jointly by UK, France and Singapore and (*4*) Hindustan Lever, controlled by Holland and UK.

Multinational Corporations in the consumer goods sector in India operate through various types of units: branches, subsidiaries and joint ventures with majority and minority equity holding (Table 5.2A and B). Of 129 companies, only one (Apple Industries Limited) is a branch of the Computerland and ARN Leading Private Limited of the USA operating in the non-food consumer goods (electronics) sector. The remaining 128 companies are either subsidiaries or joint venture companies with majority or minority foreign equity share. Thirty companies in the consumer goods sector are subsidiaries, of which 26 are UK owned. The USA has only two subsidiaries and Sweden one. Hindustan Lever, with cross-country parentage, is the other wholly-owned subsidiary, with Unilever as its parent corporation. All the 21 subsidiaries producing food and related items are tea producing companies owned by the UK. Seven subsidiaries out of a total of 30 (23.33) manufacture non-food products of which four are British (2) and American (2). Tribeni Tissues

Table 5.2A *Extent of Foreign Control in Consumer Goods Corporation*

Countries	Branches	Subsidiaries	40%-50% FE	30%-39% FE	20%-29% FE	10%-19% FE	1%-9% FE	Total
UK	-	26	21	6	6	5	-	64
USA	1	2	14	3	-	4	-	24
Switzerland	-	-	3	-	2	1	-	6
Bahamas	-	-	1	-	-	-	-	1
Japan	-	-	6	-	6	1	-	13
W. Germany	-	-	1	1	3	-	-	5
Italy	-	-	-	1	2	1	-	4
France	-	-	1	-	-	-	-	1
Holland	-	-	1	-	2	-	-	3
Sweden	-	1	1	2	-	1	-	5
Turkey	-	-	-	1	-	-	-	1
UK/France Singapore	-	-	1	-	-	-	-	1
UK/Holland	-	1	–	-	-	-	-	1
Total	1	30	50	14	21	13	-	129

Source : Computed from Company Yearbook Information FE = Foreign Equity.

Table 5.2B *Extent of Foreign Control in different types of consumer goods industries*

Countries	Branches	Subsidiaries	40%-50% FE	30%-39% FE	20%-29% FE	10%-19% FE	1%-9% FE	Total
A. Companies producing only food products :								
UK	-	21	4	1	1	-	-	27
USA	-	-	3	1	-	1	-	5
Switzerland	-	-	-	-	1	1	-	2
Bahamas	-	-	1	-	-	-	-	1
Total	-	21	8	2	2	2	-	35
B. Companies producing only non-food products :								
UK	-	4	14	4	5	4	-	31
USA	1	2	10	2	-	3	-	18
Japan	-	-	6	-	6	1	-	13
W. Germany	-	-	1	1	3	-	-	5
Switzerland	-	-	3	-	1	-	-	4
Italy	-	-	-	1	2	1	-	4
France	-	-	1	-	-	-	-	1
Holland	-	-	1	-	2	-	-	3
Sweden	-	1	-	2	-	1	-	4
Turkey	-	-	-	1	-	-	-	1
Total	1	7	36	11	19	10	-	84
C. Companies producing both food and non-food products :								
UK	-	1	3	1	-	1	-	6
USA	-	-	1	-	-	-	-	1
Sweden	-	-	1	-	-	-	-	1
UK/France/Singapore	-	-	1	-	-	-	-	1
UK/Holland	-	1	-	-	-	-	-	1
Total	-	2	6	1	-	1	-	10

Source : Computed from Company Yearbook Information

producing paper products, and Indian Schering, manufacturing cosmetics and drugs are two of the UK owned companies while both American subsidiaries are owned by two giant MNCs—Johnson and Johnson and Union Carbide. Two subsidiaries producing both food and non-food items are Glaxo (UK based) and Hindustan Lever.

Companies in the next group have equity shares held by parent corporations to the tune of 40–50 per cent. In other words, these are the joint ventures where parent corporations have majority equity participation. Britain not only has the largest number of companies in this group, their number is much higher than that of the USA, the country with the second largest number of corporations. In this group 42 per cent (21) of the corporations are British controlled; four of them produce only food and related products, Fourteen produce only non-food products and three produce both food and non-food products. Among the food manufacturers, Cadbury is significant; among the non-food producers significant names are Dunlop or International Computers; mentionable corporations producing both are Harrison Malayalam Limited (HMM). Many giant British multinationals such as Cadbury and Schwepps, Coats Paton, Gordon Woodroffe, Boots Pharmaceuticals, Dunlop, etc. have companies in the latter groups. USA has 14 (28 per cent) corporations under its control. Three of these produce food and related products and ten produce non-food consumer goods. Some of world's biggest firms operate through joint venture firms in this group. Pepsi, Colgate Palmolive, Procter and Gamble and Singer are a few examples. There is only one US controlled corporation that produces both food and non-food products—Pfizer.

Next to UK and USA comes Japan. It should be mentioned that no Japanese multinational has any branch or subsidiary in India. They operate only through joint ventures. There are six corporations in this group which are controlled by the Japanese and all are engaged in the production of non-food consumer goods. Quite a few of these, such as, Toshiba Corporation (Toshiba Anand) or Asahi Glass (Indo Asahi Glass) are included in the *Fortune* 500 list. Three corporations in this group are controlled by Swiss MNCs and all produce only non-food products. Significant ones are Bata India and Hindustan Ciba-Geigy. Bahamas (Nestlé), West Germany (Siemens), France (Coates India), Holland (Philips), Sweden (Wimco) and UK/France/Singapore (Britannia) have one corporation each in this group. In total eight corporations produce only food and related products of which 50 per cent units are from UK.

USA has three corporations and the Bahamas has one. Altogether, there are 36 corporations producing only non-food consumer goods constituting 72 per cent of the total number of corporations belonging to this group. Of these, 39 per cent are from UK, 28 per cent from USA, 17 per cent from Japan and 8 per cent from Switzerland, Germany, France and Holland.

The next group includes companies with foreign equity between 30 and 39 per cent. There are 14 such companies (10.85 per cent). UK has a much higher share (42.86 per cent) with six corporations, of which one produces only food and related products, four only non-food products and one producing both. Kissan Products Limited, a joint venture with Cadbury, is the food item producer while Crompton Greaves, Vazir Sultan Tobacco Industries and Godfrey Philips are among the non-food producing group. Only three US-controlled corporations are found in this group of which one is engaged in producing only food products (Kothari General Foods). The other two companies manufacturing electrical items and domestic appliances are Sylvania Laxman (tied-up with Sylvania Electrical Corporation) and TVS Whirlpool (tied-up with Whirlpool Corporation). Sweden has got two corporations in this group both of which are in the non-food producing sector. These are Wimco* and Facit Asia Limited. Germany, Italy and Turkey have one corporation each in this group, all engaged in the production of non-food consumer goods. Polyolefins India Ltd., production plastic products, has a tie-up with Hoechst AG of Germany. Nova Silk Limited, producing high grade variety of silk material, has a tie-up with Lotus Studio of Italy and Jai Hind Society, producing programmable washing machines, has a tie-up with Arcelic AG of Turkey.

Two corporations in this group produce only food items—one each from UK and USA. Eleven (7.9 per cent) produce only non-food items of which four are from UK, two each from USA, and Sweden and one each from West Germany, Italy and Turkey.

The next group includes corporations with foreign equity between 20 and 29 per cent. In total, 21 corporations (16.28 per cent) belong to this group, of which six are UK–controlled. One is in food production sector (Pierce Leslie India Limited engaged in cashew processing) and five non-food sector. Significant names in

* In 1991 Swedish Match AB sold off its entire stake in Wimco to an Indian company. Many such mergers followed later.

the latter group are Macneil Magor (manufacturing tea, and paper products) and Enfield India (manufacturing two and three wheelers). Japan also has an equal share with six corporations manufacturing non-food items. Listed corporations in *Fortune* 500 of 1990, such as Suzuki Motors (TVS Suzuki) or Mitsubishi Corporations (Eicher Motors) belong to this group. Germany has the next share—three in total and all producing non-food items. Some are big ones, such as Daimler Benz (Bajaj Tempo). Switzerland, Italy and Holland have two corporations each in this group of which five produce non-food items (one from Switzerland and two each from Italy and Holland). Modi Carpet has a tie-up with Arora S. of Switzerland, LML Vespa with Piaggio of Italy and Punjab Anand has a tie-up with Philips of Holland. The Swiss corporation engaged in the production of only food and related products is Consolidated Coffee Limited with a tie-up with Volkard Brothers Limited.

Among 35 food producing MNCs, two belong to this group, of which, one is UK–controlled and the other Swiss-controlled. Out of 84 non-food producing MNCs, 19 (23 per cent) belong to this group, where the largest share is claimed by Japan (31.58 per cent). UK with five corporations and West Germany with three come next while Italy and Holland have three each. There is no corporation with foreign equity between 20 and 24 per cent which produces both food and non-food products.

The last group of the foreign controlled companies in the consumer goods sector are those with foreign equity of 10–19 per cent. Thirteen corporations (10.07 per cent) are included in this group of which five are UK-tied and four are US-tied. Of the five British controlled corporations four produce non-food consumer goods such as Asian Cables (tie-up with Wilkinson Swords), National Radio and Electronics Limited (tie-up with EK Cole) etc. The remaining one, Bombay Burma Trading Corporation produces both food and non-food products such as tea, coffee, oil, rubber, etc. Of the four US-controlled corporations, one is a sole food product manufacturer: the National Cereals Products Limited. The remaining three manufacture non-food consumer goods like jeeps (Mahindra and Mahindra), air-coolers and fans (DLF Universal Limited) and domestic appliances like refrigerators or other electrical goods (Kelvinator India Ltd.). Switzerland, Italy, Sweden and Japan have one corporation each in this group. The Swiss one is engaged in the production of food and related products (India Yeast Co. Ltd.). International Ceramics tying-up with an Italian Company produces ceramic products while Uptron Electronic Devices Limited having a tie-up with LN Erickson Telephone Company of Sweden manufactures televisions and picture tubes. Giant Japanese Corporations included in the *Fortune* 500 list, such as Nissan, operate in this group through Mahindra Nissan Allwyn Limited, manufacturing light motor vehicles. Of the total 13 corporations in this group two produce food items. They constitute 6 per cent of the foreign-controlled companies producing food and related products. Out of 84 corporations producing non-food items 10 corporations share 12 per cent and of the total 10 food and non-food producing corporations only one, tying-up with an UK firm, belongs to this group.

It should be mentioned that no foreign-controlled company in the consumer goods sector has foreign equity less than 10 per cent. Further US corporations have been found to be constantly wanting to acquire higher foreign equity. It clearly indicates the keenness of the MNCs to invest in this sector.

At an inter-country level, UK-based corporations prefer to operate more through subsidiaries. Of total 64 corporations, 24 (41 per cent) are subsidiaries and 33 per cent have foreign equity between 40 and 50 per cent. In the remaining three groups, Britain has lesser number of corporations. In contrast, the USA has the largest number of corporations as joint ventures in the foreign equity group of 40–50 per cent. Fourteen out of a total 24 US-based corporations in the consumer goods sector belong to this group. The US has only 2 subsidiaries, 3 corporations with foreign equity between 30 and 39 per cent and 4 with foreign equity between 10 and 19 per cent. No US controlled corporation has foreign equity between 20 and 29 per cent. The 13 corporations from Japan are distributed in the 40–50 per cent and 20–29 per cent foreign equity groups—6 in each. One famous Japanese corporation (Nissan) has a company in the 10–19 per cent equity group. Swiss corporations have foreign equity either between 40 and 50 per cent or 20 and 29 per cent while the figure for German-controlled firms lied between 20 and 29 per cent. Sweden has more companies with equity between 30 and 39 per cent. Holland and Italy have two corporations each in the foreign equity group of 20–29 per cent. Countries which have only one corporation in consumer goods sector in India generally have equity share between 40 and 50 per cent for example Bahamas and France. Due to its early presence in plantations, UK dominates a number of foreign-controlled companies in the consumer goods sector with many wholly-owned subsidiaries. Later and recent entrants like the USA, Japan or West Germany prefer to operate through joint venture companies.

5.2 Spatial Dynamics of Multinational Corporations in the Consumer Goods Sector

Operations of multinational corporations in consumer goods industries are associated with the factors of market, labour and technology. For the production of food and related products, raw material tends to come from a wide range of suppliers distributed over a large space. Regional multiplier effects, if any, in these cases operate more through final demand and labour market conditions.

Absence of data on employment in almost all the 129 companies has partly restricted locational explanation of MNCs in India in relation to resource, market and accumulation factor. In the following analysis Level II office locations have been examined first followed by an analysis of Level III or plant locations.

5.2.1 Head office location

In 1990 among the total 129 corporations, 51 (40 per cent) have their host country head offices located in the western region. Of these 43 (51 per cent) produce only non-food products, 5 make both food and non-food products and 3 corporations produce only food products. The next highest number of head offices (38) is located in the eastern region. Of these 63 per cent (24) are corporations manufacturing only food products, 32 per cent (12) only non-food products and only two corporations produce both food and non-food products. Northern and southern regions have almost equal number of head offices—21 and 19 respectively. The northern region again has a much larger representation of corporations producing non-food consumer goods (16 out of 21) where only four produce food products. The southern region also has 68 per cent of its total number of head offices representing non-food consumer goods corporations and only four representing consumer food corporations (Fig. 5.3).

The regional distribution of head offices reveals a relationship between the products, resource and market. Among the food product manufacturing corporations, 24 (69 per cent) have head offices located in the eastern region, of which all except one are offices of tea manufacturing corporations. Most of these head offices are old establishments and initially represented branches of British corporations. In the late seventies, following the enactment of the FERA,

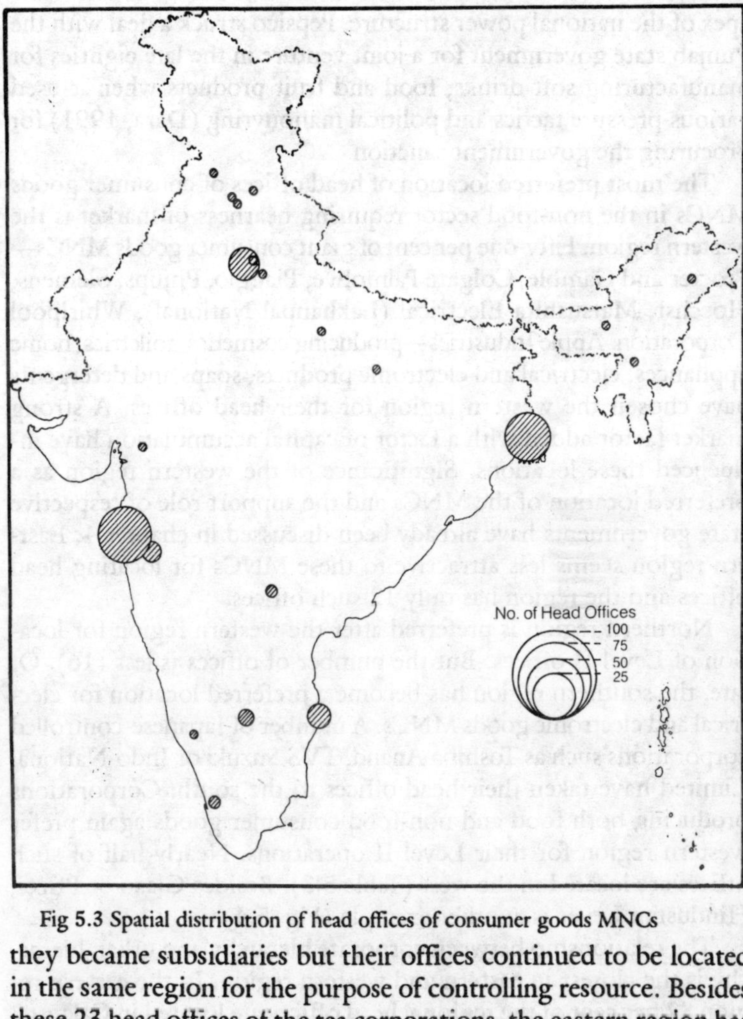

Fig 5.3 Spatial distribution of head offices of consumer goods MNCs

they became subsidiaries but their offices continued to be located in the same region for the purpose of controlling resource. Besides these 23 head offices of the tea corporations, the eastern region has only one more head office of a Swiss corporation: the Swiss yeast company. For MNCs producing food items other than tea, market becomes a factor of location in which case the choice for head office in most cases is Bombay in the western region. For example, the head office of Cadbury (India). Significant head offices in the northern region are of Nestlé and Pepsico. In both cases, the locational decisions have been influenced more by political-economic factor than by market factor. Nestlé (India) which entered India during the late 50s as the Food Specialities Limited preferred Delhi as the apex of the national power structure. Pepsico struck a deal with the Punjab state government for a joint venture in the late eighties for manufacturing soft drinks, food and fruit products when it used various pressure tactics and political manouvring (Dara, 1991) for procuring the government sanction.

The most preferred location of head offices of consumer goods MNCs in the non-food sector requiring nearness of market is the western region. Fifty-one per cent of giant consumer goods MNCs—Procter and Gamble, Colgate Palmolive, Piaggio, Philips, Siemens, Hoechst, Matsushita Electrical (Lakhanpal National), Whirlpool Corporation, Apple Industries—producing cosmetics, toiletries, home appliances, electrical and electronic products, soaps and detergents have chosen the western region for their head offices. A strong market factor added with a factor of capital accumulation have influenced these locations. Significance of the western region as a preferred location of the MNCs and the support role of respective state governments have already been discussed in chapter 4. Eastern region seems less attractive to these MNCs for locating head offices and the region has only 12 such offices.

Northern region is preferred after the western region for location of Level II offices. But the number of offices is less (16). Of late, the southern region has become a preferred location for electrical and electronic goods MNCs. A number of Japanese-controlled corporations such as Toshiba Anand, TVS Suzuki or Indo-National Limited have taken their head offices to the south. Corporations producing both food and non-food consumer goods again prefer western region for their Level II operations. Nearly half of such offices are located in the west (Table 5.3). Besides Glaxo or Pfizer, Hindustan Lever is another example (Fig. 5.4).

The relationship between corporate hierarchy and urban hierarchy is the closest in eastern and western region. In the eastern region 82 per cent of the regional head offices are located in Calcutta, the primate city of the region. Till the eighties, as no auction centre was located outside Calcutta, more than 80 per cent of the tea manufacturing corporations had their head offices there. Only 5 head offices of tea corporations are located in Guwahati and Dibrugarh in Assam. Apart from these, no head office of any consumer goods MNC is located outside Calcutta. Equally concentrated is the location

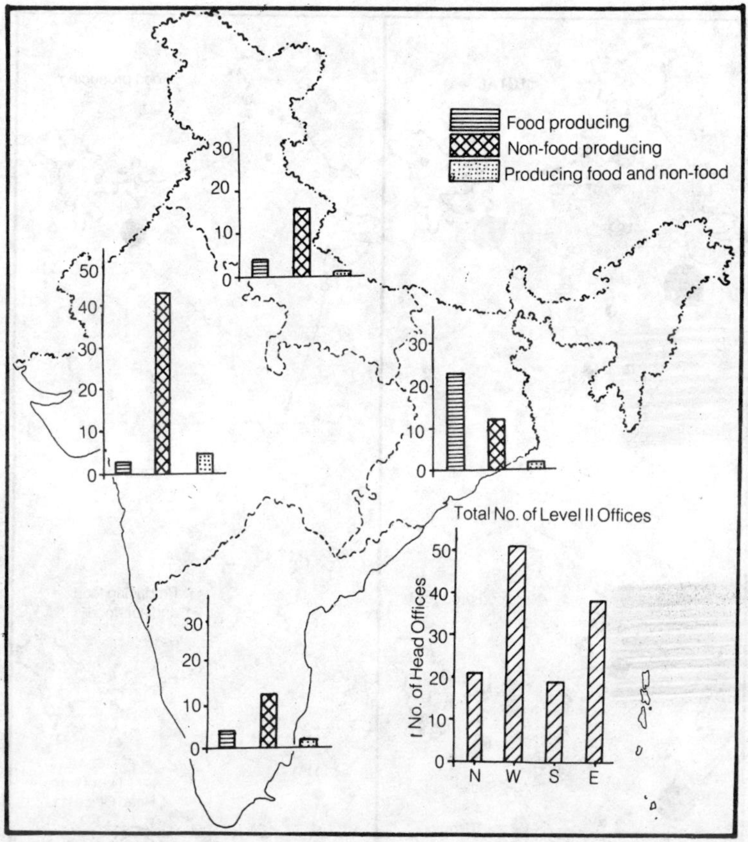

Fig. 5.4 Regional preferences of Level II offices of MNCs in consumer goods sector

of head offices in the western region. Out of a total 51 offices, 45 (88 per cent) are located in Bombay (Fig. 5.5). The remaining 12 per cent are located in the million cities of Pune, Baroda or Ahmedabad. No settlement lower than S_3 status has any Level II office. In contrast, in the north and the south, although majority of the MNC head offices are found in the biggest urban centres, offices of some corporations have been found to be located in lower order urban settlements too which are lower than even Class I cities. In the norther region, Pepsico and Mohan Meakin have located their offices in settlements with S_5 status. Fifty per cent of the head offices of food-producing MNCs are located in Delhi and

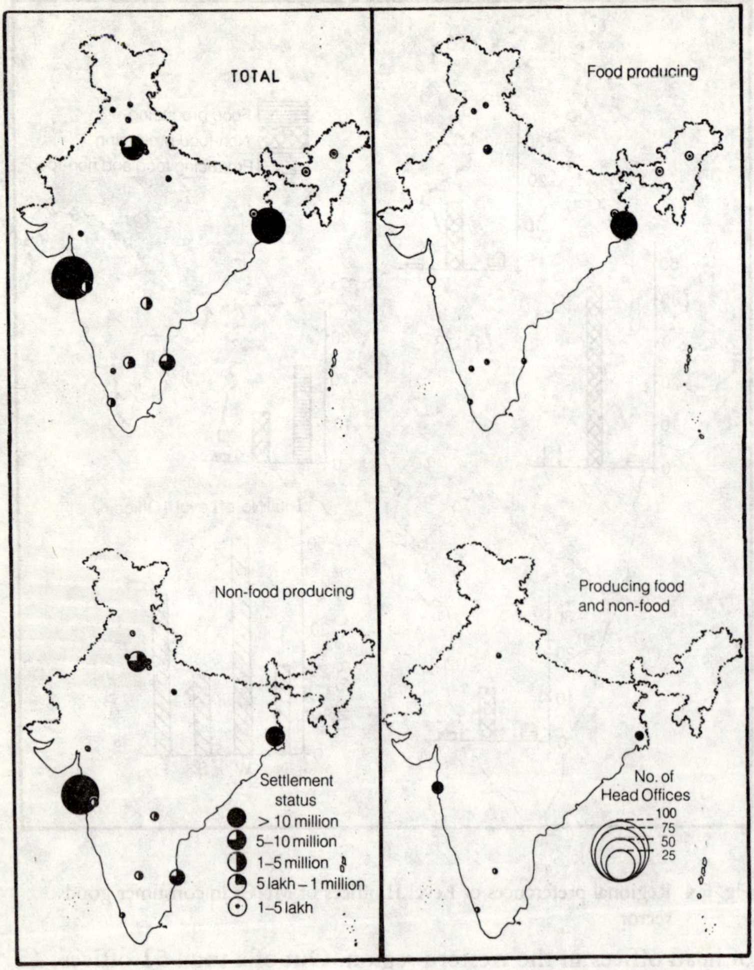

Fig. 5.5 Settlement status of head office locations of consumer goods MNCs in India

the rest is located in S_5 settlements. In case of non-food corporations, the spread of offices is more. Sixty-three per cent offices are located in Delhi proper while the rest in settlements with S_3, S_4, S_5 and even S_7 status. One head office (of Swaraj Mazda Limited) is even located in a settlement lower than a Class I city. Similarly in the south also, one Level II office of a food-producing MNC is located in an S_8 settlement. The factor deciding such location preference is the nature of the products. The head office of Consolidated Coffee Limited—a joint venture with the Swiss giant Volkard Brothers—is located in Kodagu in Karnataka. In the southern region, medium ranked million cities with population between 1 and 5 million are also preferred over Madras. Industrial policy, fiscal and tax situation, infrastructural facility and related rules prevailing in these centres are possible explanations for this shift. In the process, Bangalore has emerged as a favoured location of the recent entrants from Japan and Europe (Fig. 5.6).

5.2.2 Dynamics of plant locations

There are 319 plants of consumer goods MNCs in India. The western region dominates albeit with only 34 per cent of the total plants. In the southern and the northern regions too considerable number of plants (26 and 18 per cent respectively) are found. The 22 per cent plant locations in the eastern region is primarily due to the location of tea plantations and, therefore, cannot be said to be guided by a complex set of locational factors (Fig. 5.7).

The analysis of plant locations of different types of consumer goods brings out an interesting pattern. Of the total 68 plants in the food and related products, the largest number (33) is concentrated

Table 5.3 *Regional locations Level II operations of consumer goods MNCs in India*

Countries	Total	North	West	South	East
UK	64	3	20	10	31
USA	24	9	12	1	2
Switzerland	6	1	2	1	2
Bahamas	1	1	0	0	0
Japan	13	4	4	4	1
W. Germany	5	1	4	0	0
Italy	4	0	3	1	0
France	1	0	1	0	0
Holland	3	1	1	0	1
Sweden	5	1	2	1	1
Turkey	1	0	1	0	0
UK/France Singapore	1	0	0	1	0
UK/Holland	1	0	1	0	0
Total	129	21	51	19	38

Source : Computed from Company Yearbook Information.

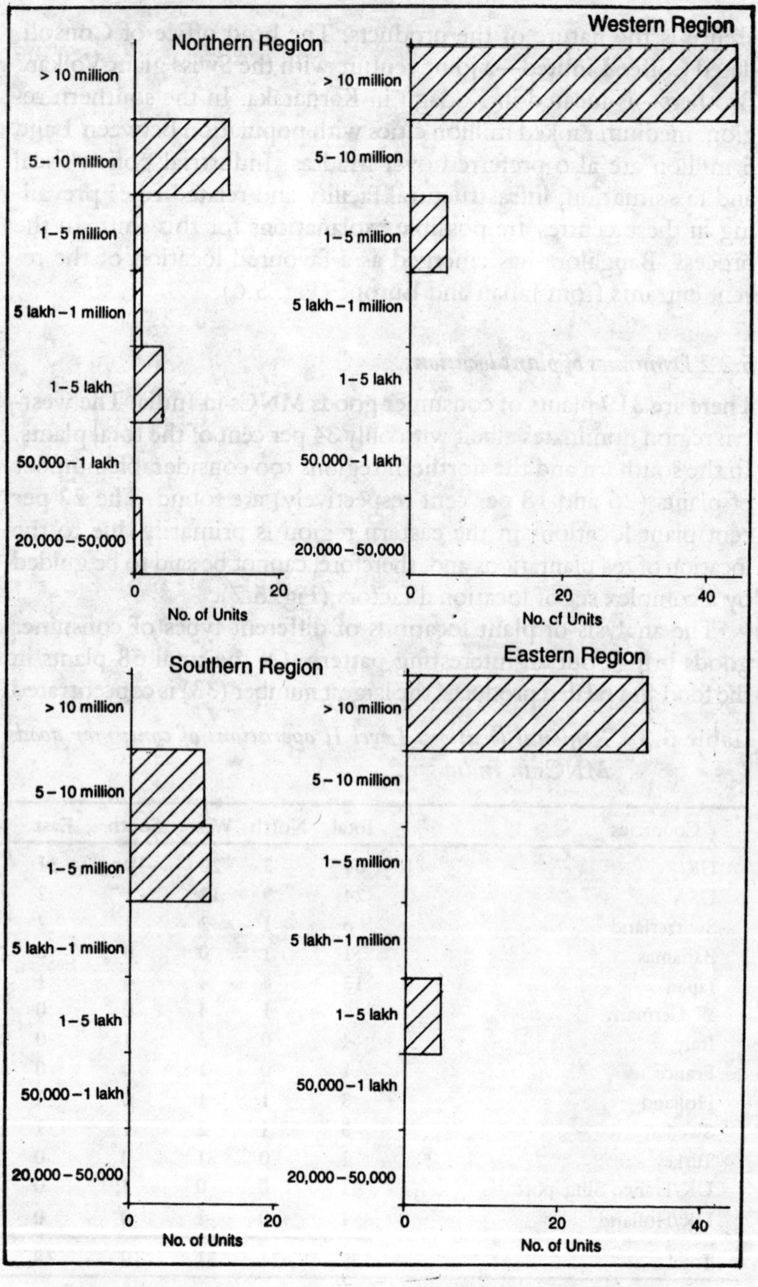

Fig. 5.6 Settlement status of Level II offices of consumer goods MNCs

in the eastern region due to the nature of location of tea plantations. Besides these, eastern region has only one plant of Indian Yeast Corporation. For the other two types of corporations, i.e., those producing non-food products and those producing both food and non-food products, the eastern region has the minimum number of plants. About 42 per cent of the MNC plants in non-food sector are located in the west. South attracts 25 per cent of the plants while 18 per cent are located in the north. About 15 per cent of the plants of the non-food consumer goods MNCs are located in the eastern region (Table 5.4). Corporations producing both food and non-food products also prefer west though the intensity of preference is somewhat less (Fig. 5.8).

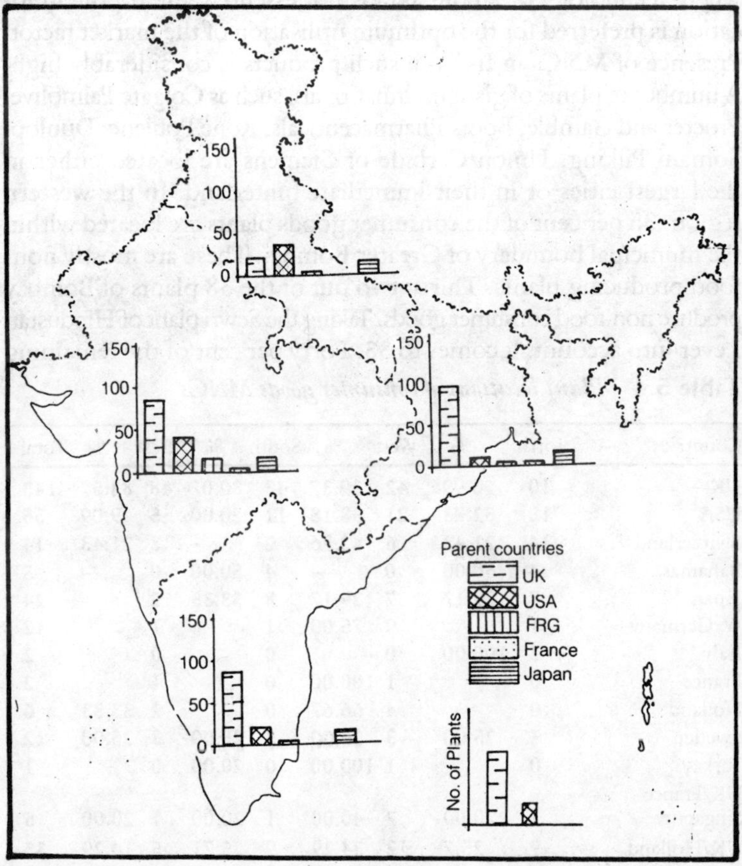

Fig. 5.7 Countrywise plant locations of consumer goods MNCs in different regions.

Within the regions, plants are located at various settlement levels. In spite of considerable spread, the largest cities dominate plant locations in western and eastern regions. Corporate and settlement hierarchies thus tend to have divergent arrangement and the horizontal spread is often restricted within metropolitan regions. The general argument,presented in the previous chapter that plants of the MNCs in India in all the four regions can afford to have metropolitan locations because of the presence of a huge army of cheap labour in the cities as opposed to a generally accepted notion of ubiquitous location (Chandler and Redlich, 1962),holds good for the consumer goods MNCs too. For many consumer goods where technology or labour skill is not essential, metropolitan location is preferred for the optimum utilisation of the market factor. Presence of MNCs in India in such products is considerably high. A number of plants of giant multinationals, such as Colgate Palmolive, Procter and Gamble, Boots Pharmaceuticals, Rone Poulenc, Dunlop, Somani Pilking, Union Carbide or Siemens are located either in the largest cities or in their immediate hinterland. In the western region, 35 per cent of the consumer goods plants are located within the municipal boundary of Greater Bombay. These are mostly non-food producing plants. Thirty-two out of the 38 plants of Bombay produce non-food consumer goods. Taking the Sewri plant of Hindustan Lever into account, it comes to 33. Forty per cent of the remaining

Table 5.4 *Plant locations of consumer goods MNCs*

Countries	North	%	West	%	South	%	East	%	Total
UK	10	6.99	42	29.37	43	30.07	48	33.57	143
USA	18	32.73	21	38.18	11	20.00	5	9.09	55
Switzerland	14	21.43	6	42.86	2	–	3	21.43	14
Bahamas	4	50.00	0	–	4	50.00	0	–	8
Japan	7	29.17	7	29.17	8	33.33	2	–	24
W. Germany	1		9	75.00	1		1		12
Italy	2	100.00	0		0		0		2
France	0		1	100.00	0		1		2
Holland	0		4	66.67	0		2	33.33	6
Sweden	3	25.00	3	25.00	3	25.00	3	25.00	12
Turkey	0		1	100.00	0	20.00	0		1
UK/France Singapore	1	20.00	2	40.00	1	20.00	1	20.00	5
UK/Holland	9	25.7	12	34.29	9	25.71	5	14.29	35
Total	58		108		82		71		319

Source : Computed from Companies Yearbook Information

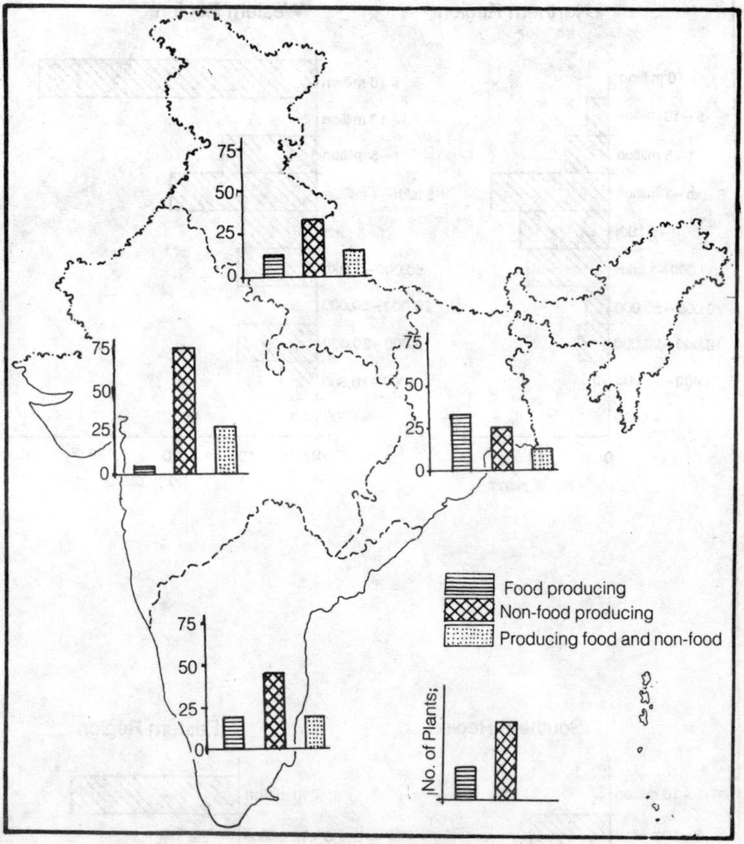

Fig. 5.8 Product specific regional preferences

plants are located in cities Class I and above. Seventy-five per cent of the plants in the western region are, therefore, located in cities with Class I status and above. Some of these are located in Pune, Baroda, Ahmedabad and in the metropolitan regions of these cities. Almost the same pattern exists in the eastern region with more concentration. Thirty-one per cent of the plants in the eastern region are located in Calcutta. The remaining 69 per cent are located mainly between Class I cities (with population between 1 lakh and 5 lakhs) and Class II towns. Twelve plants in this region are located in settlements with population between 5,000 and 10,000. But almost all of them are located in the metropolitan region of Calcutta in case of non-food products. Analogy

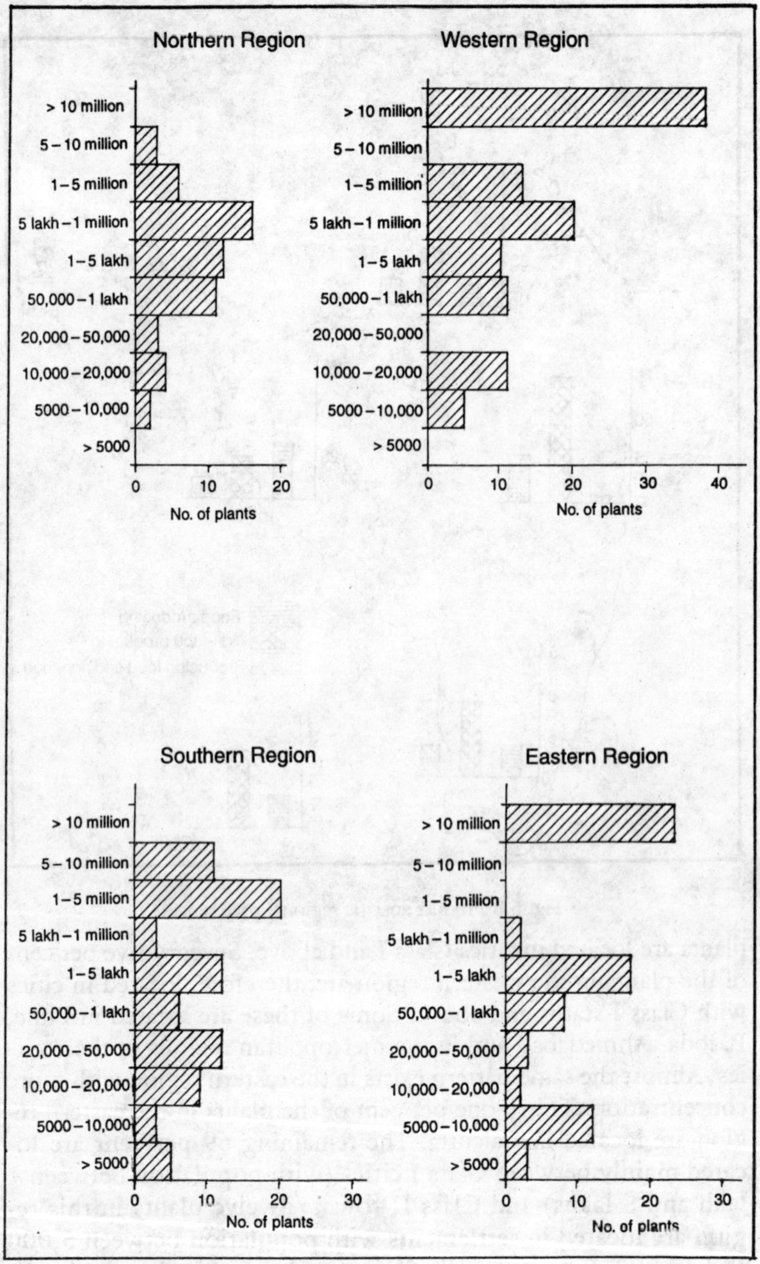

Fig. 5.9 Settlement status of plant locations of consumer goods MNCs

can again be drawn from Datta's (1977) analysis of location of 'rural banks'.

In contrast, in the northern region, 49 per cent of the total regional plants are located in cities with population between 1 lakh and 5 lakhs (21 per cent) and 5 lakh and 10 lakhs (28 per cent). Nearly 20 per cent plants of the northern region are located in Class II towns. Although a large number of these plants are found within the National Capital Region, a considerable number is located in Haryana and Punjab. In the northern region, plants producing only non-food products are more in number (57 per cent). Concentration of plants of all these corporations is more in the medium cities. Spatial spread of plants is maximum in the southern region where only 38 per cent of plants are located in the million cities. The remaining 62 per cent are concentrated in Class I cities and lower order settlements. In south non-food consumer goods MNCs are larger in number (55 per cent) located in lower order settlements. These settlements with MNC plants are found near the periphery of the metropolitan cities (Fig. 5.9). In south, plants of non-food consumer goods MNCs are more in number (55 per cent).

Plant locations of the consumer goods MNCs in general indicate a strong preference for metropolitan or higher order settlements unless otherwise guided by a necessity of nearness to resource base. It has been repeatedly found that interior locations are chosen by the MNCs in case they decide to exploit the cheap unorganised labour by sub-contracting. A number of giant MNCs like Unilever, Procter and Gamble and Glaxo have gone to the interior areas for this purpose. Besides such instances, by and large, organised sector plant locations of consumer goods MNCs in India show a distinct metropolitan bias.

5.3 Parent Countries and Regional Preference

The distribution of Level II and Level III activities of different parent countries in the four regions of India reflects convergence of some countries in a particular region and a comparative diffusion of others. In case of Level II activities, presence of the USA-controlled offices is significant (43 per cent) in the northern region whereas in the west, south and east UK-controlled offices (39, 53 and 82 per cent respectively) are noticeable. In the western region again, Level II locations of US-controlled offices have consider-

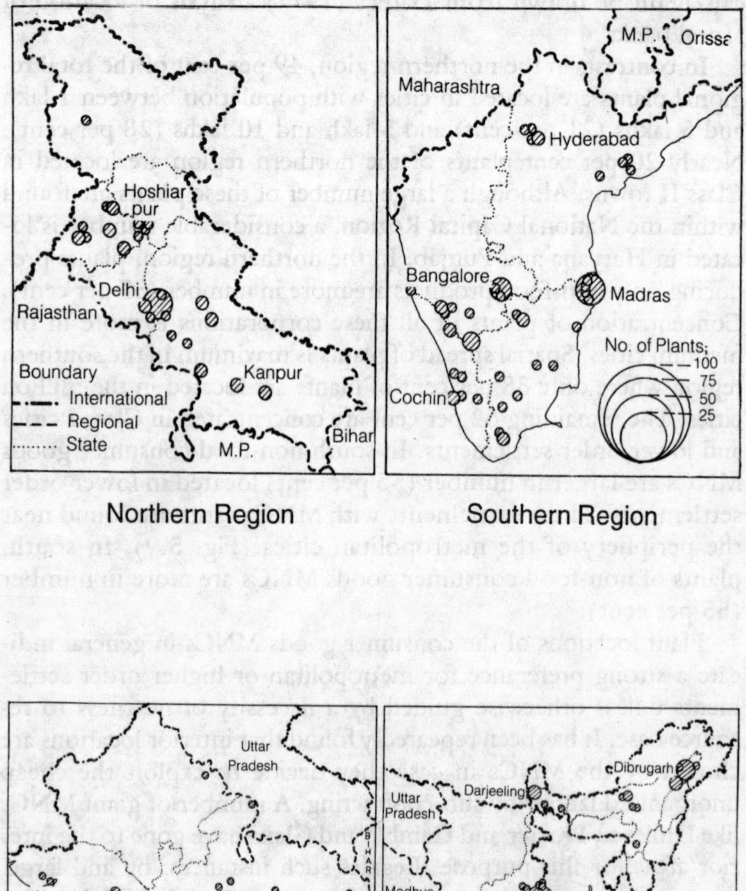

Fig. 5.10 Spatial distribution of plants of consumer goods MNCs

able importance in terms of number. Nearly one-fourth of the Level II offices in the northern region are controlled by the US multinational corporations. In the eastern and the southern regions their number is insignificant. In the western region, after USA, offices of Japanese and German subsidiaries or joint ventures are important. Japanese Level II offices have a comparable presence in the southern region (Fig. 5.10).

The picture becomes clearer when these offices are grouped under the heads of food and non-food producing corporations. East is having a large number of Level II offices (63 per cent) mainly of UK-controlled tea manufacturing corporations. In the other regions, offices of non-food producing consumer goods MNCs are larger in number (76 per cent in the north, 84 per cent in the west and 68 per cent in the south). In non-food sector western region has 40 per cent (17 in number) of the Level II offices controlled by the UK while in the south and in the east their proportion is 46 and 50 per cent respectively. It is only the western region that has Level II offices of non-food producing MNCs of all parent countries that are operating in India. Besides, the western region has five offices of corporations producing both food and non-food products while the south and the east have two each of such offices. UK again is the main parent country controlling these offices.It should be noted that in these location decisions, lifestyle and social environment, requirements of the expatriate administrative or technical personnel act as additive factors.

Germany and Italy also prefer the western region as the only location for their Level II offices. Three corporations controlled by the French, Turkish and British-Dutch group have all located their Level II offices in the west. Countries with corporations producing food and non-food products together show clear preference for the west for locating their Level II offices. It is only Japan that shows a distinctly different locational design. The MNCs (13) from Japan operating in the non-food consumer goods sector of India have an even distribution of head offices in the northern, western and southern regions with four offices in each. In the east, Japan has only one head office of the opthalmic lens manufacturer Indo-Asahi Glass.

Concentration of head offices in the western region is not due to a concentration of huge number of offices of one or two parent countries. It is rather a reflection of a systematic preference of almost all the parent countries towards this region. Regional preference of the parent countries for plant location presents a different picture. As the requirements for Level II and Level III activities are different, the acute concentration in the western region gets diluted.

It is found that most of the countries have either located their plants in all the three regions of the west, north or south or have shown clear preference for the west. In case of American controlled corporations, plants are almost evenly distributed between western (38 per cent) and northern regions (32 per cent). Only 20 per cent plants are located in the south while the share of the eastern region is negligible. Similarly, plants of Japanese and Swedish-controlled MNCs are located evenly among north (29 per cent and 25 per cent), west (28 and 25 per cent) and south (33 and 25 per cent respectively). The parent countries that show distinct preference for the western region are Germany (75 per cent of its plants are located in the west) and France (100 per cent). Hindustan Lever deserves special mention on plant location. It alone has 35 plants distributed in all four regions. Thirty-four per cent are located in the western region and 26 per cent each in the north and south. Eastern region has a small share of 14 per cent plants, numbering five.

Locational dynamics of plants of food and non-food producing corporations suggests that the food-producing MNCs of the UK prefers the southern region after the east. Besides tea plantation locations in the east, most of their southern plants such as coffee and cocoa plantations and cashew processing units are resource oriented. US-controlled food producing corporations show a clear preference for the north. The old company of National Cereal Products has its three plants in the north, mainly in the Himachal Pradesh. Asian Agro Farm, also an old company, has its plants in Faridabad. The significant entrant, Pepsi also has its plant in Punjab.

Parent countries of corporations producing only non-food products show a clear preference for the western region. Even the UK and USA, who have other regional preferences for their food-producing units, show an unambiguous preference for western region for their non-food plants.

Plants of UK-controlled corporations located in the south and the east are primarily plantations and spread in various orders of settlements. Forty-four percent of UK-controlled plants in the east are located in settlements lower than S_5 status. Similarly, 42 per cent of UK-controlled plants in the southern region are located in lower order of settlements. In the western region UK-controlled firms are primarily non-food producers, located in larger urban centres. Seventy-six per cent such plants of UK-controlled corporations are located in million plus cities while Bombay alone accounts for 45 per cent of the British plants. In the eastern and northern regions, no such USA-owned or controlled plant is located in settlements lower than S_5 status. Countries like Germany, Japan, the Bahamas, Sweden and Holland have shown locational spread to some extent in western, southern and northern regions. In the east, besides Hindustan Lever's four plants in the outer hinterland of Calcutta and Sweden's one plant in Assam, all other plants are concentrated in Calcutta city. In this region, the largest number of plants (48 out of 71) are owned by UK-controlled corporations constituting 68 per cent of the total. In the southern region again, UK-controlled plants are the largest in number (43 out of 82). In the north, USA-controlled plants are the largest in number (31 per cent) but not comparable to the plants from Britain in the east and south. In the west, UK-controlled plants are the largest in number but their share in the total is again not very high. In all the regions, till 1990, either the UK or the USA had the largest number of plants under their control. Simultaneously, a gradual increase of plants of other countries in the north, south and west is noticed. With increasing interest of German, Japanese, American and other European MNCs in India, the emerging spatial dynamics of international capital in this country will be worth examining.

5.4 Case Study of an American MNC—Procter and Gamble in India

A detailed analysis of the spatial dynamics and operational aspects of an American multinational operating in the consumer goods sector in India has been attempted in this section. The analysis is as of 1990. American multinationals have grown at a spectacular rate since the Second World War and their progressive growth rate in India has always been high. They have penetrated in all the sectors of the Indian economy and industry—right from the resource-based sectors to the market-oriented, consumer-based sectors. In the consumer goods sector, of the 129 MNCs, USA owns 23 corporations, four producing only food and related items, 18 producing only non-food items and one producing both food and non-food items. Fourteen (61 per cent) out of these 23 are included in the *Fortune* 500 list of the world's largest corporations in 1991. These are Pepsico (tie-up with Punjab Agro Foods in India) and CPC International Inc. (tie-up with Corn Products (India) Ltd.) in the food and related product sector; Apple Computer, Digital Equipments Corporation, Johnson and Johnson, Procter and Gamble, Colgate Palmolive, Chesebrough Ponds*, Whirlpool Corporation, Gillette Corporation, Ford Corporation, Chrysler Corporation and Union Carbide manufacturing only non-food products; and Pfizer producing food and related (animal products) products and non-food (health and pharmaceutical) products both.

It has been amply argued (Barnet and Muller, 1974) that US-based corporations since long have developed an increasing dependence on their foreign operations. During the early seventies, foreign income of these corporations increased to 44 per cent of the domestic income and they could insulate themselves, by geographical diversification, from recession in any one country or region. In the mid seventies, more than 20 per cent of the corporate profits of the US-based firms were derived from abroad. In order to improve efficiency, these corporations in all the host countries and especially those in the Third World have developed a huge communication networks and market control measures. The essential structures of their power by which they earn profit and control the market are based on a twofold mechanism. First is the world wide control over technology and as a result the capacity to rise above the compulsions of employing either labour-saving or labour-intensive devices. Second is their control over communication which they use to co-ordinate their organisations and market the products.

The American multinational corporation selected for the present analysis is Procter and Gamble, a manufacturer of cosmetics, health products, toiletries and drugs. In 1991, this corporation had a turnover of $ 24,376 million. Profit accrued was $ 1,602 million, constituting 7 per cent of its total sales (Hammer and Teitelbaum, 1991). Procter and Gamble had entered India in the mid-sixties.

5.4.1 History and growth

History of Procter and Gamble in India is intertwined with another American multinational, Richardson Merrill. During 1962-63,

* bought out by Unilever in 1991

its Indian subsidiary, Vicks India Incorporated, used to market Vicks Veporub manufactured by Parle and Boots. In the mid-sixties, Richardson Merrill started its subsidiary Richardson Hindustan and set up a plant at Kalwa in the MIDC industrial belt on Thane-Belapur Road. All the employees of Vicks (India) consisting of seven permanent workers and the remaining management staff were taken in as Richardson Hindustan employees.

Since July 1966 to mid-1976, Richardson Hindustan produced various products of Merrill including the primary product—Vicks. In 1969 it was bought out by Procter and Gamble which started manufacturing medicine, and health products. Richardson

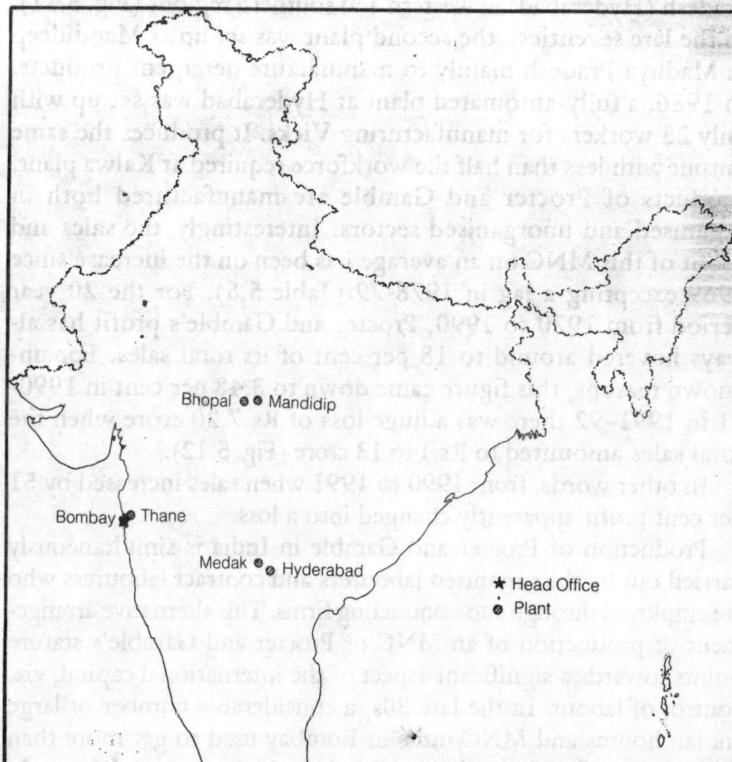

Fig. 5.11 Head office and plant locations of Procter and Gamble

Hindustan's plant at Kalwa was taken over by Procter and Gamble to set up a plant for its Indian conterpart Procter and Gamble (India) with 40 per cent of its equity owned by the parent corporation. In addition to Richardson Hindustan products, Procter and Gamble (India) now started manufacturing the home products of its parent corporation such as Clearasil lotion, Crest tooth paste etc.

5.4.2 *Spatial spread and operational norms*

In 1990 Procter and Gamble (India) had its head office located in Bombay. Plant activities were distributed over three states of Maharashtra (Kalwa) Madhya Pradesh (Mandideep) and Andhra Pradesh (Hyderabad) in western and southern regions (Fig. 5.11). In the late seventies, the second plant was set up at Mandideep in Madhya Pradesh mainly to manufacture detergent products. In 1986, a fully-automated plant at Hyderabad was set up with only 23 workers for manufacturing Vicks. It produces the same output with less than half the workforce required at Kalwa plant. Products of Procter and Gamble are manufactured both in organised and unorganised sectors. Interestingly, the sales and profit of this MNC on an average has been on the increase since 1969 excepting a lag in 1978-79 (Table 5.5). For the 20 year period from 1970 to 1990, Procter and Gamble's profit has always hovered around to 18 per cent of its total sales. For unknown reasons, this figure came down to 3.48 per cent in 1990-91 in 1991–92 there was a huge loss of Rs.7.20 crore when the total sales amounted to Rs.146.13 crore (Fig. 5.12).

In other words, from 1990 to 1991 when sales increased by 51 per cent profit apparently changed into a loss.

Production of Procter and Gamble in India is simultaneously carried out by the organised labourers and contract labourers who are employed through sub-contracting firms. This alternative arrangement of production of an MNC of Procter and Gamble's stature points towards a significant aspect of the international capital, viz. control of labour. In the late 80s, a considerable number of large Indian houses and MNC units in Bombay used to get more than 25 per cent of their products made by sub-contracting labour. In some units the entire production of certain items was carried out by them. While organised workers of Murphy had little work in the shop floor, the bulk of the production was carried out by sub-contracting firms. Plants of Rallifan or PMT Traub in Pune only undertook assembly work of the parts manufactured by sub-contracting units. At Philips, some products, such as bulbs, coating

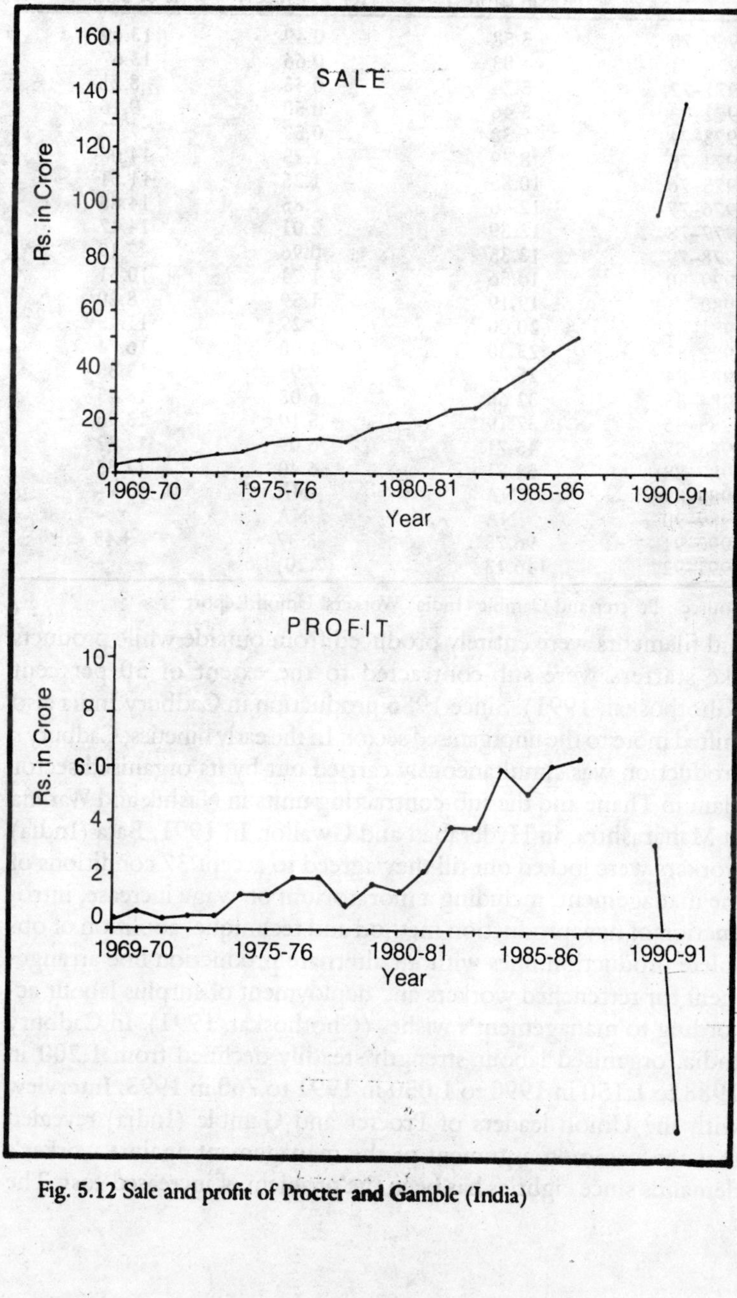

Fig. 5.12 Sale and profit of Procter and Gamble (India)

Table 5.5 *Sales and profit of Procter and Gamble (India) Limited*

Year	Sales (Rs. in Crores)	Profit (Rs. in Crores)	Profit as % of Sales
1969–70	3.58	0.49	13.69
1970–71	4.83	0.66	13.67
1971–72	5.24	0.43	8.21
1972–73	5.46	0.50	9.16
1973–74	7.38	0.57	7.72
1974–75	8.89	1.25	14.06
1975–76	10.86	1.25	11.51
1976–77	12.46	1.85	14.85
1977–78	13.89	2.01	14.47
1978–79	13.35	0.96	7.19
1979–80	16.56	1.74	10.51
1980–81	19.19	1.59	8.29
1981–82	20.00	2.29	11.45
1982–83	23.30	3.90	16.74
1983–84	25.74	3.95	15.35
1984–85	32.68	6.03	18.45
1985–86	37.19	5.19	13.96
1986–87	45.71	6.09	13.32
1987–88	51.81	6.40	12.33
1988–89	NA	NA	–
1989–90	NA	NA	–
1990–91	96.78	3.37	3.48
1991–92	146.13	(7.20) Loss	–

Source : Procter and Gamble (India) Workers' Union Report

and filaments were entirely produced from outside while products like starters were sub-contracted to the extent of 50 per cent (Ghothoskar, 1991). Since 1986 production in Cadbury India also shifted more to the unorganised sector. In the early nineties, Cadbury's production was simultaneously carried out by its organised sector plant in Thane and the sub-contracting units in Nashik and Warana in Maharashtra, in Hyderabad and Gwalior. In 1991, Bata (India) workers were locked out till they agreed to accept 37 conditions of the management, including a moratorium on wage increase, introduction of new production method and technique, abolition of obsolete production lines without alternate production line arrangement for retrenched workers and deployment of surplus labour according to management's wishes (Ghothoskar, 1991). In Cadbury India, organised labour strength steadily declined from 1,200 in 1988 to 1,150 in 1990 to 1,050 in 1991 to 760 in 1993. Interview with the Union leaders of Procter and Gamble (India) revealed that the common argument of the management against worker's demands since eighties has been the problem of increased cost. The remedy suggested by the management was increased use of contract labour and retrenchment of organised labour. It not only brings

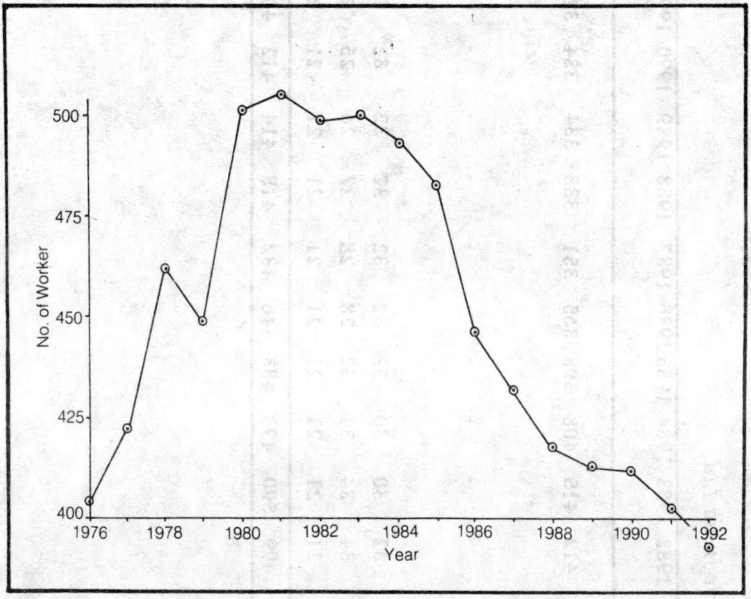

Fig. 5.13 Rate of employment charge in kalwa plant of Procter and Gamble

down the production cost and enables the corporation to earn huge profit, but also works as a permanent pressure on the organised workers who in the fear of becoming surplus become more submissive. Table 5.6 gives a clear indication of decline of permanent employment (Fig. 5.13) in the biggest organised sector plant of Procter and Gamble(I) at Kalwa (taking both shop floor and administrative workers together).

Shift of production of Procter and Gamble to the unorganised sector is thus obvious (Table 5.7). In 1992 while the Kalwa and Hyderabad plant produced only drugs and some old health products such as Vicks Veporub and Mandideep plant made soaps and detergent, contract labour produced a considerable proportion of the total sales. Forty per cent of the candy product was produced by contract labourers of the sub-contracting firms located at Surendranagar in Gujarat and Hyderabad (by two firms namely Pharmesia and Anand Food). Forty per cent of the production of Action 500, an analgesic

Table 5.6 *Employment pattern of Procter and Gamble India Ltd.*

Location of Plant	Workmen	1976	1977	1978	1979	1980	1981	1982	1983	1984	1985	1986	1987	1988	1989	1990	1991	1992
Kalwa/ Thana	Permanent	298	316	361	352	409	410	412	415	408	398	365	351	338	334	334	325	315
	Casual/ Temporary	250	300	240	60	-	-	-	-	-	-	-	-	-	-	-	-	-
	Regular but on contract																	
(1)	Canteen	45	45	42	40	35	35	32	30	30	32	32	32	32	32	32	32	32
(2)	House keeping	40	40	38	36	36	25	34	34	34	32	28	28	27	26	25	25	25
(3)	Security staff	21	21	21	21	21	21	21	21	21	21	21	21	21	21	21	21	21
	Total	654	722	702	509	501	491	499	500	493	483	446	432	418	414	412	403	393

Source : Procter and Gamble Workers' Union

drug, was undertaken by contract labourers of Hyderabad. All of the Crest tooth paste was produced by contract labourers at Vapi in Gujarat. The entire lot of Clearasil medicated cream was produced by the sub-contracting labourers of Hagel Capsul of Andheri, Bombay. Similarly, 100 per cent Ultra Clearasil facial cream was made by contract labourers in Pharmesia in Hyderabad. All of Whisper sanitary napkin was produced by contract labourers in Maharashtra and Goa.

Table 5.7 *Products of Procter and Gamble India Ltd. manufactured by Contract Labour*

Products	Contract Labour in % of total sale
1. Candy product	40%
2. Action 500	40%
3. Ultra Clearasil	100%
4. Whisper	100%
5. Crest tooth paste	100%
6. Oil of Olay	75%

Source : Primary data

5.4.3. The political economy of Procter and Gamble

The production reorganisation of Procter and Gamble is a part of the larger corporate strategies of giant multinational corporations all over the world (Massey 1984) representing a perspective relationship between production and consumption systems (Ettlinger, 1990; Aglietta, 1979).

The steady decline of permanent workers in Procter and Gamble (India) substantiates the above arguments and points at the corporations' non-Fordist strategy that did not organise sector employment, labour skill development or rise in per capita income. The gradual importance of temporary workers in the production system of the corporation and a simultaneous decline in the organised employment is also a part of the labour control strategy of the corporate sector. While organised workers' sympathy for their unorganised counterpart's plight was quite clear, their simultaneous anxiety about the latter's being a constant threat to their employment was also not hidden. During the early nineties, the organised workers in the biggest plant of Procter and Gamble (India) did not have enough production work while sub-contracting labour engaged intermittently on irregular basis produced the bulk.

The emerging geographical pattern resulting out of the above restructuration reiterates Massey's (1984) formulations and the fallacy of many spatial theories on the unidirectional inward and outward movement of capital. Example of Procter and Gamble (India) suggests that different functions of a single source capital may gravitate to different areas which, however, may not be free from hierarchy of control. It also reflects an ongoing recomposition of local social relations by MNCs by way of infiltrating the local labour market not always through organised employment. This new spatial reorganisation of capitalist production destabilises old traditional industrial heartlands (in the present case the Thane-Belapur industrial belt) and opens up new reserves of cheap labour, gender specific or region specific. It is not just capital but the working class as well which undergoes a simultaneous geographical reorganisation (Saunders, 1987). The taken-over of Godrej Soaps Limited by Procter and Gamble (with 45 per cent equity holding) and a simultaneous increase in the sub-contracting of important products reflect this reorganisation in reality. In the new corporation of Procter and Gamble and Godrej (PGG), the former concentrates more on marketing of soaps and invests less on plant and labour while the Godrej part concentrates more on manufacturing and invests less on marketing and publicity. Procter and Gamble now owns all the 12 detergent plants of Godrej and according to the merger agreement the latter receives 5 per cent profit from the total detergent sales. In 1993, the equity holding of Procter and Gamble India by the parent corporation increased from 40 per cent to 65 per cent. During 1993, Procter and Gamble set up another fully-owned subsidiary in India under the name of Procter and Gamble Home Products (PGHP) without setting up any single plant. The toilet soap, Camey, marketed by PGHP is manufactured by PGG for which PGG again receives 5 per cent of the sales proceeds. During this time Procter and Gamble also bought the total rights of a detergent soap product—Ariel of Procter and Gamble (India), researched and launched by the latter and made it a product of PGHP. Since then, Procter and Gamble (India) received only the 5 per cent manufacturing cost and the entire profit went to the parent corporation. Shares and rights of the candy products that were earlier manufactured and exported by Procter and Gamble (India) from its Kalwa plant to Australia and Japan were also taken over by the parent corporation which now became the sole exporter while production shifted from India to Indonesia. Finally, during early 1994, the parent unit of Procter and Gamble decided to close down the

Kalwa plant of Procter and Gamble (India) and force all the workers (nearing about 275) to take compulsory retirement under a voluntary retirement scheme. Closing down of the Kalwa plant in April, 1994 is actually a part of the production reorganisation strategies of the international corporate sector all over the world. Even though the analysis is of 1990 forming a part of the total analysis of chapter 4, some later developments of P&G in India have been mentioned to indicate the continuity in its spatial policy.

5.5 Unilever/Hindustan Lever : Expansion and Operation in India

Hindustan Lever, a wholly-owned subsidiary of the Unilever group is not only the biggest multinational in the consumer goods sector, it is also the biggest MNC in India among all MNCs in all sectors. Even though it operates primarily in the consumer goods sector, of all foreign controlled corporations in India including the chemical or pharmaceutical giants like Union Carbide or Hoechst, Hindustan Lever in the mid-eighties had the highest sales and total owned funds. Despite having transferred a part of its dairy products, animal feed and the vanaspati business (for dodging FERA restrictions) to Lipton and Brooke Bond—two joint venture units of Unilever—Hindustan Lever retains its position as the third largest MNC in India in terms of sales.

5.5.1. Unilever : The parent corporation

A look at the organisational structure and operational aspects of Unilever, the parent corporation, is needed here. While Lever Brothers of UK and Margarine Union of Holland had been operating way back in 19th century, their merger to form Unilever took place only in 1930. Over the next 60 years, Unilever expanded its activities steadily in almost all countries of the world. Having business and factories in 75 countries, employing nearly 3,00,000 people, this giant corporation has more than 500 subsidiaries and associated companies and more than 1,000 brands of world's best known products such as Vim cleaner, Pepsodent and Signal tooth paste, Lux and Sunlight soaps, Blue Band Margarine and Lipton tea. The worldwide turnover of this international corporation in the mid-eighties was more than £12 billion, making it the 12th among the world's largest industrial conglomerates. In 1990, Unilever ranked

19th among the world's biggest industrial corporations in terms of sales ($39.972 million) and eighth in terms of employment, with 3,04,000 employees in its payroll. The break-up of Unilever's sales turnover is distributed among various products—edible fats and dairy products (24 per cent), food and related products (23 per cent), soaps and detergents (18 per cent), chemical products (6 per cent), animal feed (6 per cent), personal products (4 per cent) and others (19 per cent). The organisational structure of the corporation is unique. Being a true Anglo-Dutch joint venture, it has two parent companies stationed in London (Unilever PLC) and Rotterdam (Unilever NV) having identical boards of directors linked by agreements of equal terms. The subsidiaries and associated companies in the erstwhile British colonies and commonwealth countries are owned by the Unilever PLC, UK. During the late eighties, Unilever acquired the famous consumer goods corporations, Chesebrough Ponds of USA (Elshof, 1988).

For many decades, Unilever concentrated its sales in Europe, especially in UK, Holland and Germany. Its capital investments were focussed in these countries with 50 per cent of its turnover and around 60 per cent of the total profits derived from them. Even though Unilever had a very strong presence in countries like India, Indonesia, Nigeria or Turkey, till the late seventies the combined turnover of the corporation in these markets could not match the turnover in Europe. During the seventies, they could contribute only to 20-25 per cent of the total profit of the corporation. With economic crises showing up in Europe since the late seventies, the strong dependence of Unilever on Europe started showing signs of problems in the form of falling profit (in 1983, Europe gave 35 per cent of the total profit on 58 per cent of total turnover), stagnation of markets due to stagnating population and economic growth and, above all, saturation of the European market for its major profit-making products (Elshof, 1989). Subsequently, the corporation decided to (*i*) select core activities and dispose of non-core activities and (*ii*) search for a more balanced global expansion in place of the erstwhile heavy concentration in Europe. This type of restructuring was taken up by many MNCs at this juncture and Unilever was the foremost. The result was a thorough restructuring of products, markets and units in Asia, Africa, Latin America as well as Europe and the United States. Since the early eighties, between 1984 and 88, it disposed of nearly 85 subsidiaries in the non-core sector in Europe but bought around 80 new companies, 50 per cent of them in Europe and all in the core sector. Mentionable ones were acquisition of Brooke Bond in 1984 and Chesebrough Ponds in 1986. In 1988, Unilever bought 55 business at a total cost of $ 3 billion. Sales nearly doubled between 1984 and 89 and profits tripled. In 1989 alone, earnings per share of Unilever rose by 15 per cent (Lowe, 1992). In most Asian countries Unilever had been operating for more than 60 years through subsidiaries in a limited range of products. Its restructuring in the eighties for Asia included (*i*) full expansion of the already existing product groups such as detergents and personal products and (*ii*) extension of market by adding products in food and related items and industrial products, especially chemicals and agri-business items like animal feed and seeds. Its penetration into newer markets brought along a whole lot of cultural changes in consumer behaviour. In addition, in its endeavour to be a low cost product corporation, Unilever started opting for computerised factories in large-scale production and a simultaneous sub-contracting for any possible product creating a deep-rooted impact on industrial employment structure of host countries. In India, Unilever had started off with a share capital of Rs. 28 lakh which increased to Rs. 344 crore by early 1990. Hindustan Lever's expansion has to be analysed with this background of its parent corporation in mind.

5.5.2. Hindustan Lever : history of growth

Lever Brothers started marketing soaps in India nearly 100 years ago. A locally registered company came only in 1934 by acquiring two Indian soap companies—the North West Soap Factory and the Premier Soap Factory. The first factory was opened in Sewri in Bombay in 1934. By the end of the Second World War, Lever Brothers commanded more than half of the soap market in India (Fieldhouse, 1978). In 1930, Unilever started another subsidiary namely Hindustan Vanaspati Manufacturing Company Limited for manufacturing vegetable hydrogenated oil popularly known as vanaspati. These two separate production branches of Unilever got integrated with United Traders Ltd., a trading company in 1944. The second phase of integration came up in 1956 with Hindustan Lever emerging as a wholly-owned subsidiary in which Unilever had an equity share of 85 per cent. In the early nineties, the face value of shares held by Unilever was 51 per cent. Hindustan Lever has interlocking management relations with other associated companies of Unilever in India like Lipton, Brooke Bond, Ponds, Naarden, etc. The mergers of the early nineties of Lipton and Brooke Bond as well as of Tomco and Hindustan Lever indicate Unilever's desire to emerge as a dominating corporate group in India, taking fullest advantage of the new economic policy and structural adjustment programmes of the Indian government. Even otherwise, India has always been very important for Unilever in terms of sales, range of products and total employment. The market and variety of economic space that India can offer are unique.

Hindustan Lever (HL) has throughout retained its high equity with its parent company. It needs mention that with every move of the government to reduce HL's foreign equity, the corporation has planned a careful expansion of production lines and of other non-manufacturing activities. In 1956, it entered into the production of synthetic detergents with the production actually starting in 1959. In 1960, another move by the government towards sale of shares induced HL for further expansion and diversification in foodstuffs, especially in cattle feed, milk products, dehydrated peas and onions, cotton seed processing etc. In 1969, the company entered into the production of the Hima range of food products, a variety of toilet soaps, personal care products such as Fair and Lovely, shaving soap/blades (Erasmic brand), talcum powder and Signal tooth paste (Agarwala, 1990). In 1977, there were pressures from the government to reduce Hindustan Lever's foreign equity share from 75 per cent to 40 per cent. The company did bring it down to 65.05 per cent but at the same time increased Unilever's paid-up capital in HL from Rs. 799.64 lakh in 1965 to Rs.1,153.45 lakh in 1977. Thus, although the ratio of Indian shares increased, the financial stake of the foreign company was increased in absolute terms. However, the way earlier government moves were thwarted, this one also was done with the help of a specific expansion plan of manufacture of fine chemicals. In 1982, the company got permission from the Indian government to retain its 51 per cent foreign equity on the ground that it was exporting more than 10 per cent of its product value and producing more than 60 per cent in sophisticated product lines. By transferring some non-core sector production to its sister company, Lipton, as mentioned earlier, the core sector production of Hindustan Lever was carefully raised. Along with Hindstan Lever, a few subsidiaries of other giant MNCs such as Siemens and Union Carbide were also permitted to retian their 51 per cent foreign equity.

5.5.3. Product diversification

During 1977-81 Hindustan Lever operated on three product lines in the core sector of Indian economy, viz., synthetic detergents, industrial machinery and fine chemicals (Table 5.8). A close look at the table reveals that the maximum value of these products as a percentage of the total production of Hindustan Lever was only 25 per cent. In 1983, by transferring a number of food items to Lipton India (which does not come under FERA regulations because of its 40 per cent foreign equity), it could show a fake increase of relative production in core sector products to 33.88 per cent. However, this was still much short of the requirement of 60 per cent imposed by the government in 1982. In the early eighties thus some careful reorganisation was undertaken by selling most of production of food items to Lipton. Moreover, the government was assured that HL produced soap used sophisticated technology by using non-edible oil as an ingredient. Secondly, it was also argued that by using non-edible oil it was releasing edible oil for mass consumption thereby helping to keep oil price under check. All these were specious arguments. Hindustan Lever's using non-edible oil for soap manufacturing was nothing unique and the technology was also nothing sophisticated. However, the company procured necessary permission from the government to retain 51 per cent foreign equity mainly on these grounds (Lieten, 1987). This ultimately gave Hindustan Lever plenty of room compared to other corporations in the consumer goods sector to manipulate its expansion in this sector that fetched for its parent corporation the highest profit due to less input costs in technology, research and development or even labour, thanks to its sub-contracting strategy. Unilever, through Hindustan Lever, Lipton and Brooke Bond thus managed to retain a dominant position in the field of soaps, detergents, tea and also [illegible] considerable extent, in hydrogenated oil.

Table 5.8 *Value of core sector products of Hindustan Lever*

(Rs. in million)

Products	1977	1978	1979	1980	1981
(a) Synthetic detergents	393	477	662	1009	1180
(b) Industrial machinery	–	0.2	0.1	0.3	0.6
(c) Fine Chemicals	1	2	2	3	2
a + b + c	394	479	664	1012	1182
(d) Total value of products	2617	2765	3326	4042	4808
Percentage of (a+b+c) to d	15.09%	17.20%	19.96%	25.02%	24.57%

Source : Annual Reports of HL in A.K. Rath, 1982

The development of the product line of Hindustan Lever in consumer goods can be followed sequentially. In 1950, it had established product line in items like toilet soap, hard soap, detergent, glycerine, tea blending, cloth printing, vegetable oil (dalda, vanaspati) etc. Following the establishment of Hindustan Lever in 1959, the company introduced a new washing soap, Rin. In 1961, Aneek Ghee, milk powder and Lever spray were introduced with the latter closing down shortly. In 1969, soaps and detergents with new formula were launched. In the mid-seventies, Hindustan Lever started manufacturing chemical products together with fine chemical blending and castor oil. Products of sulphuric acid and fine chemicals joined the line in the late seventies when another washing soap bar, 'Wheel', was launched. The older detergent powder 'Surf' was launched in 1983 in a slightly changed form, 'Ultra Surf', together with the Rin soap bar (earlier only soap cakes were available). During the same time, 'Fair and Lovely' face cream was launched. The year 1984 was significant for Hindustan Lever when it launched Vim—a washing powder for utensils, ceramics and floor and entered into the business of garments and cosmetics in a big way. Newer brands of shampoo and tooth paste were launched in the mid eighties. By that time Lifebuoy, Lux and Rexona had reached saturation points [illegible] demand and thus underwent some reformulation technique and [illegible] re relaunched in various colours and changed forms. During th[illegible] me time, men's garments were manufactured fully for export. D[illegible] g the late eighties, Hindustan Lever entered the carpet-washing [illegible] eration and prawn hatching. Its unique venture in marine fo[illegible] as a fair edge over Britannia and Chloride India. The prod[illegible] n figures of soap show that between 1974 and 1984 output had doubled. In 1983 a new soap plant was commissioned in the Kandla free trade zone, stimulating a 25 per cent increase in soap production.

Agriculture seeds and chemicals constitute the new area of attention of the company. Chemicals produced include linalol, citral, phenyl, ethyl, alcohol and linalyl acetate. Without any know-how at its disposal, Hindustan Lever also went in for producing heavy chemicals. Since the early eighties, it has been producing agro-chemicals, and plant nutrients. Mention should also be made of the Hindustan Lever Research Foundation which was started to safeguard the interest of Unilever in biotechnological research, especially in the fields of tissue culture in which giant MNCs like Hoechst (Agarwala, 1990) are the competitors.

When Hindustan Lever was first registered as Lever Brothers in 1934, it was engaged in the production of soap, vanaspati, toilet preparations and chemicals. Over the years, the product mix of the company has become a complex one. Retaining the dominance of soaps, detergents and vanaspati and introducing changed formulations in the same line, the company has diversified the core sector products together with garment, tea and leather exports. Since the late eighties, Hindustan Lever is also regarded as a major trading house. In addition to its own products, it exports footwear, garments, leather goods, tea, carpets and other small-scale sector products that constitute one-third of its exports. The Pondicherry unit installed in the early nineties is meant for only leather export. A major portion of exports is directed to free currency areas and rupee payment countries.

5.5.4. *Operational norms and organisational hierarchy*

The company in the course of about 35 years has been able to greatly increase its capital stock, diversify into various types of products, expand into newer parts of the country and also draw recognition from the government regarding its contribution towards India's economic development.

A mention of Hindustan Lever's research and development activities will not be totally out of the context here. Compared to Procter and Gamble (India), whose main research initiative was noted mainly in manufacturing and promoting the detergent soap, Ariel, Hindustan Lever's research activities cover a wider area. However, a major part of such researches aims at product differentiation, diversification or sophistication. The lower levels of researches are done at the plant level, almost as a by-product of the manufacturing process. But higher levels of research, even if undertaken at the HL Research Foundation in India, have a direct interaction with the highest management level of the parent unit to be coupled with marketing functions as an overall strategy for product development. Such researches of MNCs, in spite of being carried out at host countries to use low cost research personnel and other associative items as also for promoting regional integration, essentially form more of an enclave rather than an integrated part of the local economy (Hymer, 1972). In recent times, MNC research and development work is increasingly distributed in the host countries as a part of their regional strategy. Besides the basic research laboratories based at home and supported by smaller applied research laboratories (Warrant, 1991), regional units specialise in specific fields or stages in the research and development process. Thus Du Pont (USA) moves its agricultural research to Switzerland, Glaxo (UK) sets up research facilities for some new drugs in the USA and Fujitsu (Japan) develops computer systems business from its research and development facility in the UK. The regional research centres essentially support the global product development and control of the parent firm on them remains firm. In Hindustan Lever too, amidst all research activities, the control of the parent company remains firm. It further intensifies through a dispersal of the Indian share among 90,000 shareholders (Lieten, 1987).

At the operational level, Hindustan Lever has repeatedly violated the MRTP and FERA regulations. According to MRTP Act, it was forbidden to expand production capacity in soap, detergents, glycerine, etc. By obtaining various methods, the company continued with its expansion plans. All these methods were either detrimental to organised industrial employment or small-scale industrial sector. Special mention should be made about the company's sub-contracting practice. Even though it has been argued (Agarwala, 1990) that lack of direct employment by the company has been compensated by large scale additional employment in ancillary industry through sub-contracting, it needs to be pointed out that the latter neither creates permanent employment nor stabilises the labour process. Rather it creates large-scale destabilisation in the organised workforce. Many of Hindustan Lever's sub-contracting practices are unregistered, viz., soap units in Aurangabad and Pune in Maharashtra and Bangalore in Karnataka. In 1977 with restrictive laws which limited production of laundry soaps only in the small-scale sector, Hindustan Lever, with the permission of the government, set up an industrial machinery plant with an expressed intention to help the small-scale sector. Effectively it started controlling some small-scale sector units and got the soap produced by them through their machines. Raw material, machinery, including the stamping machine were supplied by HL which also deputed technicians and quality control personnel for streamlining the production process. Employees in these units, consisting mainly of women and children work at one-fourth the wage rate of that of the organised labour. This reorganisation, on the one hand, has reconstituted social relations by displacing skilled permanent workforce and engaging unskilled one and, on the other, has strengthened the monopoly position of the company with no additional cost on labour. And all these have been done without officially violating the government policy of protecting small-scale industry. Interestingly, Hindustan Lever does not use Indian cotton fabric as raw material in its polycotton shirt factory set up in Kandla free trade zone. This unit uses only imported fabric from the Far East to produce items for export while Indian fabric is used as raw material by innumerable small-scale, unregistered, informal sector units which produce shirts for the domestic market albeit under close supervision of Hindustan Lever.

During the late seventies and the early eighties, the value of imported raw material for HL substantially increased, thereby offsetting the positive effect of increasing exports. Actually, it is in the export-import business where drain of foreign exchange takes place and not just through repatriation of dividends which constitutes a comparatively small amount of the total outflow. When transfer pricing is taken into account, this amount increases further. Export price of Rs.0.91 of Liril soap to Australia as against the official ex-factory price of Rs.1.95 (Lieten, 1987) is one but a sufficient example of the transfer pricing technique of the MNCs. Hindustan Lever has also secured liberal loans from Indian sources under its expansion plans. In the late seventies, it was granted a subsidy (meant for indigenous entrepreneurs who are not able to raise adequate capital from the market) of Rs. 30 lakhs to expand its industrial base. The long term rupee loan was provided by the IDBI, UTI,

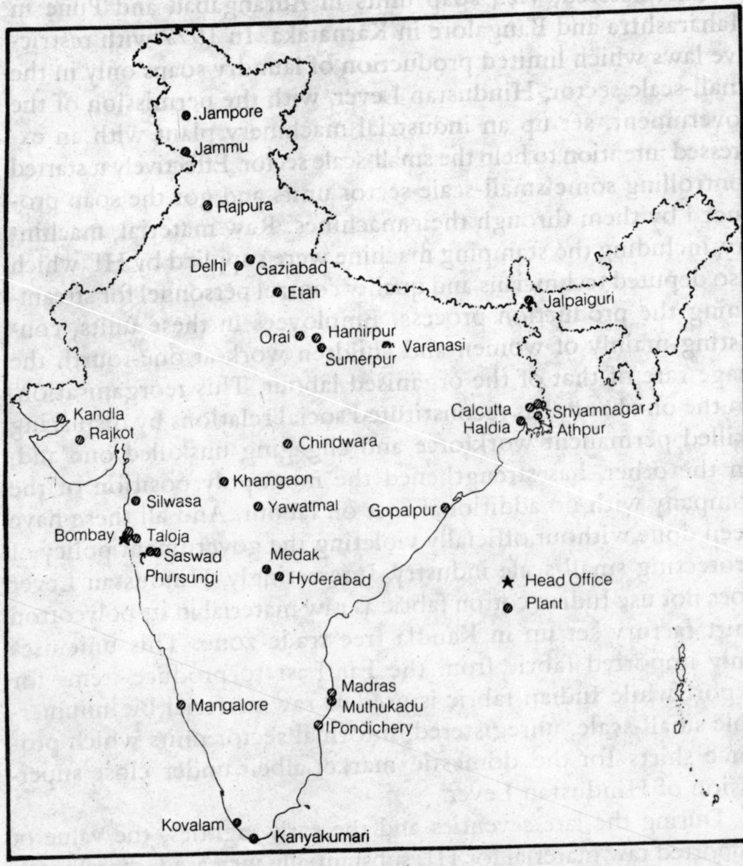

Fig. 5.14 Head office and plant locations of Hindustan Lever

LIC and other Indian financial institutions at concessional rates (Goyal, 1979). All these are examples of how a powerful MNC withstands adverse rules and laws and bypasses the official regulations of a host country. The forward and backward linkages it has established have not contributed to regional development. Rather, these have helped the corporation to move in and out of the small-scale sector in any region according to its needs.

5.5.5. *Spatial spread*

What is the nature of the spatial spread that has been achieved

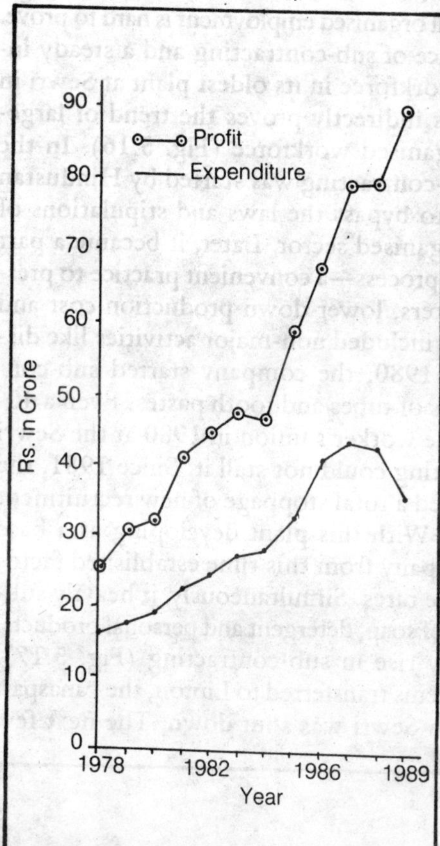

Fig. 5.15 Expenditure and profit of Hindustan Lever

by Hindustan Lever? It can be seen in two ways. First, the expansion of organised plants or factories in different parts of India and, secondly, the spreading of sub-contracting jobs and tying up several contracting firms in different parts of the country. The latter increases at the cost of the former and, therefore, is to be considered as a spatial spread of the corporation's activities without any concomitant spread of benefits for regions or rise of per capita income. Hindustan Lever has 35 plants in India (Fig. 5.14). Thirty four per cent of them are located in the western region, 26 per cent each in northern and southern regions, and 14 per cent in eastern region. In the north, 9 plants are distributed among S_2 and S_8 settlements concentrating primarily in Punjab. Few plants are also located in Delhi, Varanasi and Ghaziabad in the eastern UP. In the western region, 12 plants are scattered over Maharashtra, Gujarat and Madhya Pradesh. In south, nine plants are located in Tamil Nadu and Pondicherry while eight plants in the eastern region are mainly located in southern West Bengal, with one plant in northern West Bengal and one in Orissa. The profit curve of Hindustan Lever over the last ten years from 1980-90 shows a steady rise (Fig. 5.15). Simultaneously, there has also been a steady rise in the number of sub-contracting and temporary labour. In the absence of any temporal data on employment in all plants of Hindustan

Lever reduction in its overall organised employment is hard to prove. But the growing importance of sub-contracting and a steady increase in the temporary workforce in its oldest plant at Sewri in Bombay till early nineties indirectly proves the trend of large-scale displacement of organised workforce (Fig. 5.16). In the early seventies, when sub-contracting was started by Hindustan Lever, it was a response to bypass the laws and stipulations of the MRTP Act for the organised sector. Later, it became a part of a larger restructuration process—a convenient practice to pressurise the organised workers, lower down production cost and increase profit. It initially included non-major activities like distribution or storage. By 1980, the company started sub-contracting assembly line jobs of tubes and tooth pastes. Even a 40-day strike organised by the worker's union in 1980 at the Sewri plant against sub-contracting could not stall it. Since 1981, the Sewri plant has experienced a total stoppage of new recruitment of permanent workforce. With this plant developing as a base for unionisation, the company from this time established factories in areas with low wage rates. Simultaneously, it heavily sub-contracted the production of soap, detergent and personal products. The eighties saw a steady rise in sub-contracting (Fig. 5.17). With production of food items transferred to Lipton, the vanaspati production department in Sewri was shut down. The next few

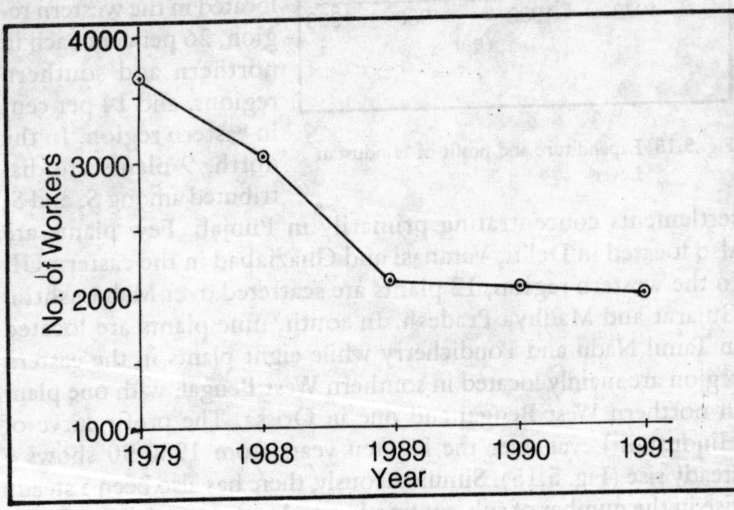

Fig. 5.16 Permanent labour force of Sewari plant

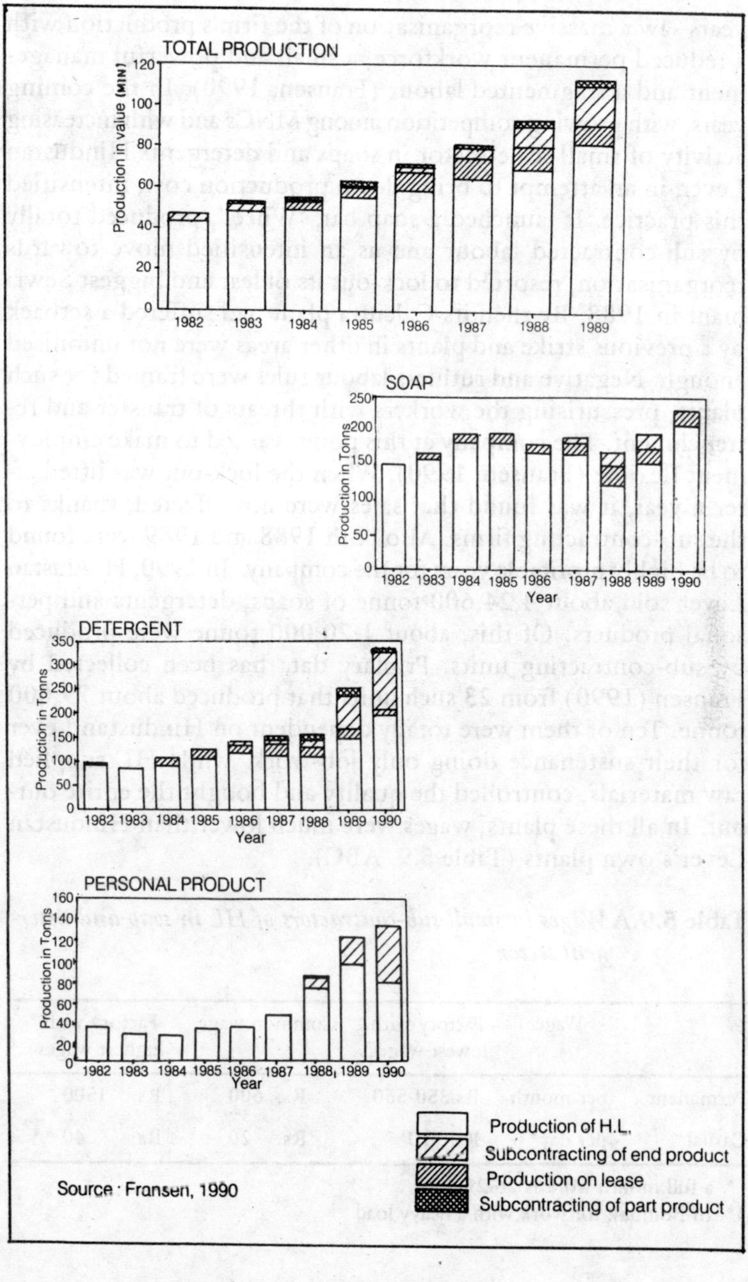

Fig. 5.17 Sub-contracting by Hindustan Lever

years saw a massive reorganisation of the firm's production with a reduced permanent workforce, a small and powerful management and a fragmented labour (Fransen, 1990). In the coming years, with growing competition among MNCs and with increasing activity of small scale-sector in soaps and detergents Hindustan Lever, in an attempt to bring down production cost, intensified this practice. It launched a soap bar, 'Wheel', produced totally by sub-contracted labour and as an intensified move towards reorganisation, resorted to lock-out its oldest and biggest Sewri plant in 1988. By then its Calcutta plant had suffered a setback by a previous strike and plants in other areas were not unionised enough. Negative and ruthless labour rules were framed for such plants, pressurising the workers with threats of transfer and retrenchment. The company at this point wanted to make employment flexible (Fransen, 1990). When the lock-out was lifted after a year, it was found that sales were not affected, thanks to the sub-contracting firms. Also both 1988 and 1989 were found to be highly profitable years for the company. In 1990, Hindustan Lever sold about 4,24,600 tonne of soaps, detergents and personal products. Of this, about 1,20,000 tonne were produced by sub-contracting units. Primary data has been collected by Fransen (1990) from 23 such units that produced about 79,000 tonne. Ten of them were totally dependent on Hindustan Lever for their sustenance doing only job-work, while HL supplied raw materials, controlled the quality and bought the entire output. In all these plants, wages were much lower than Hindustan Lever's own plants (Table 5.9. ABC).

Table 5.9.A *Wages in small sub-contractors of HL in soap and detergent sector*

	Wage	Factory with lowest wages	Common wage	Factory with highest wages
Permanent	per month	Rs.350-550	Rs. 600	Rs. 1500
Casual	per day*	Rs. 10	Rs. 20	Rs. 40 **

* a full month work is 26-27 days.

** In Bombay, for work with a heavy load

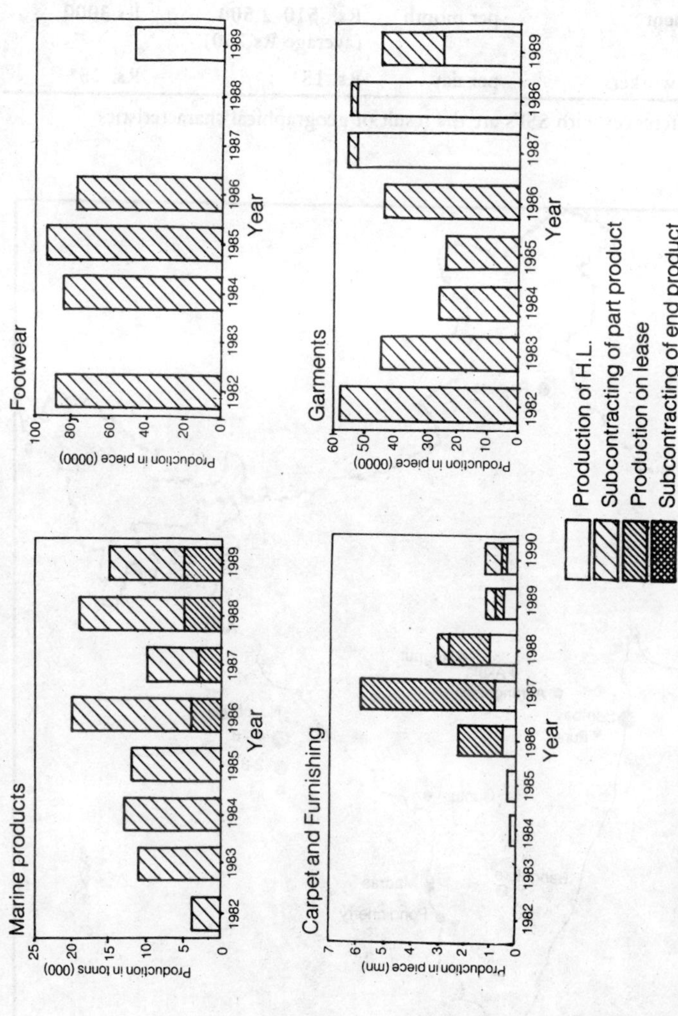

Source : Fransen, 1990

Fig. 5.18 Sub-contracting of Hindustan Lever in export products

Table 5.9.B *Wages at large sub-contractors of HL in the soap and detergent Sector*

	Wage	Factory with lowest wages	Maximum wages
Permanent	per month	Rs. 510–2,500 (average Rs.750)	Rs.3000
Casual workers	per day	Rs. 15*	Rs. 25*

* differences with SSI's are the result of geographical characteristics

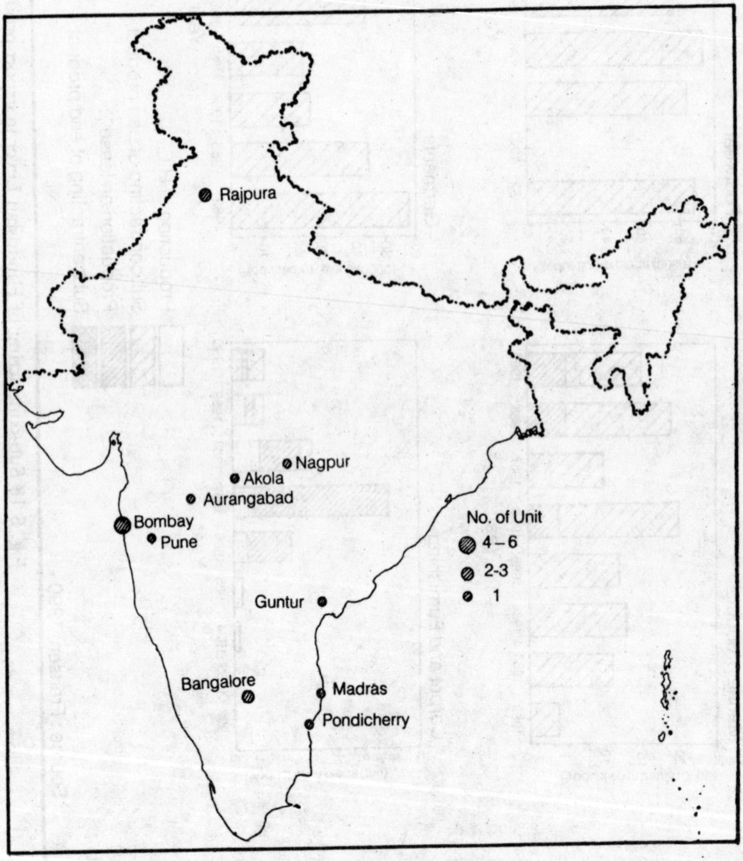

Fig. 5.19 Locations of select sub-contracting units of Hindustan Lever

Table 5.9.C *Wages at HL and sub-contractors in garment export*

	No. of workers	Wages	Wages/day	Working time/day
At HL: (workers in Madras)	90	per day	Rs. 20	8
At sub-contractors: (workers in Bombay)				
— At piece-rate *	450	piece	Rs.17–35	10–12
— Casual workers**	90	day	Rs.10–25	10–12

* Needling women are paid at piece rate. Though the work is regarded as permanent work, no security is offered to the workers.

** Workers for packaging are casual workers, paid per day.

Source: Fransen, 1990.

Apart from the above products, Hindustan lever also sub-contracts much of its export production of garments and footwear. Whereas its own garment units employ 250 workers, the sub-contracting units employ 500 workers, who work for nearly 80 hours a week and are paid on a piece-rate basis. In the footwear units of its own, Hindustan Lever employs only 54 workers while the sub-contracting units employ 350 workers. The women workers among them again are the lowest paid with a daily rate of Rs.10 (Fig. 5.18). Production norms of the sub-contracting plants of Hindustan Lever located in different districts of Maharashtra, Karnataka and Tamil Nadu (Fig. 5.19) reveal that manufacturing of soap, detergents and personal products do not require any foreign technology or skilled labour and can be produced by the unskilled labour of the informal sector too (Rupe, 1991). That hiring of sub-contracting labour is a common practice of MNCs has already been discussed. Sub-contracting units have actually emerged as a parallel production facility for many foreign-controlled companies in India (Table 5.10). A large number of these companies get most of their products manufactured by these units and only market them under their brand names (Table 5.11).

Table 5.10 *Parallel production facilities of select multinational corporations with major plants in Bombay in late eighties*

Company	Parallel Units
1. Ciba-Geigy	Goa: agro-chemicals Kandla : export
2. E. Merck	Goa Indore
3. Goeffrey Manners	Nashik (since 1980)
4. Glaxo	Thane Nashik (since 1984)
5. Hoechst	Ankleshwar: agro-chemicals, pharmaceuticals Kathmandu: pharmaceuticals
6. Rhone-Poulenc (earlier May and Baker)	Paithan
7. Pfizer	Kalyani, Ankleshwar
8. Sandoz	Paroli Kandla Ankleshwar
9. Unichem	Roha Gaziabad
10. Larsen and Toubro	Ahmednagar; switchgear (1984) Faridabad (since 1980)
11. Rallifan	Udhna (since 1981-82)
12. Ralliwolf	Ahmednagar (since 1983)
13. XLO	Nashik (7-8 companies)
14. Cadbury	Gwalior, Bangalore, Talegaon, Calcutta, Hyderabad, Kanpur (biscuits)
15. Colour chem	Roha (since 1982)
16. Hindustan Ferodo	Jalna, Paithan, Bhandara
17. Searle	Ankleshwar

Source: Ghothoskar, 1991

Table 5.11 *Select list of popular items marketed by MNCs.*

Product	Made by	Marketed by
Blue Stratos after Shave Lotion	PJM Pharmaceuticals Pvt. Ltd.	Colfax LaboraShave India Ltd.
Charmis Winter Lotion	MG Shahani & Co. (Delhi)Ltd., Delhi.	Colgate Palmolive India Ltd.
Colgate toothpowder	Crystal CosmeticsLtd., India Ltd.Hyderabad.	Colgate Palmolive India Ltd.
Halo shampoo	MG Shahani & Co. (Delhi) Ltd., Delhi.	Colgate Palmolive India Ltd.
Palmolive shampoo	-do-	-do-
Colgate toothpaste	Sunshine Cosmetics Pvt. Ltd.	-do-
Colgate Trigard toothbrush	Advani Industries, Maharashtra	-do-
Colgate tooth brush	United Bristles & Brushes Pvt. Ltd., Bombay.	-do-
Colgate Plus adult toothbrush	Dye-Azo Pvt. Ltd.	-do-
Palmolive Brilliantine	MG Shahani & Co. (Delhi) Ltd., Delhi.	-do-
Palmolive soap	Godrej Soaps Ltd.	-do-
Lacto Calamine skin lotion	Lacto Cosmetics (Vapi) Pvt. Ltd.	Duphar Interfran Ltd.
Index Burn Spray	Accra Pac India, Vapi.	Eskayef Ltd.
Cibaca toothpowder	Kent Labs (Bombay) Pvt. Ltd.	Hindusthan Ciba-Geigy Ltd.
Signal toothpaste	Int. Healthcare Products Pvt. Ltd., Bombay.	Hindustan Lever Ltd. Ltd.
Liril Freshness talc	International Healthcare Products Ltd., Bombay	Indexport Ltd. s/o. Hindustan Lever Ltd.
Liril Freshness talc	Saina Industires, Silvassa	-do-
Clinic shampoo	International Healthcare Product Ltd., Bombay	-do-
Close-up tooth paste	Mul Healthcare Products Pvt. Ltd.	-do-
Sun Silk Shampoo	International Healthcare Products Ltd., Bombay	-do-
Fair & Lovely Cream	-do-	-do-

Product	Made by	Marketed by
7 O'clock Ejtek shaving cream	Lucky Laboratories Ltd., Sikanderabad	Indian Shaving Products Ltd.
Tiara Balsam shampoo	Fiora Cosmetics Pvt. Ltd.	JK Helene Curtis Ltd.
Nivea after shave lotion	Cosmopac, Silvassa	JL Morison India Ltd.
Nivea body talc	Kaivan Cosmetics, Daman	-do-
Nivea shaving cream	-do-	-do-
Nivea shaving brush	Herman Plastic Industries.	-do-
Addis shaving brush	Crystal, Bombay	-do-
Nivea fine talc.	Saina Industries, Silvassa	-do-
Cuticura prickly heat powder	Lakshmi Cosmetics, Pondicherry	Muller & Phipps India Ltd.
Flush Up	Walsons Laboratories, Calicut	-do-
Cuticura International Classic	Anand Cosmetics, Bangalore	-do-
Cuticura Lavender Mist (Lage)	Alpha Cosmetics	-do-
Cuticura International Classic	Venus Products	-do-
Cavisan	Chemicure Laboratories Pvt. Ltd., Udaipur.	-do-
Cuticura Lavender Mist	Pavitra Cosmetics, Madras.	-do-
Pomade (Vaseline)	JB Advani & Co. (Mysore) Ltd.	Ponds India Ltd.
Ponds sandal talc.	International Healthcare Products Ltd., Bombay	-do-
Ponds conditioning shampoo.	Care Treat, Bharuch	-do-
Pond's soap	Godrej Soaps Ltd.	-do-
Rallicoil (Mosquito coil)	Senio Chemicals Pvt. Ltd., Hyderabad	Rallis India Ltd.
Dettol antiseptic lotion	Universal Generics Pvt. Ltd., Bombay.	Reckitt & Colman of India Ltd.
Dettol soap	Godrej Soaps Ltd., Bombay	-do-
Kissan milk biscuits	Premier Biscuits Pvt. Ltd.	Kissan Products Ltd. (Licensee)

Source: Chandra Shekhar, 1992, pp 67, 68, 69.

Apart from employing sub-contracted labour in separate locations, MNCs increasingly make use of contract or casual labour in the organised plants. Wages and service conditions of these workers are much inferior to those of permanent workers, a fact which proves them as exploited partners of the larger rationalisation programme of the international corporations. Initially, in the late seventies, contract labour was used for services like canteen, transport, sweeping, loading or unloading etc. In the early nineties, contract labour was found to constitute a major portion in the shop floor in companies like Parke-Davis, Johnson and Johnson, Siemens, Hindustan Lever, Colour Chem., etc. (Ghothoskar, 1991). All these point towards a deepening crisis in the labour market and an unequal competition between the formal and informal sectors. For the multinational corporations, these contribute towards more flexibility of operation and organisation.

The well-organised schemes of reorganisation and labour control of Unilever and Procter and Gamble in India reveal that the current production practices of the MNCs in host countries enable a diversified use of people and space. With the power of flexibility, the MNCs locate their activities at different locations in either large organised sector with modern technology and less workers or in depressed areas within a labour-intensive system using the unorganised workforce. Such movements cause regional unemployment directly and general unemployment indirectly by means of a reduction in worker income, a lack of mass market, a lower overall rate of economic growth and thus, a lack of demand for workers (Peet, 1983). Hindustan Lever in this process generates a spatial hierarchy not with a uniform rigidity of Level II and Level III operations but with a mixed status. Level II remains rigidly fixed with the levels of urban hierarchy while Level III activities become not just footloose and flexible but also non-capitalist in form.

5.6. Socio-Cultural Effects of Consumer Goods MNCs

The above analysis based on the operations of MNCs in consumer goods sector implies far reaching effects of such operations. These, besides having economic import also have social and cultural bearing. They establish a producers' sovereignty over consumers', belying the claim of the latter and also influence the pattern of their daily life, societal habits, behaviour and cultural psyche. This is done as a requirement for the MNCs themselves, to ensure a steady sale of their products. While selling their products, the MNCs require to sell a specific socio-economic order (Peet, 1982) for which they again need to shape the market. This task of shaping the market involves an attack on the consumers' mind or, the already developed cultural and social institutions of the consumers' society. Hence the impact of consumer goods MNCs on the society and culture of the host countries tends to become a sensitive and an ideological issue and attains a wider quality.

Two crucial aspects of this socio-cultural impact have been discussed here. First, products of the consumer goods MNCs tend to raise the general propensity to consume and create a distinct demonstration effect on the societies of the Third World host countries acting as an obstacle to capital formation and development (Hirschman, 1968). Also their products wage an unequal competition with indigenous producers including the small-scale sector. The competition is unequal not for technology or production system but mainly because the financial power and the advantage due to global operations that the MNCs enjoy make them flexible in organising production. This is in no way attainable by the indigenous producers. It gives a wide leverage in price fixing and control of market. For example, Hindustan Lever's pricing of 'Wheel' soap bar very cheap to push out 'Nirma' a product of the small-scale sector, from the soap market, at least partly, is an apt example.

The market share of the consumer goods MNCs in India during the mid-eighties shows how efficiently they have penetrated the market of specific products for which they do not necessarily use any sophisticated technology or the like (Table 5.12). Hindustan Lever alone controlled 70 per cent of the toilet soap market, while four foreign-controlled companies—Colgate Palmolive, Hindustan Ciba-Geigy, Geoffrey Manners and Hindustan Lever—together controlled 72 per cent of the tooth paste market (Sachdeva, 1989). A specific consumption pattern is thus created at the cost of erosion of an indigenous production base. Let us take the case of dairy industry. In new economic policy this industry has been delicensed. So now the National Dairy Development Board confronts Nestlé or Glaxo as its competitors in the Indian market. But what is the nature of that competition? The Board sets up a condensed milk plant in 1991 under the instruction of the Indian government as Nestlé earlier had refused to do so. After the plant starts functioning, Nestlé decides to set up a similar plant. Earlier the Board had to take up the manufacture of baby food when Glaxo had declined on the ground that too many bacteria were present in the Indian air. Once the Board started its production, Glaxo decided to launch their baby food plant. In both cases, the MNCs could secure necessary support from the Indian government. And both the MNC plants were high-cost ventures than those launched by the Board. Kurien (1991) argues that any public or co-operative venture involves low input cost than any MNC venture including salary of the highest personnel. For example, the salary of the managing director of Amul—the largest dairy corporation of India—is one-tenth of his counterpart in Nestlé.

Table 5.12 *Market shares of foreign controlled companies in India (1984)*

Product & Companies	% share in the market	Total % share of FCCs
I. *Toilet Soap*		50.3
1. Hindustan Lever ltd.	50.3	
2. Tata Oil Mills Co. Ltd.,	25.7	
II. *Synthetic Detergents*		62.6
1. Hindustan Lever Ltd.	58.1	
2. Tata Oil Mills Co. Ltd.	12.7	
3. Reckitt & Colman of (I) Ltd.	4.5	
III. *Cosmetic and Toilet Preparation*		85.2
1. Colgate Palmolive (I) Ltd.	44.4	
2. Ponds (I) Ltd.	24.1	
3. Hindustan Lever Ltd.	8.5	
4. Lakme Ltd.	7.6	
5. Hindustan Ciba Giegy Ltd.	6.7	
6. Tata Oil Mills Co. Ltd.	3.5	
IV. *Milk Products and Baby Foods*		49.5
1. Food Specialities Ltd.	25.6	
2. Glaxo Laboratories (I) Ltd.	18.5	
3. Lipton (I) Ltd.	3.3	
4. Hindustan Lever Ltd.	2.1	
V. *Malted Foods*		77.0
1. HMM Ltd.	57.3	
2. Hindustan Cocoa Products Ltd.	19.7	
VI. *Wheat and Cereal Products*		93.5
1. Food Specialities Ltd.	93.5	
2. Mohan Meakins Ltd.	6.5	
VII. *Biscuits*		31.8
1. Britannia Indutries Ltd.	31.8	
VIII. *Confectionery*		15.0
1. Hindustan Cocoa Products Ltd.	15.0	
IX. *Instant Coffee*		100.0
1. Brooke Bond (I) Ltd.	60.8	

	2. Food Specialities Ltd.	39.2	
X.	*Dry Cells*		47.7
	1. Union Carbide (I) Ltd.	47.7	
XI.	Storage Batteries		64.6
	1. Chloride (I) Ltd.	48.7	
	2. Standard Batteries Ltd.	15.9	
	3. Willard India Ltd.	9.3	
XII.	*GLS Lamps*		52.4
	1. Peico Eln. & Electricals Ltd.	29.3	
	2. Sylvania & Laxman Ltd.	11.6	
	3. Electric Manp (I) Ltd.	11.3	
	4. Geep Industrial Syndicate	0.2	
XIII.	*Fluorescent Tubes*		16.6
	1. Electric Const. & Eqpt. Co. Ltd.	10.4	
	2. Peico Eln. & Electricals Ltd.	6.2	

Source : 'Economic Intelligence Service' Market and Market Shares Centre for Monitoring India Economy, March 1980.

This brings us to the second aspect of the socio-cultural effects. To sell the products and to ensure their future sale,the MNCs carefully plan an attack on the consumers' psyche of the poor host countries through colonially structured advertisement campaign. These campaigns are totally based on the concept of cultural hegemony of the West launched by the MNCs as a corporate manipulation tactic. Advertisements of Nestle's Nescafé inducing people to drink it because elites in Paris drink it, or of Cadbury's chocolates asking children to buy the product with the aid of European fairy tales, etc. are good examples. Even a Japanese MNC like Nippon Electric company advertises in leading Indian dailies with pictures of western viewers gathered in front of their television sets (Times, 1989). For a better understanding, let us look at the development of a world synthetic consciousness and culture that is increasingly structuring the minds and actions of world managers, workers and consumers alike (Peet, 1982). The relative autonomy of the MNCs to mobilise this concept in any part of the world helps create a consciousness of a false reality in the consumers' minds in countries like India. The reality is that the advertisement project is not one generated from within the cultural and social development processes of the host country, but a disembodied one exported from the West where again it is encouraged and deliberately constructed by the international corporations for commercial purposes. This false or fantacised culture gets transported to the host countries and sets in the stratified social ethos. It destroys the actual image of reality of the general mass vis-a-vis their productive placement and creates a feeling of universality through consumption with which people even think of overcoming the class barrier.

In poor host countries with chances of altering their position in the production system being remote, larger sections of the people may prefer the easier option of this fantacised consumption approach and attempt at consuming it at any cost and means. Increasing criminalisation and illegalisation of urban economic base in metropolitan cities of India are the reflections of this process. Multinational corporations with their parentage in core countries do make the Third World believe that the culture traded by them is the most modern one, which can be imbibed by just buying their products. It creates a large-scale propensity to consume. Even though a small section with higher purchasing power actually can fulfil this desire, a systematic wave of desire percolates down the cross-section of the soceity which is the ultimate goal of the MNCs. This is reflected by the huge expenditure of consumer goods MNCs in India on advertisement (Sachdeva, 1989). In the existence of a competition with indigenous producers, they obviously win and reach the consumers more (Table 5.13).

Table 5.13 *Advertisement expenditure of Hindustan Lever Ltd. and its percentage share in the expenditure by different categories of companies*

Category	1976	1980	1984
1. Advertisement expenditure of Hindustan Lever Ltd. (Rs. crores)	2.98	2.91	8.09
2. Per cent share of the expenditure by Hindustan Lever Ltd. in the advertisement expenditure by			
(i) Consumer goods producing companies	13.30	7.89	12.19
(ii) FCCs	17.22	10.81	15.96
(iii) Total advertisement expenditure	10.75	6.22	9.83
(iv) Top 10 advertisers	26.80	17.90	25.42
(v) Top 50 advertisers	13.47	7.68	11.95

Source : Sachdeva, 1989

They also devise various ways of approaching buyers at different levels. In rural markets, they bring elephants to the buyers' homes or station a big regiment of active workers for publicity during village festivals and fairs. In 1984, Hindustan Lever accounted for 25 per cent of the total advertisement budget of the top ten commercial advertisers in India as in the United States Unilever emerged as one of the three largest advertisers. The branch managers of Hindustan Lever regularly spend a fortnight every month in an Indian village to ensure familiarity of villagers with HL products. Resultantly, the eight million rural consumers (just a 1.4 per cent of the total rural potential buyers) buy almost 35 per cent of the 14 inch black and white television sets, 72 per cent of portable radios and 49 per cent of quartz wrist watches (Fernandes, 1991) of the country while 98.6 per cent remain below the affordability status. Further, through advertisements, sales of brands and not the generic products get ensured. Unifying the world in a cobweb of a market structure is a calculated move of the international capital. Markets of the largest cities of India have become the bases of this unification in the country with the help of their supportive infrastructure and communication facilities. Thus the products of the MNCs can reach any corner of the country including the rural markets. It is a regional integration obtained through selective hierarchical diffusion (Chapman, 1979) at the behest of the world commercial power and in effect an integration of markets of different regions and not the people. The hierarchical operation of markets in consonance with the corporate hierarchy, in which television has contributed enormously, reveals the imposed and superficial nature of this integration. Higher the hierarchical placement of a market in the settlement system, more will be its control, range of products and also influence on lower order markets or settlements. The people of different regions and settlements get totally structured by this hierarchical integration, get alienated from a real integrative system and gradually get disjointed from the people of other regions. All the time, it is a two-way process. There is a market integration with a simultaneous reduction in regional integration. Goods move fast, goods of the powerful MNCs move faster but at the cost of the mobility of the people at large. Their freedom to interact with the environment declines as many parts of their own country become economically inaccessible and tourism becomes global. In this commercially structured and restricted parameter, the larger section with less economic power becomes more regionalist with select exposure for which again they look up at the MNCs—the only purveyor of exposure, interaction and modernisation. International capitalism breaks regional barriers and boundaries to spread an unbroken market surface while their activities contribute to the process of creation of myriads of absolute spaces and disintegration of people. To sell products, MNCs even promote myth of antiquated social traditions or religious fanaticism and use them in advertisements. In the process, they encourage to develop an 'ultra-culture' (Peet, 1986) based on old beliefs but manufactured by the highest technology of the West and thereby ensure again another market for their products. People of different regions of the host country thus get directly or indirectly connected with the international market. Procter and Gamble while explaining the reasons for their renewed interest in India banks on this false consciousness and states that a class is emerged in India which can become a partner to the multinationals in all their activities (Das, 1991). But the matrix on which the MNCs intend to work is hopelessly unequal with the top ten per cent of the society actually participating (Bose, 1994) in it. It depends on the pockets of affluence in India's 23 metropolitan centres, four mega cities and about eight per cent of rural population (RUPE, 1994).

Operations of multinational corporations in the consumer goods sector in India or, for that mater, in any Third World host country subject the people to three kinds of domination (Peet, 1986). First, resource becomes degraded and destroyed. Second, the production system is kept unutilised and third, a huge human waste is created that is excluded from the network of production and purchase. The latter can hardly be expected to help in raising productivity in either industry or agriculture or in expanding market and thereby increasing long-term profitability of investment (Bagchi, 1994). The above spatial strategy of international capital in its attempt to maintain profit aggravates the tension of overcoming space by production of space (Harvey, 1985) and intensifies uneven space-economies. The related mechanism of manufacturing and sale of products of the MNCs thus perpetuates a process of dependent capitalism and obtains an ideological phenomenon.

6

Multinational Corporations and Uneven Development in India

Operation of the multinational corporations on Indian economic space and its resultant ramifications have been discussed in detail. There is a need to summarise and relate it to the basic structuration of the Indian economy and society. The spatial pattern of the economic and social development in India in the early nineties is obviously what the planning mechanism of the country over the years has shaped it to be. This becomes the geographical premise (Harvey, 1982) of the multinational corporations to operate on and influence. A detailed analysis of the spatial distribution of social and economic well-being in India in the early nineties is, therefore, attempted briefly but historically.

6.1. Uneven Development in India

This section does not attempt to undertake a full-length historical-geographical study of the development experience of India. On the basis of the existing material it would rather highlight the basic points in the trajectory of Indian development in colonial and post-colonial period. A detailed spatial analysis of the uneven development has been taken up from 1981, concentrating on 1991 as the end point. The aim is to aid the analysis of the spatial organisation of MNCs in India and not develop a parallel body of text.

Any study on India's developmental experience cannot be complete 'without referring to the historical fact of the protracted colonial domination' (Bharadwaj, 1982) and the differential in its impact on various regions and segments of the economy. Hierarchic placement of regions in the metropolitan economy along with their locally-generated economic conditions largely decided the regional trajectories of economic development of colonial India. The exhaustive literature (Bagchi, 1972, 1973 and 1976a, 1976b, Patnaik, 1972, Basham, 1954; Chandra, 1966; Chattopadhyay, 1973; Chicherov, 1971; Desai, 1972; Dutt, 1906; Habib, 1975; Thorner, 1962; Chowdhury, 1971) on colonial underdevelopment and the resultant regional disparity clearly suggests that in colonial India large-scale differentiation was created between and within regions in agriculture, industry and public investment. The imperial policy differed considerably from region to region in terms of land settlement and commercial penetration in agriculture. This was coupled with the differential policy towards public investment in railways, irrigation (Bharadwaj, 1982) and industry. All these later got associated with the disparate rise of regional bourgeoisie in different regions.

In agriculture, the eastern region suffered the most through the zamindari system instituted by the British. Land was controlled by a class having no primary interest in productive cultivation. Productive investment in agriculture in the eastern region hence did not grow as reflected in the slow growth of output and low yield per acre. Large tracts of food crops were converted into cash crop areas, disrupting the sustaining bases of the poor subsistence farmers and inducing unproductive commerce. In the ryotwari and mahalwari areas of the west and the north-west, in contrast, some mitigating factors that existed, such as, direct connection between producers and the state (instead of the middlemen system of the east) or proper legislation of occupancy rights led to more productive investment in Punjab, Madras, Bombay and their hinterlands in contrast to that in Bengal, Bihar, Orissa and Uttar Pradesh. In public investments sector, Punjab and the west received preference in irrigation and other related works while in Bengal even the privately-owned minor irrigation works were dismantled (Whitcombe, 1971). In the hinterland of ryotwari areas, a significant survival of handicraft and small-scale industry was noticed in contrast to the total destruction of the handicraft industry in northern and eastern India. Punjab, being a military base, a number of small-scale enterprises developed here to shape an economic base at a later period.

It has been mentioned earlier that due to the geographical location, the western India, especially Bombay, remained quite inaccessible to the British till the late eighteenth century when rapid expansion of trade between India and China started in raw cotton and later in opium. Indigenous traders, in the absence of British monopoly in the region, specialised in the trade with the help of opium grown in Malwa plateau and other nearby places and established a monopoly. It became their major source of capital accumulation that led to further investments in industries, housing and real estate (Munsi, 1993). In contrast, in the eastern region, the dominant indigenous trading class of Marwaris, originally hailing from Rajasthan, initially were not interested in investing in industries because of their organic alienation from the region. However, the general picture in the organised industrial sector, including in western India, represented a total absence of forward or backward linkages and a heavy dependence on import of capital and consumer goods. Together it gave rise to rural-urban imbalance and a dualism between the pockets of manufacturing and traditional agricultural areas (Bharadwaj, 1982). The railways, initiated during the middle nineteenth century by the same rule, converted many interior parts of the country into raw material suppliers instead of augmenting a process of capital accumulation.

Regionally speaking, a pattern of agglomeration economy grew in India without any positive role of the core centres in generating regional balance (Hoover, 1971). This reorganisation of the space economy was a crucial feature of the colonial rule by which port enclaves prospered and got alienated from their hinterlands. At the end of the rule, Bihar, the richest state in minerals, became the poorest in terms of per capita income.

Calcutta's eminence as a commercial city was created out of this process at the cost of its hinterland centres. In the western region, with an assertive regional bourgeoisie who obviously abetted with the colonial powers through a systematic network of investment and industries, consolidated themselves with their centre in Bombay while Punjab experienced the emergence of a rural elite in its rich agricultural areas. In 1948, Bombay, Madras and Calcutta accounted for 77 per cent of the total industrial workers of the country, 82.2 per cent of the value of engineering and electrical goods and 87.2 per cent of the value of total chemical goods. The corresponding figures of the mineral-rich states of Bihar, Orissa and M.P. were 9.61 per cent, 9.54 per cent, and 5.1 per cent respectively (Bharadwaj, 1982). Southern and western regions by all means were thus better placed and had a better start in both agriculture and industry on the eve of the planning era.

Development course in the national planning era was not marked by any basic change. Later, it exhibited a process of perpetuation, if not an aggravation, of the above disparateness. In spite of promises made to develop backward regions and uplift less privileged classes (Planning Commission, 1956), the 'mixed economy' that developed in India with a combination of public and private sectors essentially accentuated imbalance. Rapid industrialisation with special emphasis on the development of basic and heavy industry that had prevailed in early years of planning (Chatterjee and Sen, 1988) strengthened the growth of industrial and urban enclaves. This was followed by technology-based agricultural development that created *nouveau riche* rural pockets in the sixties which even in the field of productivity failed to contribute in the long run (Bagchi, 1984). Centralisation and concentration thus became the key words of Indian space economy. With the help of principal component analysis, Dasgupta in the seventies identified divergent development status among states with Bihar and Orissa emerging as the two least developed ones. The Sixth Plan document also admitted that regional imbalance in industrial development was a reality with very little trickle-down effect (Planning Commission, 1980). Though literacy rate gradually improved, 40 per cent of the population, according to the Planning Commission, remaind below poverty line as late as in the eighties while inter-state and intra-state disparities widen. In spite of a possible increase in the real wage of workers in some regions, the general pattern indicates towards an intensification of inequality of incomes and 'a rising conspicuous expenditure by the rich on luxury items as against the near starvation levels' of the unemployed and underemployed workers in the poorer regions (Bagchi, 1984). The large cities of the country with little integration with their hinterlands also exacerbated regional inequalities (Banerjee-Guha, 1985; Chakraborty, 1978).

In 1981, the spatial pattern of development, therefore, for obvious reasons, indicated towards polarisation as a dominant process. Spoils of development were concentrated in small enclaves making the hiatus of developed cores and impoverished periphery a spatial reality. The few dominating cities followed by a large number of sub-regional centres at a secondary level surrounded by a host of smaller centres and the rural periphery at local levels (Dasgupta, 1984) reflected a discordance between distribution and redistribution. The curve of socio-economic well-being in 1981 peaked at the metropolitan centres and at select pockets, such as Punjab, declined steeply at the level of smaller towns and rural periphery (Banerjee-Guha and Dasgupta, 1989). A standard score additive model (Smith, 1973) using 22 variables (Dasgupta, 1984) reflects the pattern of regional disparity in India in 1981. It shows the northern region dominated by the national capital of Delhi and marked by great disparity. With affluence of Delhi and Punjab at one extreme and poverty and deprivation of the eastern Uttar Pradesh and western Rajasthan at the other, this region also comes out as a major area of

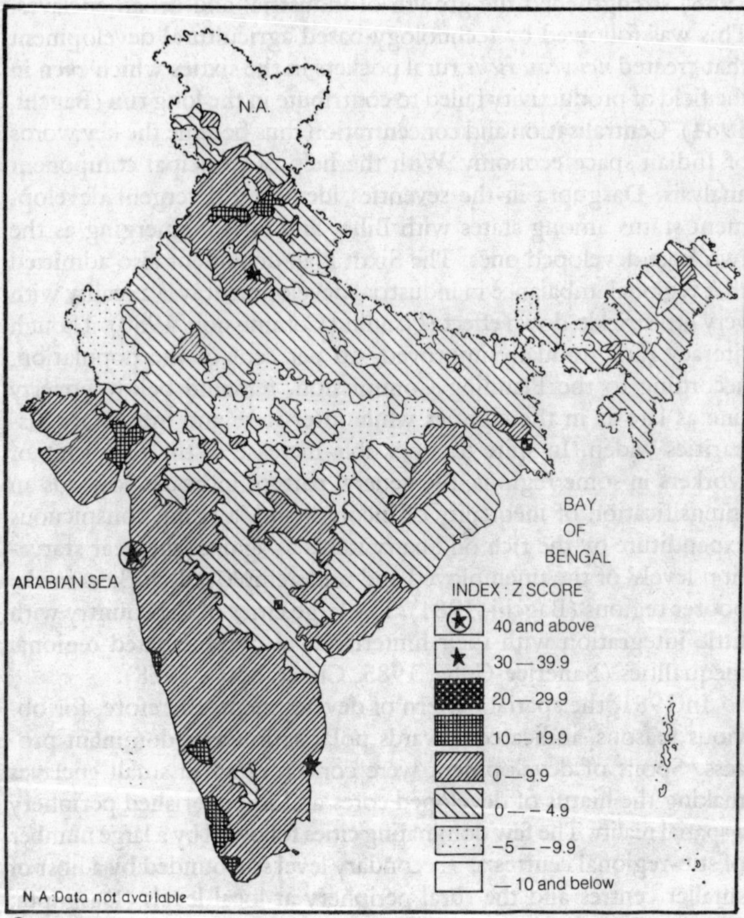

Source: Dasgupta, 1984

Fig. 6.1 Spatial pattern of socio-economic well-being in India

social deviance (Fig. 6.1). It needs mention that the productivity increase and the resultant increase of wealth of Punjab that created its economic alienation from the region owes considerably to the provision of infrastructural facilities by the state at subsidised rates—a common practice among landlords and rich farmers in ex-colonial countries of using the state apparatus to subsidies irrigation and transport facilities. Examples can be drawn from Barzil and Argentina. In the post Independence India also, initially co-operative banks and later commercial banks have provided cheap credit to large landowners (Bagchi, 1989) although Punjab had been receiving larger share since the British period. 'From 1860 to 1947 the government expenditure for irrigation in Punjab was 32.6 per cent of the total spent in the country on that account' (Bharadwaj, 1982)—the reason being Punjab provided members for the British army. Although 80 per cent of this irrigated land went to West Pakistan during the time of partition and Punjab received a large number of refugees, it was compensated by the plan share of the central government in contrast to that of West Bengal. In the first five year plan, Punjab (including Haryana) received a per head assistance of Rs. 152 while Bihar and Uttar Pradesh received Rs. 14 each and West Bengal Rs. 40. With a strong irrigation base built over a long period and large-scale self-cultivated land, Punjab became the centre of green revolution in India in wheat and later in rice (Johl, 1974) albeit creating social differentiation among farmers. The affluence of Delhi (Z–score + 34.7) as the centre of the National Capital Region (NCR) is of a different nature. It owes to Delhi's being the administrative and defence centre of the country and also to the later policy decision to industrialise the surrounding region. The infrastructural advantages that Delhi enjoys is unmatched in the country which has been further aided by its unhindered horizontal expansion in the circular umland. The western region is also marked by a high degree of urban-rural and intrarural disparity in 1981. It accounts for a very affluent core of Bombay as well as some poorest districts of the country located in eastern Maharashtra. Absence of correspondence in the rank ordering of the states in 1970s on the basis of per capita net product in urban and rural areas corroborates this pattern. It reflects disjunction between industrial and agricultural growth. While Maharashtra and West Bengal have the highest rank in urban consumption, they are way down in rural consumption (Bharadwaj, 1982). Dynamic and modern, the urban industrial core of Bombay has an extended umland in western Maharashtra and Gujarat. Nonetheless, it fails to integrate with the region and remains a feature of alienated urbanisation with mounting intra-regional inequality and intra-city social deviance. The curve of social and economic well-being in western India exhibits a sharp distance decay. While Bombay has a Z-score of +34.35, Thane and Pune located in the outskirts, have scores of + 7.85 and 3.59 respectively. Z-scores of south and south-western districts of Gujarat also express intra-state disparity. These districts generate higher income from agriculture and industry and stand in contrast to the backward areas of north, northeast and east. Madhya Pradesh stands out as one of the poorest and low score states of western India and the country as well. Sugar belt of south-eastern Maharashtra at another plane brings out intra-rural disparity as a manifest reality in the rural sector of western India. In the eastern region, the pattern of concentration is more intense than that of western region with Calcutta enjoying an acute primacy (with Z-score of +28.58) amidst the vast impoverished periphery of the Northeast, Bihar and Orissa having a few industrial pockets and agricultural sub-cores. In contrast, the southern region exhibits signs of more balanced development. Although in Kerala it mainly shows a distribution of social inputs without a strong production base (as exemplified by the high outmigration rate of the state), in the eastern part, in Tamil Nadu and Karnataka a spread of economic activities is identified responsible for the growth of alternate medium centres at Tiruchirapalli, Kodagu or Dakshin Kannad. The importance of alternate cores of Bangalore (Z-score +9.00) or Hyderabad (Z-score +3.45) like, Pune and Ahmedabad in the western region is, however, an extension of the old pattern of metropolitan dominance. Districtwise data of 1979 on concessional finance corroborates it by bringing out the location of main recipient districts in southern and western regions in the vicinity of the existing industrial and metropolitan centres (Banerjee and Ghosh, 1988). Dasgupta's (1971) arguments of the alienation of imposed industrial centres from their hinterland is well-suited here. The 1981 national space thus is marked by a simultaneous development disparity syndrome (Fig. 6.2). With the exception of two states of Punjab and Kerala with high socio-economic well-being and low disparity, the general trend is a synchronisation of high composite index and high disparity indicating a continuity of uneven development. Correlation matrix of 22 variables shows high positive 'r' values between metropolitan cities and level of urbanisation, improved

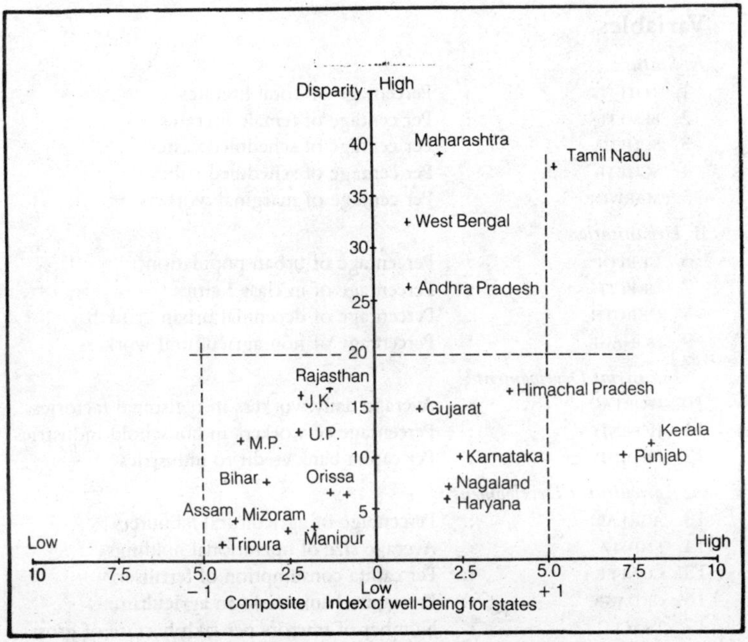

Fig. 6.2 Grouping of states based on composite index

infrastructure, non-agricultural workers and cognisable crime suggesting a distinct urban bias in the development and planning process.

Spatial pattern of development in 1991 reinforces the above process of centralisation and metropolitan hegemony despite trends of agricultural changes in selective districts of Maharashtra, Karnataka, Tamil Nadu and Andhra. A factor analysis with 23 variables (district level data) of economic and social development has been used to examine the nature of development as a geographically variable condition. Variables originally selected were 30. Seven were rejected due to non-availability of information for many states. Significant among them were on employment, income and consumption of essential commodities. The selected 23 variables, despite the nonavailability of information from a few states on two variables, in aggregate do represent the essence of economic and social development. The variables have been grouped under the heads of basic ingredients of development in the following manner.

Variables

A. *Status* :

1. TOTLIT	:	Percentage of total literates
2. FEMLIT	:	Per centage of female literates
3. SCHECA	:	Per centage of scheduled castes
4. SCHETB	:	Per centage of scheduled tribes
5. MARWOR	:	Per centage of marginal workers

B. *Urbanisation* :

6. URBPOP	:	Percentage of urban population
7. URBCIT	:	Percentage of in class I cities
8. URBGTH	:	Percentage of decennial urban growth
9. NONAGR	:	Percentage of non-agricultural workers

C. *Industrial Development* :

10. WORFAC	:	Average daily workers in registered factories
11. HOSIND	:	Percentage of workers in household industries
12. CRDIND	:	Per capita bank credit to industries

D. *Agricultural Development* :

13. AGRLAB	:	Percentage of agricultural labourers
14. LNDSIZ	:	Average size of operational holdings
15. CONFER	:	Per capita consumption of fertiliser
16. CRDAGR	:	Per capita bank credit to agriculture
17. TRACLC	:	Number of tractors per lakh hectare of gross cropped area
18. IRICRP	:	Percentage of irrigated area to gross cropped area

E. *Quality of Life* :

19. VILELC	:	Percentage of village electrified
20. HOSBED	:	Number of hospital beds per 1,00,000 people
21. BNKDEP	:	Per capita total bank deposit
22. BNKCRD	:	Per capita total bank credit
23. COGCRM	:	Number of cognisable crime per 10,000 people

Data on the above variables have been collected from the Centre for Monitoring Indian Economy (CMIE), Bombay, Statistical Abstracts, Handbooks, Digests of Statistics and Economic Reviews of various States, Bureau of Economics and Statistics, Government of Maharashtra, Times of India, Bombay (Reference Section) and 1991 Census of India. The entire data is not from 1991. It varies between 1988 and 1991. The emerging pattern has been considered as of early nineties.

Linkage analysis derived from the correlation coefficient (r) values produces three major typal groups representing the basic structure of the Indian economy.

The first group shows very high positive correlation between per capita bank credit and organised industry with a coefficient value of 0.85, indicating the significance of investment in organised industrial sector in large cities especially in capital intensive production lines. It hence reflects the new industrial policy of India. The second typal group is a manifestation of polarisation in large urban centres. Based on high positive 'r' values among variables denoting levels of urbanisation, population in large cities, non-agricultural workers, household industry workers, marginal workers and cognisable crime, the typal group speaks of concentration of people into a disproportionately small area in the largest cities causing concentration of wealth and power on the one hand and over-crowding and squalor on the other. It also focuses a bi-polarism in the urban economy with preponderance of household and marginal workers. None of these coefficients, all highly significant, falls below 0.60. The third typal group brings out the significance of the input based technology in the agricultural sector with high positive 'r' values (0.56) between irrigated area and fertiliser consumption or agricultural bank credit and incidence of tractors (0.51). The group also focuses on the convergence of wealth and high quality of life in selective rural pockets (Fig. 6.3) of the country.

Factor analysis brings out two significant aspects. Factor I, explaining 63 per cent of the variance is loading high on urban population (URBPOP), total bank credit (BNKCRD) and deposit (BNKDEP), bank credit for industries (CRDIND), population in class I cities (URBCIT), average daily workers in registered factories (WORFAC), total literates (TOTLIT), female literates (FEMLIT), number of hospital beds (HOSBED), cognisable crime (COGCRM) as well as consumption of fertiliser (CONFER), number of tractors (TRACLC), bank credit to agriculture (CRDAGR) and villages electrified (VILELC). The first six variables reflect the association between industrial and urban concentration and the associated social deviance while the last four indicate the role of increased agricultural productivity and surplus in the recent new urbanisation trends as seen in Punjab, exemplified by factor scores of Chandigarh (12.63), Ludhiana (5.71) and Patiala (3.98). This factor can be interpreted as the factor of industrialisation and urbanisation. It is negatively associated with variables like percentage of agricultural labourers (AGRLAB) or percentage of scheduled tribe population (SCHETB).

Factor scores of all the districts have been divided into eight categories. Group I includes the single unit of the metropolis of Bombay (17.39) standing out as an index of polarisation. In Group II are included the metropolitan districts of Calcutta (14.57) and

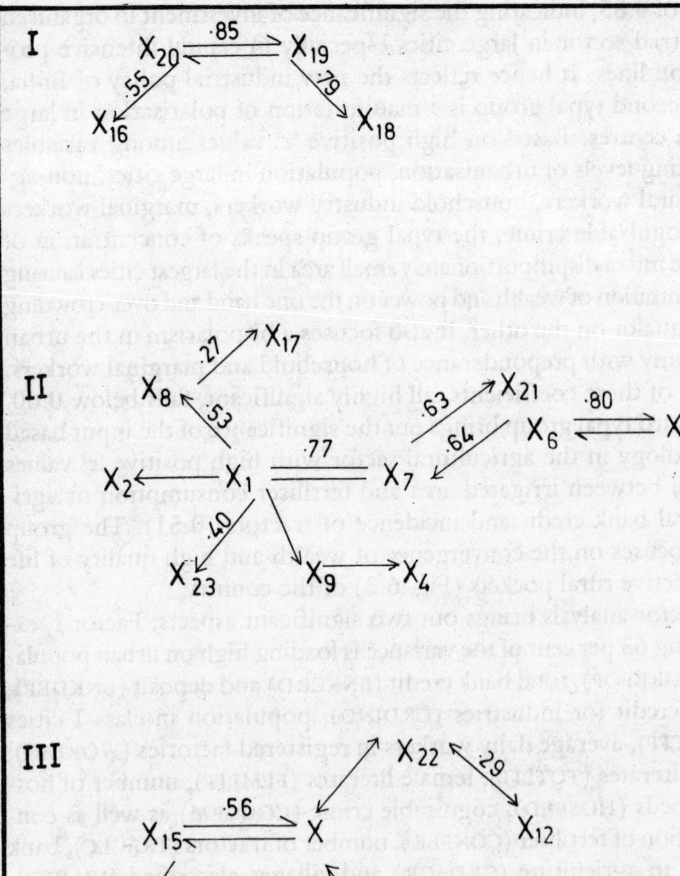

Fig. 6.3 Typal structures obtained by linkage analysis

the union territory of Chandigarh (12.63) indicating, again, the concentration of urban-industrial activities in primate cities but also focussing on the hierarchy of operations. Group III includes the national capital of Delhi (11.00) and also Madras (11.10) followed by the second-order metropolitan districts of Bangalore (8.90), Hyderabad (8.08), Ahmedabad (6.58), Bhopal (6.60), Lucknow, Ernakulam (6.17), Ludhiana (5.71) and Kanpur (5.11) in Group IV. Semi-urban districts of Pune (4.45), Thane (4.18) hinterland districts of Bombay, Nagpur (3.66), Baroda (3.49), districts with old urban centres, such as Gwalior (3.05), hinterland districts of Calcutta, and almost the entire state areas of Kerala and Punjab are included in Group V. Group VI with factor scores ranging from 1.00 to 2.90 includes large tracts of Tamil Nadu, western Karnataka, eastern Andhra, sugarcane areas of southeastern Maharashtra, industrial estate areas in central Maharashtra, southern Gujarat, large parts of Jaipur and its hinterland, western districts of Uttar Pradesh as well as eastern districts, such as, Allahabad (0.10) Varanasi (0.92) and their adjoining areas, districts with major cities of Bihar and Orissa, resource rich areas of Bihar and West Bengal. Negative scores with values ranging from 1.00 to 2.90 representing the characteristic scores of the country are found in the geographical heartland of the country consisting of vast tracts of Rajasthan, eastern Uttar Pradesh, Bihar, central and eastern Maharashtra, eastern Karnataka, western Andhra, almost entire Orissa and the Northeast. Lowest negative scores ranging from 2.9 and less than that are found in Bastar areas of Madhya Pradesh, some parts of eastern Uttar Pradesh and eastern Bihar (Fig. 6.4).

The factor of urbanisation and industrialisation exemplifies the process of how capital operates (Smith, 1984) in India. That following the general tendency, it has produced uneven development and capitalised space, especially of the largest cities. Once growth starts taking place in these locations along capitalist lines, it tends to attract resources even at the cost of depriving other regions (Bagchi, 1989). Capital gravitating in their choice locations has generated local capital, growth of industries including ancillary and consumer goods and initiated a multiplier effect. Funds have been diverted to these points for developing basic and social infrastructure and a skilled labour force has sprung up at such nodes. Multiplier being an important factor contributing towards uneven distribution, the other areas remain out of the minimum threshold line and do not generate growth or associative factors of reproduction. Thus the process of accumulation operating in large urban or industrial centres turns out to be essentially a cumulative causation process generating backwash and outmigration (Mydral, 1957) in other regions. This is proved by the expenditure of large cities on consumer durables,

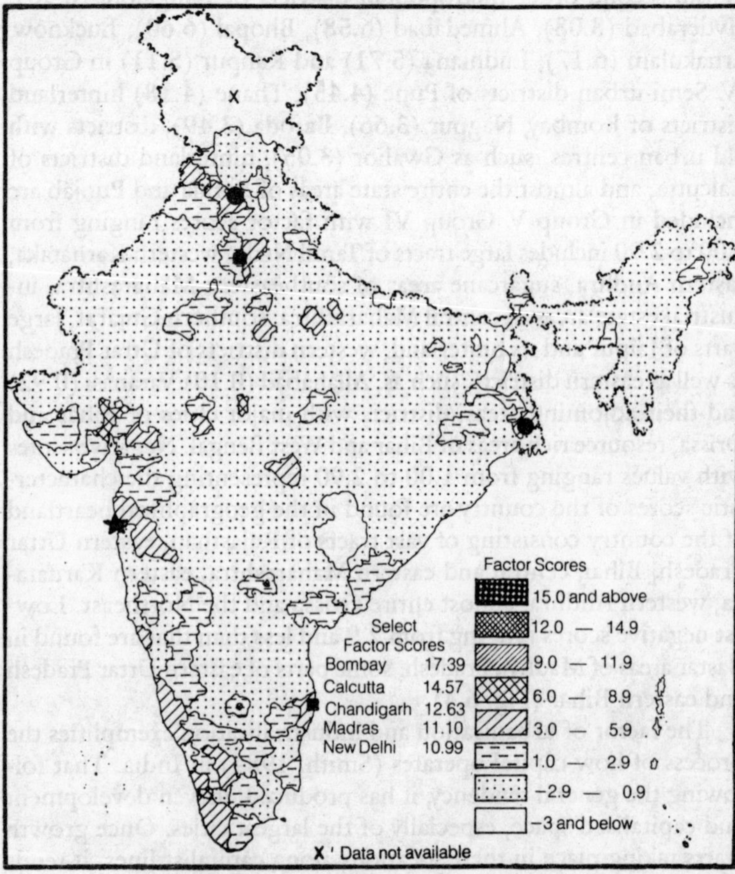

Fig. 6.4 Factor I : Urbanisation – industrialisation factor

infrastructure or by their share in bank deposit. The following statistics are apt examples. In 1991, Bombay accounted for 61 per cent of the total deposits in the scheduled commercial banks of the western region while the four combined largest cities (Bombay, Calcutta, Delhi, Madras) account for 34 per cent of the national total. For the same reason, in the mid-eighties, Delhi cornered 40 per cent of the budget outlay earmarked for national urban planning expenditure. The present predatory and expansive nature of large cities is also brought out by the higher factor scores in the umland of these centres than in interior urban units. For example, the high scores of Thane adjoining Bombay is an expression of the latter's dominance through expanded urban space (Castells 1977). The recent concentration of state investment of Maharashtra in the Raigad district that happens to be the backyard of Bombay and an officially recognised backward region of the state, part of which is located in the newly-developed metropolis of New Bombay, is a more contemporary example of expansion of dominant urban space. The very same process thwarts movement of capital and development beyond the limit of this expanded space and reconstructs a primacy of agglomerations than of single urban units. The spatial colonial order of control over capital and space that had generated acute primacy in Indian settlement system gets reconstructed and extended contributing to regional disparity at various scales.

The second-order placements of Calcutta and Chandigarh show a two directional and temporal pattern. On the one hand, it distinctly distinguishes Calcutta as a declining core (reasons for which have been discussed earlier) and on the other, it identifies the emerging trend of a rising capitalist class in Punjab and along with it a highly differentiated class structure in rural areas. A new trend of a symbiosis of agricultural surplus and urban growth in a number of states, besides Punjab, is also brought out by the factor.

Placement of Delhi and Madras at the subsequent level, however, represents two divergent processes operating in the north and the south respectively. Delhi had a much later start in industrial expansion compared to Calcutta, Bombay and Madras. During the planning era, especially since the sixties, Delhi and its surrounding got privileged patronages for industrial development, thanks to the making of the National Capital Region (NCR). The newly emerged capitalist class of Punjab, Haryana and nearby areas have invested large proportion of their agricultural surplus into these industrial estates to make the regional investment factor significant. But the declining supremacy of Madras is associated with a positive trend of spread of benefits during the plans. Development of centres, such as Bangalore, Hyderabad, Ernakulam, Tiruchirapally, Kodagu, Trivandrum etc. are indicators of this trend. The regional urban system of southern India thus has less acute primacy in its structure (Banerjee-Guha, 1985). Thus, Factor I represents the forces of market and the process of centralisation and brings out the role of political economy in the country's development.

Factor II (explained variance 21%) is loading high on fertiliser consumption (CONFER), number of tractors (TRACLC), irrigated area under cultivation (IRICRP), agricultural bank credit (CRDAGR), agricultural labourers (AGRLAB), electricity in villages (VILELC), and average size of operational holdings (LNDSIZ). Because of the combination of these variables, Factor II can be interpreted as agricultural development factor. Factor scores are divided into seven groups; entire Punjab stands out singularly with the highest scores (ranging from 3.5 to 7.00) while rice regions of Andhra have scores ranging from 3.5 to 6.00. These regions in Group II cover districts of West Godavari (4.17), Nizamabad (3.64), Nellore (3.5) and East Godavari (3.18). While in Punjab variables of agricultural and industrial activities have shown synchronisation leading to higher total score, significant variables in other districts with high scores represent only agricultural development. Punjab's prominence in both Factor I and II, as mentioned earlier, is an expression of convergence of agriculture and industry in contrast to their earlier divergent status. Symbiosis of the two sectors and interflow of capital between them have made Punjab a distinct case. Simultaneously, this pocketed and concentrated nature of the 'success areas' of Green Revolution also brings out the fact that input-based agriculture introduced in the late sixties, failed to raise the income of rural poor in India in general. In many parts, real earnings of agricultural labourers and poor peasants in the early seventies were lesser than what it was in the early sixties (Bagchi, 1989). In Punjab itself, it gave rise to social inequality. The Bhalla Chadha study (1983) reveals that about one-third of the marginal farmers (cultivating upto 2.5 acres), one-fourth of the small farmers (cultivating 2.5–5 acres) and one-fifth of the medium level farmers (cultivating 5–7.5 acres) were living below poverty line in Punjab in the eighties. Together they constituted 16.48 per cent of the total sample. If 16 per cent households of landless labourers are added with it, then 32 per cent of the rural households in Punjab in the eighties were living below poverty line. Pockets of agricultural development included in Group III, with factor scores ranging from +1 to 3.5 located in southeastern Maharashtra in the sugar belt of Kolhapur (2.07) and Central Gujarat, are also indicators of the same trend. The other contiguous areas in Tamil Nadu, including districts of Chengal Pattu (2.80), North Arcot (2.74) Thanjavur (2.73), South Arcot (2.34), Periyar (1.71), Dindigul (1.41) and Madurai (1.36) indicate a specific regional process of resource utilisation added with an active participation of the state government in price subsidisation and supply of inputs for food and cash crops. Further, there is no zero-industry district in Tamil Nadu with its level of urbanisation much higher than the national average. The contiguous districts of Chikmagalur (1.42) and Chitradurga (1.27) in south Karnataka forming parts of the old Mysore state, have been agriculturally and industrially developed since long. Coorg had a well-developed plantation economy with a favourable man-land ratio. Most of the districts have nearly 100 per cent villages electrified. In Andhra, districts in Krishna and Godavari deltas stand out. While Kurnool benefits from the Tungabhadra multipurpose project, Nellore and Chittor get water of lower Pennor. Other districts harness water from the Nagarjunsagar project. In Uttar Pradesh, mainly the districts of Meerut (2.08), Jaunpur (1.92), Agra (1.58) in the west, Varanasi or Allahabad (1.87), Gorakhpur, (1.33), Mirzapur (1.26) in the east and a few districts of Bihar such as Gaya (1.43) and its adjoining districts have factor scores between 1.00 to 3.5. Interestingly, all districts located close to large urban centres have higher scores in bank credit to agriculture indicating an urban-biased diffusion of agricultural credit operations. In West Bengal, districts standing out are Bardhaman (2.24) (the only region in the state where input based agriculture achieved a partial result) and the adjoining districts of Birbhum (2.21) and Malda (1.20). The latter also shows high scores in bank credit to agriculture. Huge contiguous areas in Rajasthan, Madhya Pradesh, Orissa, Maharashtra and Gujarat have negative factor scores (Fig. 6.5).

The above factor analysis exposes the basic socio-economic process of India and shows how space has been a factor to it. Industrial growth and urbanisation are found to have a very limited spatial expansion as shown by the very high factor scores of selective urban centres. Factor II simultaneously brings out the import of capital intensive agriculture and focusses on the increasing degree of rural disparity characterised by a mass of poor peasants, landless agricultural labourers, sizeable minority of middle peasants and a small minority of rich peasants and landlords. The latter control a major part of land, private capital goods, credit, public infrastructure and government patronage and get enriched by increasing commercialisation of agriculture and use of non-labour inputs in land (Bagchi, 1984). Following this, many new urban and rural pockets of affluence represent a process of double convergence of industry, agriculture and infrastructure while large old urban centres focus on industry. The very low, negative scores of the majority of the districts bring out the status of the mass in abject poverty focussing on areas of double conjunction of poverty and underdevelopment in both agriculture

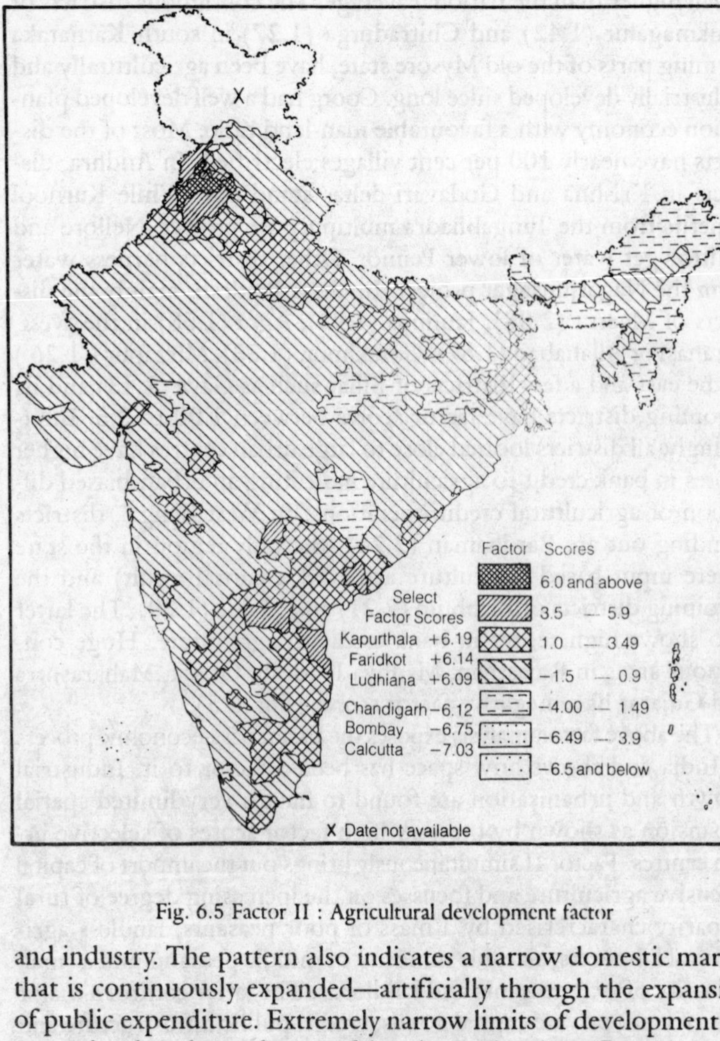

Fig. 6.5 Factor II : Agricultural development factor

and industry. The pattern also indicates a narrow domestic market that is continuously expanded—artificially through the expansion of public expenditure. Extremely narrow limits of development on space also show how advance of the advanced regions (Bagchi, 1989) is restrictive and very few efforts are there to redistribute income. Anti-monopoly measures in this structure are meagre with the large-scale industry inclining more towards export-oriented growth. The state in such situations, becomes more repressive following the dictates of international finance organisations. Analogy can be drawn from Brazil or Mexico.

Spatial organisation of multinational corporations in India needs to be understood in the backdrop of the above fragmented socio-economic space.

6.2 Integrating Polarisation : Space Economy of MNCs

Spatial organisation of multinational corporations generally has an integral relationship with uneven economic space. Uneven development happens to be the geographical premise (Smith, 1984) as well as the product of international capital. The distinct spatial scales that MNCs create differentiates the relative space in minute levels, changing constantly with the nature and orientation of their operations. Their regional concentration aggravates the disparity while their metropolitan bias aggravates settlement primacy and rural-urban divide.

In India, during the colonial period, the spatial economic system changed from an inward oriented, partially regionally linked system to an export and metropolitan oriented one, promoting port enclaves and collection centres. As in Brazil, the imposition of imperial control was characterised by a shift of urban settlements to the coast and a rising eminence of colonial cities as administrative and economic centres (Armstrong and McGee, 1985). In Nigeria also the first class towns were created by the colonial power on the coast or railway lines (Mabogunje, 1968) to facilitate export. In India too significant inland and sea ports declined with the rise of Calcutta, Bombay and Madras as a part of the colonial spatial policy. Among the three colonial port enclaves Bombay gradually became the major centre of capital accumulation. In post colonial period, it developed a more conducive environment towards generating an export sector, a centralised consumer market and a rapidly growing labour force. Advantages of diversification in manufacturing that it had, established a link between urban development and international capital (Armstrong and McGee, 1985). Obviously, therefore, the largest number of the Level II offices of the MNCs are found in Bombay. The pattern is similar to the concentration of foreign investment in the United Kingdom near Heathrow International Airport (Hoare, 1975) or sea ports in Holland (De Smith, 1966). Bombay's eminence vis-a-vis Calcutta's decline as an economic centre owes largely to political-economic factors. What is mentionable here is that Calcutta is still a second preferable location for Level II offices of MNCs in India and the existing locational decisions in Calcutta can be explained more by geographical inertia and old colonial ties than by contemporary factors of capital accumulation. The locational shift of MNCs from the eastern to the western and later to other regions of India can be said to be a result of a simultaneous process of accumulation and devaluation which is place-specific but not symmetrical. Devaluation of old sectors is geographically fixed to regions where previous rounds of investment had been concentrated. But new investment is footloose and is located wherever the conditions of production and operation are most suitable and profitable. The recent investment pattern of MNCs in various locations of Punjab or South India corroborates this. Regions in this process acting as territorial platforms for production get transformed and tightly linked with the rhythm of fixed capital investment and subsequently with the larger rhythm of economic cycles. They actually represent the scale at which systems of production are organised and get differentiated from each other (Smith, 1986). This explains the extreme concentration of MNC regional headquarters in the western region, especially in Bombay and the declining status of Calcutta and the eastern region (Fig. 6.6). By the same mechanism, other metropolitan locations of Madras, Bangalore, Pune or Hyderabad in western and southern regions become significant, especially for Japanese, German or Dutch MNCs. Metropolitan bias in the head office location of MNCs is also obvious for factors of communication and infrastructure for which location of Level II activities in smaller settlements and away from metropolitan centres is less. The few locations that have been identified are also generally found within the umland of metropolitan centres reinforcing the concept of metropolitan corporate heirarchy. Simultaneously, the division of functions between units and settlements follows a scheme of corporate structural organisation which is adaptive and ever-changing.

Spatial distribution of MNC plants in India presents a pattern of convergence and centralisation. Following the logic of uneven development, MNC plants coverage heavily in the western region centering round Bombay, making the city and its extended hinterland in the western Maharashtra and south Gujarat the most significant cluster of MNC plants in India (Fig. 6.7). The eastern region in contrast to all other regions has the minimum number of plants and a zone of convergence is observed in Calcutta and its hinterland. The above type of spatial organisation based on the profitability of capital either transforms a regional space economy

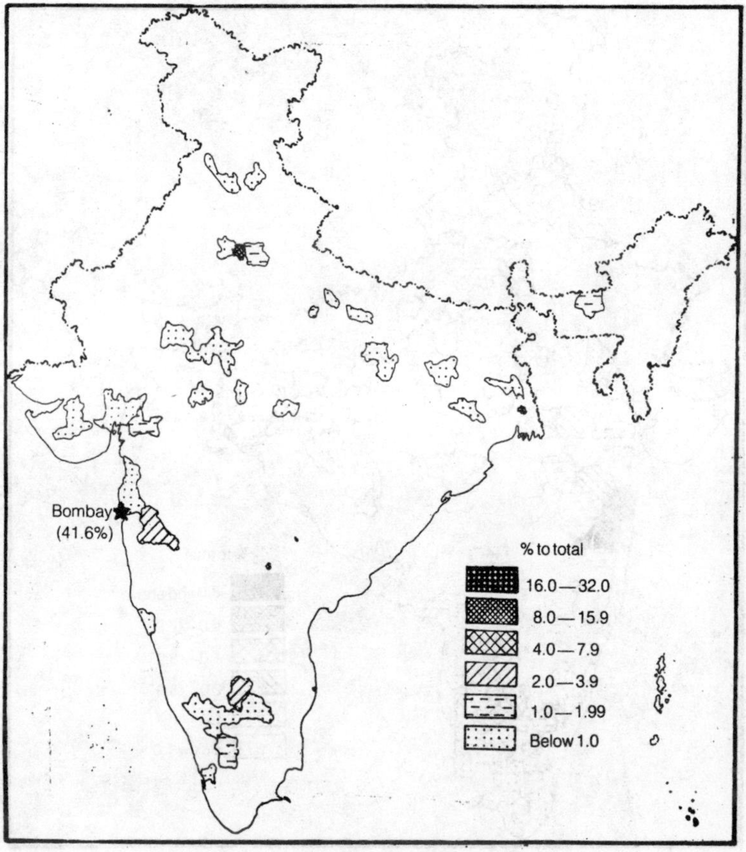

Fig. 6.6 Spatial concentration of MNC head offices in India 1990

or reinforces the status quo of space hierarchy, as needed (Smith, 1986). In India, preference given to the metropolitan districts of Bombay, Bangalore or Delhi to the interior areas by MNCs for locating plants valorises the current pattern of spatial inequality and reinforces uneven development. Inherently geographical, by this process the respective regions are placed at specific development scales in a fashion that is less than accidental. Further, the 'spatial fix' (Harvey 1982) it resultantly creates may lead to a genuine problem of devalorisation of labour and consequent decline of a region which may not be overcome by mere production of newer space or sectors. In order to tackle this constraint and increase profit,

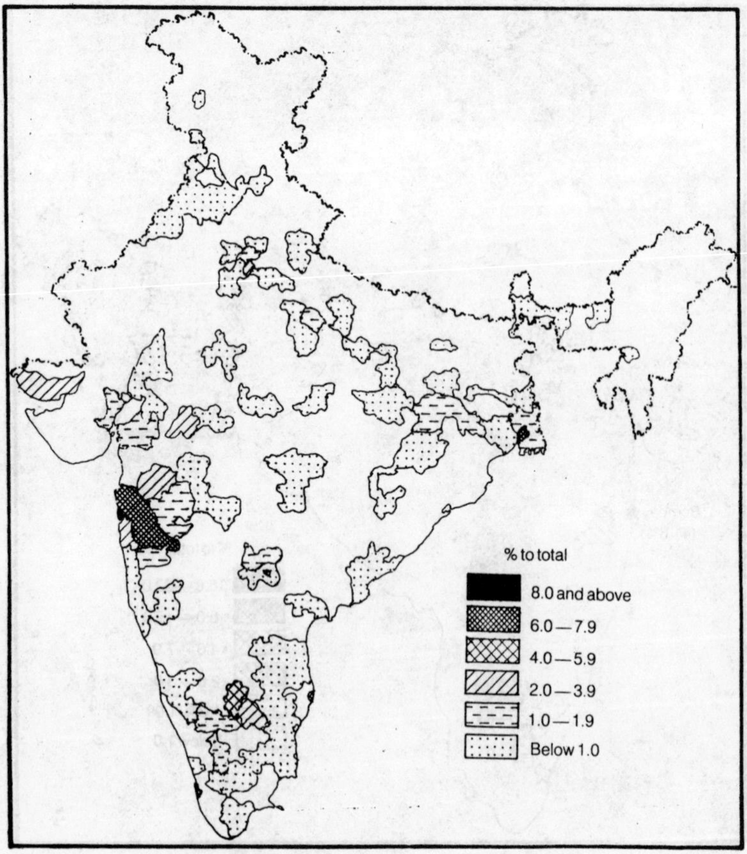

Fig. 6.7 Spatial concentration of MNC plants in India

simultaneous strategies of restructuration and reorganisation thus may be adopted by international capital. In India and in many other Third World countries, multinational corporations since the eighties have been adopting a dynamic strategy of spatial reorganisation of production that operates on the above line. Spatial division of labour under this system does not remain associated with only a division of work but gets intrinsically associated with international pricing system, wage differentials and the relative immobility of labour, in other words with the entire socio-economic fabric of labour at various scales. By this, production becomes more fragmented and suited to spatially separated sub-processes (again due to the improvement in transport and communication technology). Highly skilled and priced organised labour are simultaneously engaged with less or semi-skilled cheap unorganised contract workers in devalorised form. This inherent structural but spatial reorganisation is easier to achieve than devalorising an entire region or reduce the cost and wage rate of its organised sector (Harrison, 1984). More so, it naturally aids to bring down the size of organised labour (who are projected surplus as considerable production work is given to the unorganised ones) and hence reduces cost. The above strategy, known as the non-Fordist strategy, has worked towards an absolute exploitation of surplus without any associated cost of reproduction and, therefore, reaps profit. The gradual reduction of organised labour force of Hindustan Lever or, for that matter, the closure of Procter and Gamble (India) plant at Thane in Maharashtra and a simultaneous increase in their unorganised labour are pertinent examples. This is a part of the global policy of international capital as exemplified by the drastic reduction of their organised labour force in parent country units, as against the rapid increase of their workforce in the organised sector in poor countries. This geographical see-saw has become a favoured strategy of the MNCs in order to overcome the constraints of time and space.

Metropolitan bias in MNC plant locations also follows the primary logic of centralisation and accumulation. Plants in India are mainly located in large cities, occasionally, however, spilling over to adjoining umlands or extended hinterland with a distinct distance decay rule. Intensification of the structural concentration that it leads to is again a part of the global spatial policy of MNCs. In Brazil, out of some 103 MNC plants, only 14 are found located outside the states of Sao Paulo and Rio de Janeiro and more than one-third of all the plants are located in the municipality of Sao Paulo alone. The metropolitan area of Sao Paulo has more than 50 per cent of the total MNC plants (Cunningham, 1981). In South Africa, in the eighties, the greatest absolute concentration of MNC plants occur in the national core area of Pretoria-Witwaterstand-Vereeniging Complex. Secondary cores are found in the metropolitan Cape Town, Durban or Port Elizabeth regions. Together these four metropolitan areas account for more than 83 per cent of the foreign controlled jobs (Rogerson, 1982). Spatial convergence of American firms in Belgium (Mingrat, 1970), or in Britain's (Dunning, 1958) select industrial estates tell the same story in different forms and time scales. In India, more than 90 per cent of the MNC plants are located in the metropolitan cities and their immediate peripheries. All parent countries follow this pattern. Excepting the plantations located in the Northeast and the South, very few plants are located in the interior districts of India.

Implications of the locational preference of the MNCs are significant for regional and national economic development. At the aggregate macro level MNCs have contributed to industrial concentration in old and new metropolitan areas of India. They have not entered into the geographical heartland of the country in Madhya Pradesh, Bihar, eastern Maharashtra, Western Andhra, northern Karnataka, eastern Rajasthan, Orissa and the Northeast. These areas constituting the economic hinterland of the country is kept reserved and only explored through non-Fordist method as and when needed. The ambivalence existing in the regional industrial policy in India has been essentially utilised by them as a functional premise. Apart from the immediate income and employment implications, the above concentration pattern has created multiplier effects in and around the metropolitan areas that eventually has aggravated regional inequality. The above exposition brings to the fore some significant policy issues related to distributive justice and balance development.

6.3 Dynamics of Foreign Corporate Space and Uneven Development in India

Structural aspects of multinational corporations have been found to be intrinsically associated with their spatial organisation. Together they go to make a corporate hierarchy that links space and sector of MNCs at various levels. A corporate hierarchy also binds the innumerable subsidiaries and collaboration units and various local, regional and national economies in a close net of 'interdependency' inducing flows of goods, capital, technology and services of specific types. Although the movement takes place between one country and another, it is actually an internal movement between one department of a corporation and another. Thus, more the activity of multinational corporations, greater is the globalisation of economies. In this globalised economy, the constituent units are not similar or homogenous. Rather it is important that the global economy is conceptualised as consisting of heterogenous units with different agenda (Kurien, 1993). The corporate aspect in totality tangibly represents a contradictory, uneven often crisis-ridden process that continually explores the possibility of reorganising and restructuring production and space relations to create more surplus. The above developmental dynamics of multinational corporations simultaneously produces efficient production complexes (Harvey, 1982) with skilled labour and better infrastructure and growth peripheries (Storper and Walker, 1989), of less developed status—both as their necessary spatial correlates—and gives rise to territorial differentiation aggravating geographically uneven development in poor host countries. In other words, uneven development becomes a natural product and a basis of MNC operation. The geographic landscape experiences a tension between forces making for agglomeration and forces making for dispersal. Both work towards MNCs' accumulation. Thus market expands in terms of purchasing capacity but not in terms of number of consumers; and so increases the distance of the periphery from the centre (Harvey, 1985) thereby aggravating the spatial gap. Tehnological and organisational changes create further place-specific disintegration. With the changing pattern of capital's self-expansion, depressed areas go to form the basis of conversion of surplus value into new variable capital while the established production complexes continue to offer the benefits of scale economy and infrastructure (Harvey, 1982). The vast impoverished periphery of central India or western Rajasthan may not match with Greater Bombay's credibility as a vantage location for foreign investment in organised industries or real estates but they offer immense possibilities for unorganised operations in the name of dispersal. Innumerable 'sweat shops' of multinational corporations thus abound in the interior areas of Madhya Pradesh, Gujarat or West Bengal (Fig. 6.8). Geographical fixation of use value and fluidity get translated into tendencies towards differentiation in one case and equalisation in another (Smith, 1984). By exploring the dynamics of space, multinational corporations break the existing political boundaries as barriers to international production and by the very same process generate and perpetuate unevenness. Hence they internalise the tensions between fixity and movement of capital and organise their operations on space according to specific needs of profit in a given framework. A particular place specific devaluation results from this process forming a part of an internationally operative human cost, social wear and tear (Harvey, 1982) and accumulation through underdevelopment. Poor areas with cheap and less skilled labour are thus as indispensible for MNC operation as agglomeration economies are (Fig. 6.9).

The above disaggregation of production, a hallmark of MNC op-

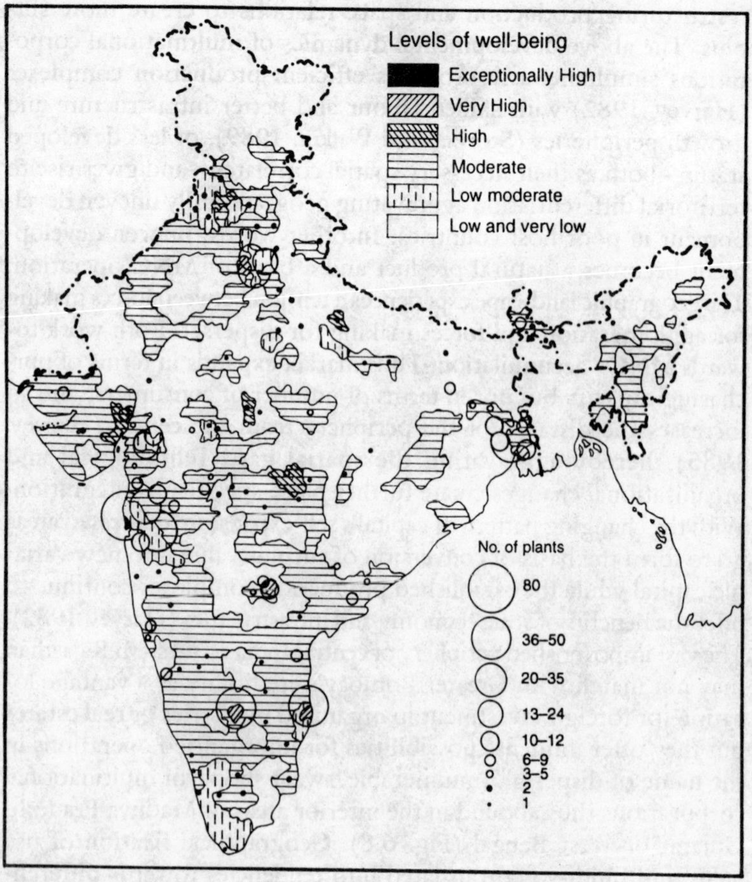

Fig. 6.8 Spatial pattern of well-being and location of MNc plants, 1990

eration since the eighties (which has been elaborated in Chapter 2), is not only related with unevenness in space, but also inequality among sectors and social groups, especially labour. In the less developed regions of India where majority of the workforce is unorganised having little bargaining power, the social fabric of labour is disrupted with such operations of the MNCs. Female and children, being the cheapest workforce, are systematically engaged by large corporations in their sub-contracting units located in interior places in preference to adult male workers. In no way this practice contributes towards the organised strength of labour. On the contrary,

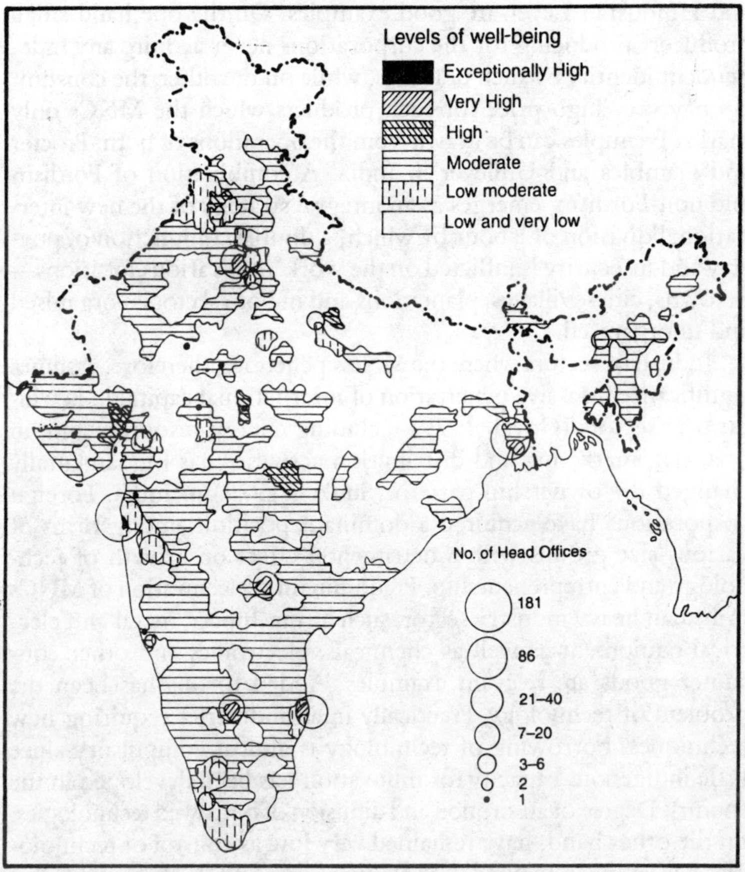

Fig. 6.9 Well-being status and MNC head office locations, 1990

it is used as a constant threat of an alternate production system to the organised labour who gradually lose their bargaining capacity and control on their own labour power. With this new labour divide increased productivity and profit get dissociated from employment and the concept of labour aristocracy gets diluted with expendability of labour. Almost all the organised factory units of multinational corporations whose employment data was made available show a decline of permanent workforce. Specific examples can be drawn from Procter and Gamble and Unilever. Increased production of MNCs in the unorganised sector also indicates an exploitation of both small producers and consumers. Bata, Procter and Gamble and Hindustan Lever are good examples. On the one hand small producers producing for the corporations never acquire any independent identity by such practices, while on the other, the consumers pay very high price for such products which the MNCs only market Examples can be drawn from the operations of both, Procter and Gambles and Unilever in India. A combination of Fordism and non-Fordism, emerges as an integral strategy of the new international division of labour by which, a double conjunction of poverty and insecurity is inflicted on the workers at various locations—in towns, cities, villages, plantations and in both sectors—organised and unorganised.

Industrial sectors where the MNCs penetrate, therefore, assumes significance. Massive penetration of international capital in key industrial sectors (Goyal, 1979) including energy, resources and, in financial, marketing and distribution activities has fundamentally changed the ownership pattern (Sunkel, 1979) in India. Foreign corporations have acquired a dominant position among firms of various size groups with a detrimental effect on growth of technology and entrepreneurship. Predominant concentration of MNCs in Indian heavy industry sector, such as machinery, metal and electrical equipment as well as chemicals, electronics and other consumer goods are relevant examples. Added to this has been the problem of technology. Practically in all industries requiring new techniques, borrowing of technology is almost compulsory since little indigenous capacity for innovation has been developed in the country. Degree of absorption and diffusion of borrowed technologies, on the other hand, have remained very low as control of technologies has largely remained with foreign firms and the narrow base of Indian market has not allowed a high degree of utilisation of the technologies (Bagchi, 1989). As explained in Chapter 2, like many Latin American (Furtado, 1968) and African countries (Mabogunje, 1978) import of technology by MNCs has thwarted the indigenous technological development in India and usurped the technological base. Increasing import of capital goods and transaction of raw materials (at various levels) within the foreign corporate structure, bypassing the market, has further frustrated regional development initiative and its very base of forward and backward linkages. Backward linkages especially with coal, steel and other similar inputs have drastically fallen with the decline of capital goods sector which is again connected with the reduction of the price of imports and withdrawal of production for domestic industries. Resultantly, production activities on a large scale have been curtailed (RUPE, 1994). The pattern of the final output emerging from forward linkages in recent times often consists of an evergrowing list of commodities and services relating to conspicuous consumption such as perfumes, cosmetics, televisions, video, instruments, luxury hotels, breweries, etc., fulfilling the demand of a very small section of the society keen to measure its consumption levels in terms of international standards (Chatterjee and Sen, 1988).This also has a detrimental effect on the development of local entrepreneurial class in different regions. Instead of entrepreneurs, a new managerial class has been emerging in each region whose allegiance to regional economic development is negligible compared to their zeal to become part and parcel of the MNC structure. Increasingly, they participate in all kinds of multinational activity (Das, 1991) and define their identity as a new breed.

At various levels of space, society and economy the operations of multinational corporations in India thus can be associated with unevenness, inequality and distorted growth. At the level of production, these are expressed through capital intensive, imposed technologies, extraordinary foreign control of key industrial sectors and expendability of labour through Fordist and non-Fordist Methods; at the cultural level, through promotion of conspicuous consumption and the resultant demonstration effect (Hirschman, 1958); at the fundamental level of development, through creation of regional inequality, pocketed development, export-oriented industrialisation and extreme rural-urban and class-divide (Sunkei, 1979).

This brings us to the issue of the role of state in combating unbalanced development and the prevailing political economy in India. Official planning mechanism in India has largely belied the goal of balanced, equitable or independent development. In sector and space, inequality reigns supreme. In the course of 40 years of national planning, disjunction of economy—in agriculture, industry, trade and other sectors—has intensified rather than reduced. A large and diverse terrain of precapitalist relations exist in the economy along with a modern capitalist sector, generating a mix of capitalist and pre-capitalist forms of exploitation (Chatterjee and Sen, 1988). Capital-labour relations in this bi-polar system are extended along complex lines which the international capital exploit to its benefit. State initiative has been miserably inadequate to redefine these two sectors and reduce the gap between the two. A viable line of action has never been initiated to augment productivity of workers in both, especially in the traditional village industries on which millions of people depend for employment and livelihood. On the other hand, over the years regional imbalance in the country has intensified for which ambivalent development policies are considerably responsible. For example, in many pronouncedly backward eastern states, with little industry, tax revenues have remained woefully inadequate even for servicing central debt. Drastic squeeze of state finances has gradually led to a reduction of resources for development expenditure in these states and hence has aggravated their backwardness. During 1992-93, per capita income in Orissa fell by 4.6 per cent while in Rajasthan during 1993-94, it fell by 8.9 per cent (RUPE, 1994). Even banks in these regions lend less than they receive as deposits. A number of states, such as Bihar, Uttar Pradesh, Madhya Pradesh, West Bengal or Assam, falling in relatively backward category show steep shortfalls in plan expenditure indicating place-bound retrogression in an overall retrogressive national economy. The only states that show some growth features are the ones that are relatively developed and capable of attracting foreign capital (Fig. 6.9). In the present situation while individual states, irrespective of their professed political manifesto, tend to woo foreign capital with a hope to tide over the predicament or grow more, the existing spatial gap creates a fragmentation of economic and social space of the country. Since macro-level administrative divisions in India are based on linguistic and ethnic lines on which investment decisions are made, economic unevenness readily gets manipulated into broad socio-cultural issues by various interest groups thereby blurring the diverse trajectories of political economy. The narrow structured base of regionalism thus created is further mystified and reinforced by the body politic and lends an aura of verisimilitude because it functions across class boundaries and offsets class antagonisms and grass root instability. Tensions generated therein are again controlled in a manner that is region and place specific which does not hinder the smooth flow of international capital. Falsity of such notions is only exposed when the matrix of consumption of different economic classes is studied (Table 6.1).

It indicates a process of deepening poverty and channelisation of wealth into the pockets of a narrow segment of non-producing population. With 46 per cent of the population below poverty line and an extremely skewed curve of consumption, it also exposes the presence of a nested hierarchical structure characterised by all kinds of intra-regional and inter-regional overlaps and discontinuties. In addition, as explained earlier, in India there is an increased tightening of control by the central government, with a greater degree of centralisation of financial and economic power. This goes hand in hand with a greater degree of internationalisation of the economy. Multinational corporations through their integrated corporate structure take advantage of all these and accelerate the pattern. Depending on the poverty matrix of respective regions, they plan their spatial strategy of production and other operations and thereby use the dynamism of space in a convoluted manner.

Table 6.1 *Pattern of consumption (in %) by various expenditure groups per capita per month, 1989-90*

Per capita per month expenditure class (Rs.)		% of persons	% share of total consumption				
			Total consumption	Agricultural	Industrial	Cloth	Consumer durable
1a	Very poor (Rs.00-110)	17.58%	7.56	9.82	5.47	1.28	0.57
1b	Poor (Rs.110-160)	28.48%	18.18	22.17	14.53	8.43	2.78
1.	Total poor	46.06%	25.74	31.92	20.00	9.71	3.35
(2a)	Just above poverty line (Rs.160-215)	22.32%	19.90	21.92	18.05	14.88	4.35
(2b)	Middle class (Rs.215-385)	26.92%	38.32	36.46	40.03	43.29	21.57
(2c)	Rich (Rs.385 +)	4.70%	16.04	9.63	21.92	32.11	70.73
2.	Total above poverty line	53.94%	74.26	68.01	80.00	90.28	96.95
	Total India:	100.00	100.00	100.00	100.00	99.99	100.00

Source : Sarvekshana, July-Sept, 1992, NSSO
As cited in Bose, 1994.

Spatial dynamics of multinational corporations is a complex phenomenon integrated in the aspects of spatiality, production relations, social reproduction, politics, power and the state (Soja, 1985). Their quest for exploiting the spatial diversity in order to intensify disparity and unevenness and exploit it further is essentially a condition of capitalist spatiality. It is again a product and at the same time a begetter of specific social relations. As much of these particularities are spatially structured, the impact of the operations of multinational corporations is not clearly exposited unless more studies on the spatial dynamics of international capital are taken at all levels—national, regional and local. These studies will establish links with local and global factors of capitalism and draw a line joining society with space. Geography of uneven development and the spatial dynamics of multinational corporations will then be exemplified as an integral parameter of economy, polity and society.

REFERENCES

Abumere, S.I. (1978) : 'Multinationals, Location Theory and Regional Development : Case Study of Bendel State of Nigeria', *Regional Studies,* Vol. 12, pp 651–664.

——(1981) : 'Multinationals and Industrialisation in a Developing Economy : The Case of Nigeria, in M.J. Taylor and N.J. Thrift (eds)., *The Geography of Multinationals*, Croom Helm, London.

Agarwala, P. N. (1990) : *The Role and Impact of Multinationals*, New Delhi.

Aglietta, M. (1979) : *A Theory of Capitalist Regulation : The U.S. Experience*, New Lift Books, London.

Aliber,. R.Z. (1970) : 'A Theory of Foreign Direct Investment', in Kindleberger, C.P. (ed), *The International Corporation*, MIT Press, Cambridge.

Amin, S. (1974): *Accumulation on a World Scale*, Monthly Review Press, New York.

——(1976) : *Unequal Development*, Monthly Review Press, New York.

—— (1977) : *Imperialism and Unequal Development*, Monthly Review Press, New York.

Armstrong, W. and McGee, T.G. (1985) : *Theatres of Accumulation : Studies in the Asian and Latin American Urbanisation*, Methuen, U.K.

Associated Chambers of Commerce (1959) : *Report of the Committee of the Bombay Chamber of Commerce and Industry for the year 1958*, Bombay, 1959, pp 45–46.

Aydalott, P. (1980) : *Dynamique Spatiale et Development Inegal*, Economica, Paris.

Bacha, E.L. (1983) : 'Vicissitudes of Recent Stabilisation Attempts in Brazil and the IMF Alternative' in J. Williamson (ed)., *IMF Conditionality*, MIT Press, U.K., pp 323–340.

Bagchi, A. K. (1963) : *Private Investments and Partial Planning in India*, Doctoral Dissertation, Cambridge University, U.K., Ch.8.

——(1972) : *Private Investment in India 1900–1939*, Cambridge University Press, U.K.

——(1972) : 'Some International Foundations of Capitalist Growth and Underdevelopment', *Economic and Political Weekly*, Vol.7, Special no., pp 1559–1570.

——(1976) : 'Reflections on the Pattern of Regional Growth in India During the Period of the British Rule', *Bengal : Past and Present*, Vol. XLV, Part I, No. 180, pp 28–33.

——(1976) : 'Deindustrialisation in India', *Journal of Development Studies,* Vol. 12(2), pp 135–164.

——(1982) : *The Political Economy of Underdeveloped*, Cambridge University Press, U.K.

——(1984) :'Towards a Political Economy of Planning in India' *Contributions to Political Economy,* Cambridge University Press, U.K., No.3., pp 15–38.

——(1986) :'Foreign Collaboration in Indian Industry', *Economic and Political Weekly*, Vol.XXI(21), pp 915–918.

——(1987) : 'Foreign Capital and Economic Development in India : A Schematic View' in K. Gough and H.P. Sharma (eds), *Imperialism and Revolution in South Asia*, Monthly Review Press, New York.

——(1987) : *Public Intervention and Industrial Restructuring in China, India and Republic of Korea,* I.L.O. (ARTEP), New Delhi.

——(1993) : 'Foreign Capital and Economic Development in India : A Schematic View', in K. Gough and H.P. Sharma (eds.), *Imperialism and Revolution in South Asia*, Monthly Review Press, New York.

——(1994) : Export-led Growth and Import Substituting Industrialisation', in D. Nayyar, (ed), *Industrial Growth and Stagnation : The Debate in India,* O.U.P., New Delhi, pp 78–88.

Bagchi-Sen, S. and Wheeler, J.O. (1989) : 'A Spatial and Temporal Model of Foreign Direct Investment in the United States', *Economic Geography*, Vol.65, pp 113–129.

Bambrick, S. (1979) : *Australian Minerals and Energy Policy*, Australian National University Press, Canberra.

Banjeree, D. and Ghosh, A. (1988) : 'Indian Planning and Regional Disparity in Growth', in A.K. Bagchi, (ed), *Economy, Society and Polity*, O.U.P., Calcutta, pp 104–165.

Banerjee-Guha, S. (1985) : *Colonialism, Neo-Colonialism and Regional Disparity : The Indian Experience*, Unpublished Monograph, Department of Geography and Environmental Engineering, The Johns Hopkins University, Baltimore, U.S.A.

——(1990) : 'Spatial Spread of Multinational Corporations in Third World Countries and Some Related Aspects', *Social Scientist*, Vol. 18 (1–2), pp 55–68, New Delhi.

Baran, P. and Sweezy, P. (1966) : *Notes on the Theory of Imperialism*, Monthly Review Press, pp 15–31.

Barlett, C.A. and Ghoshal, S. (1989) : *Managing Borders : The Transnational Solution*, Harvard Business School Press.

——(1968) : *Monopoly Capital*, Monthly Review Press, New York.

Barnet, R.J. and Muller, R.E. (1974) : *Global Reach : The Power of the Multinational Corporations*, Simon and Schuster, New York.

——(1975) : *Global Reach*, Jonathon Cape, London.

Basham, A.L. (1954) : *The Wonder That was India*, Sidgewick and Jackson, U.K.

Bater, J.H. and Walker, D.F. (1974) : 'Aspects of Industrial Linkage : The Example of the Hamilton Metal Working Complex, Ontario', *Revue de Geographie de Montreal*, Vol. 243, 28, pp 233–23.

Bennett, D. and Sharpe, K.E. (1984) : 'The World Auto Industry and its Implications for Developing Countries in Latin America', in R. Newfarmer (ed), *Profits, Progress and Poverty,* Notre Dame.

Bettelheim, C. (1971) : *India Independent*, (Translated from French by W.A. Caswell), Monthly Review Press, New York, pp 234.

Bhalla, G.S. and Chadha, G.K. (1983) : *Green Revolution and the Small Peasant : A Study of Income Distribution Among Punjab Cultivators*, Concept Publishing Co., New Delhi.

Bharadwaj, K. (1982) : 'Regional Differentiation in India : A Note', *Economic and Political Weekly*, Vol. XVII (14–16), pp 605–614, Bombay.

Bhusan, B. (1983) : 'The New Deals', *Business India Cover Features*, pp 50–64, May 9–22, 1983.

Blackbourn, A. (1974) : 'The Spatial Behaviour of American Firms in Western Europe, F.E.I. Hamilton (ed), *Spatial Perspectives on Industrial Organisation and Decision-Making*, John Wiley, London, pp. 245-65.

——(1978) : 'Multinational Enterprises and Regional Development : A Comment', *Regional Studies*, Vol. 12, pp 125–127.

Blake, D.H. and Walters, R.S. (1976) : *The Politics of Global Economic Relations*, Prentice Hall Inc., USA.

Bose, A.N. (1994) : 'In Search of an Alternative Industrial Structure', *Indian Journal of Regional Science*, Vol.XXVI(1), pp 29–48, Kharagpur.

Brewer, A. (1980) : *Marxist Theories of Imperialism*, Routledge and Kegan Paul, London.

Britton, J.N.H. (1976) : 'The Influence of Corporate Organisation and Ownership on the Linkages of Industrial Plants : A Canadian Enquiry', *Economic Geography,* Vol., 52, pp 111–114.

Britton, J.N.H. and Gilmour, J. M. (1978) : *The Weakest Link*, Science Council of Canada, Ottawa.

Brookfield, H. (1975) : *Interdependent Development*, Methuen, London.

Brown, A.J. and Burrows, E.M. (1977) : *Regional Economic Problems : Comparative Experiences of Some Market Economics*, Allen and Unwin, U.K.

Buckley, P. J. and Casson, M. (1976) : *The Future of Multinational Enterprise*, Macmillan, London.

Carney, J., Hudson, R. and Lewis, J. (1990) : 'New Perspectives in European Regional Theory' in Carney, J. et. al. (eds), *Regions in Crisis*, St. Martin's Press, New York, pp 15–24.

Castells, M. (1983) : 'Crisis, Planning and the Quality of Life', *Environment and Planning* 1(1), pp 3–22.

Caves, R.E. (1983) : *Multinational Enterprise and Economic Analysis,* Cambridge University Press, Cambridge.

Chakraborty, S.C. (1978) : 'Urban Economic Base : A Review of Contemporary Indian Experience', *Nagarlok*, Vol. X(4), New Delhi.

Chalapati Rao, K.S. (1985) : 'A Study of Interconnections under MRTP Act', *Corporate Studies Group Working Paper I.I.P.A.*, New Delhi.

Chandler, A.D. (1962) : *Strategy and Structure : Chapters in the History of Industrial Enterprises*, Macmillan, London.

Chandler, A.D. Jr. and Redlich, F. (1961): 'Recent Developments in American Business Administration and their Conceptualisation', *Business History Review*, pp 103–128.

Chandoke, N. (1991) : 'The Post Colonial City', *Economic and Political Weekly*, December 14, pp. 2868–2873.

Chandra, S. (1966) : 'Some Aspects of the Growth of Money Economy in India during the 17th Century', *Indian Economic and Social History Review*.

Chang Kang-isung (1989) : 'Japan's Direct Manufacturing Investment in the United States', *The Professional Geographer*, Vol. 41(3), pp 314–328.

Chapman, K. (1979) : *People, Pattern and Process : An Introduction to Human Geography*, Arnold Heinemann, London.

Chatterjee, P. and Sen, A. (1988): 'Indian Planning and Regional Disparity in Growth' in A.K. Bagchi (ed)., *Economy, Society and Polity : Essays in the Political Economy of Indian Planning*, O.U.P., Calcutta.

Chattopadhyay, P. (1973) : *Trends in India's Economic Development*', in K. Gough and H.P. Sharma, eds.

Chaudhuri, S. (1979) : 'Financing Growth of Transnational Corporations in India, 1956–75', *Economic and Political Weekly*, August 18, pp 1431–1435.

——(1979) : 'FERA : Appearance and Reality', *Economic and Political Weekly*, April 29, pp 734–744.

Chicherov, A.I. (1971) : *India : Economic Development* in 16th–18th Centuries, Moscow.

Chossoudovsky, M. (1978) : 'Is the Canadian Economy Closing Down ?' in F. Caloren, et. al. (eds)., *Is the Canadian Economy Closing Down* ? Black Rose, Montreal.

Chowdhury, P. (1971) : 'India : Objectives, Achievements and Constraints' in P. Chowdhury (ed.),*Aspects of Indian Economic Development*, London.

Clairmonte, F.C. (1991) : 'Global Services : Shifting Galaxy of Imperialism', *Economic and Political Weekly*, February 23, 1991.

Clairmonte, F. C. and Cavanagh, J. (1987) : 'Global Economic Debacle and Corporate Power, *Economic and Political Weekly*, Vol.XXII (13), pp 559–563, Bombay.

Clarke, I. J. (1985) : *The Spatial Organisation of Multinational Corporations*, Croom Helm, London.

Clarke, I.M. (1992) : 'Inside Unilever: The Evolving Transnational Company', *Harvard Business Review*, Vol. 70(5), pp. 46–52.

Clarke, G.L. (1981) : 'The Employment Relation and Spatial Division of Labour: A Hypothesis',*Annals of the Association of American Geographers*, Vol. 71, pp. 412–424.

Cohen, J.D. (1979) : 'The Changing Transaction Economy and its Spatial Implications', *Ekistics*, 46, No. 272, pp 7–15.

——(1981) : 'The New International Division of Labour, Multinational Corporations and Urban Hierarchy', in M.J. Dear and A.J. Scott (eds.)., *Urbanisation and Urban Planning in Capitalist Society*, Methuen, U.K., pp 287–315.

Cohen, R.B., Felton, N., Nkosi, M. and Van Liere, J. (1979): Introductory Chapter in R.B. Cohen, et. al. (eds)., *The Multinational Corporation : A Radical Approach,* Cambridge University Press, Cambridge, pp 1–27.

Collins, L. and Walker, D.F. (eds)(1975) : *Locational Dynamics of Manufacturing Activity*, John Wiley, London.

Cunningham, S.M. (1981) : 'Multinational Enterprises in Brazil : Locational Patterns and Implications for Regional Development', *The Professional Geographer*, Vol. 33(1), pp 48–62.

Damette, F. (1980) : 'The Regional Framework of Monopoly Exploitation' in J. Carvey and R. Hudson (eds), *Regions in Crisis : New Perspectives in European Regional Theory*, Croom Helm, London, pp 76–92.

Dara, R. (1991) : *The Real Pepsi : The Real Story*, Asian Games Village, New Delhi.

Das, G. (1991) : 'Press Ahead with Economic Reforms' *Times of India*, December 27, 1991, Bombay.

Dasgupta, B. (1971) : 'Socio-economic Regionalisation of India', *Economic and Political Weekly*, August 5, 1971, Bombay.

Dasgupta, N. (1984) : *A Geography of Socio-Economic Well-Being in India*, Unpublished M. Phil Dissertation, Department of Geograpny, University of Bombay.

Dasgupta, S. (1964) : 'Underdevelopment and Dualism', *Economic Development and Cultural Change*, Vol.XII(2).

Datta, B. (1977) : *The Contents of Economic Growth and other Essays*, Research India Publication, Calcutta.

Deo, S. (1986) : *Multinational Corporations and the Third World*, Ashis Publishing House, New Delhi.

Department of Industrial Development (1969) : *Report of Industrial Licensing Policy Inquiry Committee*, Government of India, Manager of Publications, Delhi.

Desai, A.R. (1972) : *Social Background of Indian Nationalism*, Popular Prakashan, Bombay.

de Smidt, M. (1966) : 'Foreign Industrial Establishments located in the Netherlands', *Tijdschrift Voor Economische en Social Geografie*, Vol. 58.

Dhar, B. (1984) : Foreign Controlled Companies in India : An Attempt at Identification, *Corporate Studies Group Working Papers*, I.I.P.A., Delhi.

Dickens, P. (1994) : The People Lecture in Economic Geography : Global-Local Tensions : Firms and States in the Global Space Economy', *Economic Geography,* Vol.70(2), pp 101–128, Massachusetts, USA.

Dicken, P. and Lloyd (1976) : 'Geographical Perspective on United States Investment in the United Kingdom', *Environment and Planning*, Vol. 8, pp 685–705.

Dietvorst, A.G. J. and Wever, E. (1977) : 'Changes in the Pattern of Information Exchange in the Netherlands', *Tijdschrift Voor Economische on Sociale Geografie*, Vol. 68, pp 12–82.

Dill, W.R. (1958) : 'Environment as an Influence on Managerial Autonomy', *Administrative Science Quarterly*, Vol. 2, pp 409–443.

Dunning, J. (1958) : *Americal Investment in British Manufacturing Industry*, Allen and Unwin, London.

——(1973) : 'The Determinants of International Production', *Oxford Economic Papers*, 25(3), pp 289–336.

——(1977) :'Trade, Location of Economic Activity and the MNE : A Search for an Electric Approach' in B. Ohlin, et al. (eds)., *International Allocation of Economic Activity*, Macmillan, U.K.

——(1981) : *International Production and the Multinational Enterprise*, George Allen and Unwin, London.

——(1983) : Changes in the Level and Structure of International Production' in M. Casson (ed)., *The Growth of International Business*, George Allen and Unwin, London.

Dunning, J.H. and Norman, G. (1979) : *Factors Influencing the Location of Offices of Multinational Enterprises*, Location of Offices Bureau and Economists Advisory Group Ltd., London.

Dutt, R.C. (1906) : *India Under Early British Rule*, London.

Elridge, P.J. (1969) : *The Policies of Foreign Aid in India*, Vikas Publications, New Delhi.

Elshof, P. (1988) : *Unilever in Asian and Pacific Region*, Somo, Amsterdam.

——(1989) : *Unilever in Asia : The Big Leap Forward*, Conference paper presented for the IUF affiliated Trade Unions in Asia/Pacific Region, Hongkong.

Enzenberger, H.M. (1975) : 'The Industrialisation of the Mind', *Urban Review*, Vol. 8, pp 68–75.

Estall, R.C. and Buchanan, H. (1961) : *Industrial Activity and Economic Geography,* Hutchinson, New York.

Ettlinger, N. (1990) : 'Worker Displacement and Corporate Restructuring: A Policy Conscious Appraisal', *Economic Geography*, Vol. 66, pp 67–80.

Evans, A.W. (1973) : 'The Location of the Headquarters of the Industrial Companies', *Urban Studies*, Vol. 10, pp 387–395.

Fernandes, A. (1991) : 'When Villages Awake', *Times of India*, March 21, 1991, Bombay.

Fieldhouse, D.K (1978): *Unilever Overseas : The Anatomy of a Multinational*, Croom Helm, London.

Fitzgerald, T.M. (1974) : *The Contribution of the Mineral Industry to Australian Welfare*, Australian Government Publishing Service, Canberra.

Forbes, D. (1986) :'Spatial Aspects of Third World Multinationals', Direct Investment in Indonesia in M.J. Taylor and N.J. Thrift (eds), *The Multinationals and the Restructuring of the World Economy*, Croom Helm, London.

Fortune (1990) : 'The Worlds' Biggest Industrial Corporations', *Fortune International*, pp 43–46.

Frank, A.G.(1967) : *Capitalism and Underdevelopment in Latin America*, Monthly Review Press, New York.

——(1969): *Capitalism and Underdevelopment in Latin America*, Modern Reader Paperbacks, New York.

——(1977) : 'New International Division of Labour', Review Article, *Economic and Political Weekly,* December 17, 1977, pp 2093–2096.

——(1978) : *Dependent Accumulation and Underdevelopment*, Macmillan, London.

Franklin, J.L. (1975) : 'Down the Organisation : Influence Processes Across Levels of Hierarchy', *Administrative Science Quarterly*, Vol. 20, pp 153–164.

Fransen, J. (1990) : 'Subcontracting and Inequality : The Case of Unilever in India' *Occasional Paper No.26*, University of Amsterdan, Holland.

Frobel, F., Heinricks, J. and Kreye, O. (1980) : *The New International Division of Labour*, Cambridge University Press, U.K.

Fuchs, V. (1962) :*The Changing Location of Manufacturing in the United States since 1929*, Yale University Press, New Heaven.

Fujita, M. and Ishigaki, K. (1986) : 'The Internationalism of Japanese Commercial Banking' in M.J. Taylor and H.J. Thrift (eds) *The Geography of Multinationals*, Croom Helm, London.

Gabriel, P.P. (1972) : 'The Multinational Corporations on the Defensive', *Fortune,* New York.

Galeano, E. (1974) :*Open Veins of Latin America*, Monthly Review Press, New York.

Gaurishankar, A. (1980): *Taming the Giants*, Vidya Vahini, New Delhi.

Ghosh, B.N. (1985) : *Political Economy of Neo-Colonialism in Third World Countries*, Sterling Publishers, New Delhi.

Ghothoskar, S. (1991) : *Management Strategies in the 1990s and the Case for Eroding New Union Strategies*, Workers' Solidarity Centre, Bombay.

Gilbert, (1974) : *Latin American Development*, London.

Goddard, J.B. (1975) : 'Organisation Information Flows and the Urban System', *Economic Applique*, Vol.28, pp 125–64.

——(1977) :'Urban Geography: City and Regional Systems', *Progress in Human Geography*, Vol.1(20), pp 296–303.

——(1978) : 'Multinational Corporations in India : The Need for a Realistic Policy Framework', *Working Paper* No.1, P.A. New Delhi,

——(1979) : 'Foreign Private Investment in India : Myth and Reality', *Man and Development*, No.4, New Delhi.

——(1980) : 'Some Aspects of the Operations of Multinational Corporations in India', *Social Action*, Vol. 30(4).

——(1980) : *MNCs and Indian Economic Development: Some Basic Issues*, August, 1980, Link, New Delhi.

Goddard, J.B. and Morris, D. (1976) : *The Communication Factor in Office Decentralisation*, Oxford, Pergamon Press.

Goodwin, W. (1965) : 'The Management Centre in the United States', *Geographical Review*, Vol. 55, pp 1–16.

Gordon, M. J. and Fowler, D. J. (1984) : 'Performance of the Multinational Drug Industry in Home and Host Countries : A Canadian Case Study', P. Kindleberger and D.B. Audretshch (eds.), *The Multinational Corporation in the 1980s*, The MIT Press, USA.

Goyal, S. K. (1979) : *The Impact of Foreign Subsidiaries in India's Balance of Payments*, I.I.P.A., New Delhi.

Graham, E.M. and Krugman, P.R. (1991) : *Foreign Direct Investment in the United States*, Institute for International Economics, Washington, D.C., USA.

Graham, R. (1968) : *Britain and the Outset of Modernisation in Brazil, 1850–1914*, Cambridge University Press, U.K.

Gramsci, A. (1988) : *Prison Notebooks*, Lawrence and Wishart, London.

Hakanson, L. (1979) : 'Towards a Theory of Location and Corporate Growth' F.E.I. Hamilton and G.J.R. Linge (eds).', *Spatial Analysis, Industry and the Industrial Environment*, Vol. I, John Wiley & Sons, London.

Hamer, A. (1973) : *Industrial Exodus from the Central City*, Lexington Books, Lexington, Massachusetts.

Hamilton, F.E.I. (ed) (1974) : 'Spatial Perspectives on Industrial Organisation and Decision Making', John Wiley & Sons, London.

Hamilton, F.E.I. and Linge, G.J.R. (eds) (1979) : 'Spatial Analysis, Industry and the Industrial Environment', *Industrial Systems, Vol. I* , John Wiley & Sons, London.

Hammer, S. and Teitebaum, R.S. (1991) : 'The World's Biggest Industrial Corporations : How They Performed in 1990', *The Fortune Global*, New York, Vol.124(3), pp 66–108,.

Hansen, N. (1981) : 'Mexico's Border Industry and the International Division of Labour', *Annals of Regional Science*, 15(2), pp 1–12.

Harrison, B. (1984) : 'Regional Restructuring and Good Business Climates' in L. Sawers and W.K. Tabb (eds), *Sunbelt/Snowbelt : Urban Development and Regional Restructuring*, Oxford University Press, U.K.

Harvey, D. (1982) : *Limits to Capital*, Basil Blackwell, London.

——(1985) : *The Urbanisation of Capital*, Basil Blackwell, London.

Hathi Commission (1975) : *Report of 1978*, Government of India, New Delhi, pp 90.

Helleiner, G.K. (1975) : 'The Role of Multinational Corporations in the Less Developed Countries" Trade and Tchnology' *World Development* 3(4).

Hirsch, P.M. (1975) : 'Organisational Effectiveness and the Institutional Environment', *Administrative Science Quarterly*, Vol. 20, pp 327–44.

Hirschman, A.O. (1958) : *The Strategy of Economic Development*, Yale University Press, USA.

——(1974): *The Strategy of Economic Development*, Yale University Press, USA.

Hoare, A.G. (1975) : Foreign Firms and Air Transport : The Geographical Effect of Heathrow Airport', *Regional Studies*, Vol.9, pp 349–367.

Holland, S. (1976) : *Capital Versus the Regions*, Macmillan, London.

Hoover, E. (1971) : *An Introduction to Regional Economics*, Alfred Knopf, New York.

Hoover, E.M. (1948) : *The Location of Economic Activity*, McGraw Hill, New York.

Howelles, J and Wood, M. (1991) : 'The Globalisation of Production and Technology, Commission of the European Communities', *Commission Dossier* 2, pp 77–78.

Hymer, S. (1960) : *The International Operation of National Firms*, MIT, Massachusetts.

——(1971) : 'The Multinational Corporation and the Law of Uneven Development', in J.W. Bhagwati (ed), *Economics and World Order*, Macmillan, New York.

——(1972) : 'The Internationalisation of Capital', *Journal of Economic Issues*, Vol.6 (1), pp 91–111.

——(1972) : 'Multinational Corporation and International Division of Labour' in R.B. Cohen, et.al (eds), *The Multinational Corporation : A Radical Approach*, Cambridge University Press, U.K., pp 140–164.

——(1975) : 'International Politics and International Economics' in L.N. Lindberg, et. al. (eds), *Stress and Contradiction in Modern Capitalism*, Lexington Books, Massachusetts, pp 355–372.

——(1976) : *The International Operation of National Firms : A Study of Direct Foreign Investment*, The MIT Press, Cambridge, Massachusetts.

IDPAD, (1984) : *Political Dimensions of MNCs in India*, IIPA, New Delhi.

I.L.O. (1981) : *Employment Effects of Multinational Corporations on Developing Countries*, Geneva.

ILPIC (1969) : *Report of the Industrial Licensing Policy Inquiry Commission, Main Report*, pp 15.

I.M.F. (1964) : *Balance of Payments Year Book : Concepts and Definitions*.

——(1977) : *Balance of Payment Manual*, Fourth Edition, quoted by UNCTC, Salient Features and Trends in Foreign Direct Investment, United Nations, 1983, p 26 cited in B. Dhar (1984) pp 7.

Isard, W. (1956) : *Location and Space Economy*, MIT Press, Cambridge.

Jenkins, R. (1984) : *Transnational Corporations and Industrial Transformation in Latin America*, Macmillan, London.

——(1987) : '*Transnational Corporations and Uneven Development : The Internationalisation of Capital and the Third World*, Methuen, London,

Jo, S. (1976) : 'The Impact of Multinational Firms on Employment and Income : The Case of South Korea', World Employment Programme Research, *WEP*, ILO, Geneva, pp 2–28.

Johl, S.S. (1974) : 'Green Revolution and What Next' in S.S. Johl (ed), *Green Revolution—The Unfinished Task*, Minerva Associates, Delhi.

Johnston, R.J. (1968) 'Commercial Leadership as an Urban Function : Some International Comparisons', *Proceedings of 5th New Zealand Geography Conference*, Auckland.

Johnston, R.J. and Rimmar (1967) : 'Commercial Leadership in New Zealand', *New Zealand Geographer*, Vol. 23, pp 765–768.

Keeble, D. (1976) : *Industrial Location and Planning in the United Kingdom*, Methuen, London.

Kidron, M. (1965) : '*Foreign Investments in India*, Oxford University Press, New York.

Kindleberger, C.P.(1969): *American Business Abroad*, Yale University Press, New Haven.

Kindleberger, C.P. and Audrestch, D.B. (eds) (1983): *The Multinational Corporation in the 1980s*, MIT Press, Cambridge.

Knickerbocker, F.(1973): *Oligopolistic Reactions and Multinational Enterprise*, Harvard Business School, Cambridge, Massachusetts.

Kochanek, S.A. (1974) : *Business and Politics in India*, University of California Press, Berkeley, USA.

——(1980) : *United States Expropriation Policy and South Asia : A Case Study in Policy Implication*, Concept, New Delhi.

Kumar, Nagesh (1982) : 'Regulating Multinational Monopolies', *Economic and Political Weekly*, May, 1982.

——(1984) : *Multinational Corporations in India*, Sage, Delhi.

——(1990) : *Multinational Entërprises in India*, Sage, New Delhi.

Kumar, Nagesh and Chenoy, K.M. (1982) : 'Multinationals and Self Reliance : A Case Study of the Drugs and the Pharmaceuticals Industry', *Social Scientist*, No.107.

Kurien, V. (1991) : 'Don't Milk our Dairies Dry', *Times of India*, September 29, 1991, Bombay.

Lall, S. (1973) : 'Transfer Pricing in Multinational Manufacturing Firms', *Oxford Bulletin of Economics and Statistics*, Vol.35, pp 3–21.

——(1980) : 'Monopolistic Advantages and Foreign Involvement by U.S. Manufacturing Industry', *Oxford Economic Papers*, 32, pp. 102–122.

——(1980) : *The Multinational Corporation : Nine Essays*, Macmillan, London.

Lall, S. and Streeten, P. (1977) : *Foreign Investments, Transnationals and Developing Countries*, Macmillan, London.

Landsberg, M. (1979) : 'Export-led Industrialisation in the Third World: Manufacturing Imperialism', *Review of Radical Political Economy*, Vol.11(40), pp 50–63.

Langdon, S. (1978) : 'The Multinational Corporation in the Kenyan Political Economy', R. Kaplinsky(ed)., *Readings on the Multinational Corporations in Kenya*, OUP, Nairobi.

Lefebrre, H. (1993) : *The Survival of Capitalism*, Allison and Busky.

Le Heron, R.B. (1977): 'Patterns of Company Control and Regional Development in New Zealand', *Pacific Viewpoint*, Vol. 18, pp 58–78.

Lenin, V. I. (1950) : 'Imperialism : The Highest Stage of Capitalism', *Selected Works*, Vol.1, Foreign Language Publishing House, Moscow.

——(n.d.) : Imperialism, the Highest Stage of Capitalism,' *Selected Works*, Vol.6, Martin Lawrence, London.

Levine, S and White, P.E. (1961): 'Exchange as a Conceptual Framework for the Study of Inter-organisational Relationships', *Administrative Science Quarterly*, Vol. 5, pp. 583–601.

Lieten, G.K. (1987) : The Dutch Multinational Corporations in India, New Delhi.

Losch, A. (1954) : *The Economics of Location*, Yale University Press, New Haven.

Lowe, J. (1992) : *The Secret Empire : How 25 Multinationals Rule the World*, Business One Irwin, Illinois, USA.

Mabogunje, A. (1978) : *On Developing and Development*, University of Ibadan Lectures, Ibadan, Nigeria.

Maini, J.S. (1990) : *The Growth of Foreign Investments in India*, Unpublished Report, New Delhi.

Malecki, E.J. (1982) : 'Industrial Geography : Introduction to the Spatial Issue' *Environment and Planning,* 14, pp, 1571–1575.

Malecki, E.J. (1985) : 'Industrial Location and Corporate OrganiSation in High Technology Industries', *Economic Geography*, Vol. 01(4), pp 345–369.

Mandel, E. (1975) : *Late Capitalism*, Verso, London.

Markusen, A.R. (1983) : 'Profit Cycles, Oligopoly and Regional Transformation', *Working Paper No.397*, Institute for Urban and Regional Development, University of California, Berkeley.

Marshall, J.N. (1982) : 'Organisational Theory and Industrial Location', *Environment and Planning*, A 14, pp 1667–83.

Martinussen, J. (1988) : *Transnational Corporations in a Developing Country*, Sage Publications, New Delhi.

Massey, D. (1977) : 'Towards a Critique of Industrial Location Theory' in R. Peet (ed), *Radical Geography*, Marouffa Press.

——(1979) : 'The Geography of Industrial Reorganisation', *Progress in Planning*, 10, pp 115–123.

——(1979) : 'A Critical Evaluation of Industrial Location Theory', F.E.I. Hamilton and G.J.R. Linge (eds) *Spatial Analysis, Industry and Industrial System* John Wiley & Sons, London.

——(1980) : 'Industrial Location in Context', *IBG Industrial Location and Area Activity Conference*, London.

——(1984) : *Spatial Divisions of Labour : Social Structure and the Geography of Production*, Macmillan, U.K.

——(1984) : *Spatial Divisions of Labour : Social Structure and the Geography of Production*, Macmillan, U.K.

Massey, D. and Meegan, R. (1978) : 'Industrial Restructuring Versus the Cities', *Urban Studies*, Vol. 15, pp 273–88.

——(1979) : 'Labour Productivity and Regional Employment Change', *Area,* Vol.11, pp 137–45.

——(1982) : *The Anatomy of Job Loss: The Why and Where of Employment Decline*', Methuen, New York.

MIC (1964) : *Report of the Monopoly Inquiry Commission*, Vol.I, pp 5.

Mingret, P. (1970) : 'Les Investments American en Belgique' *Revue de Geographie de Lyon*, pp 243–78, France.

Mckern, R.B. (1976) : *Multinational Enterprise and National Resources*, McGraw Hill, New York.

McNee, R.B. (1958) : 'Functional Geography of the Firm', *Economic Geography*, Vol. 34, pp 321–337.

Monthly Review (1972): 'Globalisation - To what End' Part I, *Review of the Month*, Monthly Review, Vol.43(9) pp 1–18.

Mogdoff, H. (1972) : 'Notes on the Multinational Corporations', in P.M. Sweezy and H. Mogdoff, *The Dynamics of American Capitalism*, Monthly Review Press, New York, pp 88–112.

MRTP (1974) : *Report to MRTP Commission on Philips India Ltd.*, October, 1974, New Delhi.

Mukherjee, S. (1988) : 'The Private Sector and Industrial Policy in India 1946–1956' A.K. Bagchi (ed), *Economy, Society and Polity.*

Muller, R. (1973) : The Multinational Corporations and Underdevelopment in the Third World, in C.K. Wilber (ed.), *The Political Economy of Development and Under-development*, Random Book House, New York.

Munsi, S.K. (1993) : 'An Enquiry into the Historical Roots of Indian Urbanisation, *Geographical Review of India*, Vol. 55 (3), pp 1–3, Calcutta.

Nafziger, E.W. (1978) : *Class, Caste and Enterpreneurship : A Study of Indian Industralists*, East West Centre, Honolulu, Hawaii.

Nair, V. and Kasbekar, S. (1975) : *'Multinationals', Times of India, Annual Number*, Bombay, pp 123–131.

Nakase, T. (1981) : 'Some Characteristics of Japanese Type Multinationals Today', *Capital and Class*, Vol.13, pp 61–98.

Negandhi, A.R. (1962) : *Foreign Private Investments Climate in India*, Asia Publishers, New Delhi.

Nehru Jawahar Lal, n.d.: *Planning and Development, Speaches of Jawaharlal Nehru* (1952–56). New Delhi.

Newfarmer, R.S. (1984): 'Multinationals and Market Place Magic in the 1980s', in C.P. Kindleberger and D.B. Audretsch (eds)., *The Multinational Corporation in the 1980s* the MIT Press, USA, pp 162–197.

——(1985) : 'International Oligopoly and Uneven Development', in R. Newfarmer (ed), *Profit, Progress, Poverty : Studies of International Industries in Latin America,* Notre Dame University Press, Notre Dame.

Newfarmer, R. and Marsh, L. (1981) : *Industrial Interdependence and Development : A Study of International Linkages and Industrial Performance in Brazil*, University of Notre Dame.

Nofal, B. (1983) : *Dynamics of the Motor Vehicle Industry in Argentina*, Ph.D. Thesis, Department of Geography and Environmental Engineering, The Johns Hopkins University, Baltimore, USA.

Nofal, B and Shoenberger, E. (1984) : *Research Proposal on International Firms in Argentina*, Department of Geography and Environment, The John Hopkins University, Baltimors USA.

North, D. (1955) : 'Location Theory and Regional Economic Growth', *Journal of Political Economy*, Vol. 63, p 243–58.

Noyalle, T. J. (1983) : 'The Rise of Advanced Services : Some Implications for Economic Development in U.S. Cities', *Journal of the American Planning Association*, Vol.25, pp 280–90.

Nurkse, R. (1959) : *Patterns of Trade and Development*, Almqvist and Wikesell, Stockholm.

O'hullachain, B. (1985) : 'Spatial Pattern of Foreign Direct Investment in the United State', *The Professional Geographer*, Vol. 37(2), pp 155–163.

Ouchi, W.G. (1977) : 'The Relationship between Organisational Structure and Organisational Control', *Administrative Science Quarterly*, Vol. 22, pp 95–113.

Pak, J.A. and Solo, S. (1990) : The Global 500, *Fortune International*, pp 43–46.

Palloix, C. (1973) : *Les Firmes Multinationales et le Process d' Internationalisation*, Francois, Maspero, Paris.

——(1975) : 'The Internationalisation of Capital and the Circuit of Social Capital', in H. Radice (eds), *International Firms and Modern Imperialism*, Harmondsworth, Penguin.

——(1977) : 'The Self Expansion of Capital on a World Scale', *Review of Radical Political Economics*, Vol.9, pp 1–28.

Patnaik, P. (1972) : Imperialism and the Growth of Indian Capitalism', in R. Owen and B. Sutcliffe (eds.), *Studies in Theory of Imperialism*.

Peet, R. (1978) : 'Materialism, Social Formation and Socio-spatial Relations : An Essay in Marxist Geography' *Cahiers de geographie du Quebec*, Vol.22.

——(1981) : International Capital, International Culture' in M.J. Taylor and N.J. Thrift (eds). *The Geography of Multinational Corporations*, Croom Helm, London. pp 274–302.

——(1983) : 'Relations of Production and the Relocation of the United States Manufacturing Industry since 1960', *Economic Geography*, Vol. 59(2), pp 113-143.

——(1986) : 'The Destruction of Regional Cultures', R.J. Johnston and P.J. Taylor (eds), *A World in Crisis*, Basil Blackwell, New York.

Perloff, H., Dunn, E., Lampard, E. and Muth, R. (1960) : *Regions Resources and Economic Growth*, The Johns Hopkins University Press, Baltimore, USA.

Pfoffer, J. and Salancik, G.R. (1978): *The External Control of Organiations: A Resource Dependence Perspective*, Harper and Row, London.

Planning Commission (1956) : *Second Five Year Plan*, Government of India, New Delhi.

——(1958) : *The New India*, pp 387–396

——(1980) : *Sixth Five Year Plan*, Government of India, New Delhi.

Pred, A.R. (1973) : 'The Growth and Development of Systems of Cities in Advanced Economies', in A.R. Pred, et al. (eds), *Systems of Cities and Information Flows, Lund Studies in Geography,* Series B 38, Gleerup, Lund.

——(1974) : 'Major Job-providing Organisations and Systems of Cities', *Resource Paper No. 27*, Association of American Geographers, Commission on College Geography.

Rao, A. (1994) : 'Making of the New Democrat', *Mainstream*, New Delhi, January 15, pp 12–14.

Rees, J.(1972) : 'The Industrial Corporation and Location Decision Analysis', *Area*, Vol. 4, pp. 199-205.

—— (1978) : 'On the Spatial Spread and Oligopolistic Behaviour of Large Rubber Companies', *Geoforum*, Vol. 9.

Research Unit For Political Economy (1991) : *Aspects*, No.4, pp 39–70.

Reserve Bank of India (1950) : *Report on the Census of India's Foreign Liabilities and Assets* as on 30.6.93.

——(1973) : RBI *Bulletin*, October, 1973.

——(1978) : 'India's International Investment Position, 1963–64 and 1973–74', *RBI Bulletin*, Bombay.

——(1985) : 'Foreign Collaboration in Indian Industry'; *'Fourth Survey Report*, Bombay.

——(1993) : Occasional Papers, 1993, Bombay.

Reuber, R. (1973) : *Private Foreign Investment in Development*, Oxford University Press, London.

Robbins, S.A. and Stobaugh, R.B. (1973) : *Money in the Multinational*, Basic Books, New York.

Rogerson, C.M. (1981) : 'Multinational Corporations in Southern Africa : A Spatial Perspective', in M.J. Taylor and N.J. Thrift (eds), *The Geography of Multinational Corporations,* Croom Helm, London.

Roychowdhury, P. (1981) : *The Transnationals*, Firma KLM Private Ltd., Calcutta.

RUPE (1991) : 'Subcontracting High Tech Soap', *Aspects No.5.*

Soja, E.W. (1985) : 'The Spatiality of Social Life : Towards a Transformative Retheorisation' in D. Gregory and J. Urry (eds), *Social Relations and Spatial Structures*, Macmillan, U.K.

Rupe (1994) : 'Redistributing Income Upwards', *Aspects*, No.12, pp 11–25.

Sachdeva, S. (1989) : *Advertising in India : Some Characteristics and Trends*, Corporate Studies Group, I.I.P.A., New Delhi.

Saini, M.K. (1981) : *Politics of Multinationals*, Gitanjali Prakashan, New Delhi.

Sample, E.K. (1975) : 'Recent Trends in the Spatial Concentration of Corporate Headquarters', *Economic Geography*, Vol. 49, pp 309–18.

Sau, R. (1986) : 'Economic Consequences of a Dominant Coalition, *Economic and Political Weekly*, Vol. XXI (24).

Schemenner, R.W. (1982) : *Making Business Location Decisions,* Prentice Hall, New Jersey.

Schoenberger, E.(1984): *Foreign Manufacturing Investment in the United States: Implications for the U.S. Economy*, Ph.D. Thesis, Department of City and Regional Planning, University of California, Berkeley, USA.

Shekhar, Chandra (1992) : *Political Economy of India, ISID*, Vikas Publishing House, New Delhi.

Simon, M. (1967) : 'The Pattern of New British Portfolio Investment, 1865–1914', J.H. Adler (ed.), *Capital Movements*, London, pp 40–41.

Smith D.M. (1973) : *The Geography of Social Well-Being in the United States*, McGraw Hill, New York.

Smith, I.J. (1978) : 'Ownership Status and Employment Change in Northern Region Manufacturing Industry, 1962–73', *Discussion Paper 7*, Centre for Urban and Regional Development Studies, University of Newcastle-upon Tyne.

Smith, I.J. (1985) : 'Foreign Direct Investment and Divestment Trends in Industrialised Countries', in M. Pacione (ed), *Progress in Industrial Goegraphy*, Croom Helm, London, pp 142–173.

Smith, N. (1984) : *Uneven Development*, Basil Blackwell, London.

——(1986) : 'On the Necessity of Uneven Development', *International Journal of Urban and Regional Research*, Vol. 10, pp 87–104.

Sohn-Rethel (1971) : 'Mental and Manual Labour in Marxism' in S. Hall and P. Walton (eds), *Situating Marx Human Context Books*, London.

Soja, E., Morales, R. and Wolff, G. (1983) : *Urban Restructuring : An Analysis of Social and Spatial Change in Los Angeles*, Vol. 59, pp 195–230;

Spencer, W.I. (1972) : *Newsweek*, November 20.

Srinivasa-Raghavan (1991) :'Walking the Tight rope', *The Economic Times*, July 15, 1991, Bombay.

Stephens, J.D. and Holly, B.P. (1981) : *City System Behaviour and Corporate Influence : The Headquarters Location of Urban Studies*, Vol. 10, pp 102–18.

Storper, M (1992) : The Limits to Globalisation : Technology District and the International Trade', *Economic Geography*, Vol. 68, pp 60–93.

Storper, M and Harrisons, B (1991) : *Flexibility, Hierarchy and Regional Development : The Changing Structure of Industrial Production Systems*, Department of Geography and Environmental Engineering, The Johns Hopkins University, Baltimore, USA.

Storper, M. and Walker, R. (1981) : 'The Spatial Division of Labour : Labour and the Location of Industries', in L. Sawers and W.K. Tabb (eds), *Sunbeld-Snowbelt Urban Development and Regional Restructuring*, Oxford University Press, New York.

——(1983) : 'Theory of Labour and the Theory of Location', *International Journal of Urban and Regional Research*, Vol. 7(1), pp 1–43.

——(1989) : *The Capitalist Imperative : Territory, Technology and Industrial Growth*, Blackwell Publishers, Cambridge.

Subrahmanian, K.K. (1972) : *Import of Capital and Technology*, People's Publishing House, New Delhi.

Subrahmanian, K.K. and Pillai, M.P. (1978) : *Multinational and Indian Export, Mimeograph*, Sardar Patel Institute of Economic and Social Reserch, Ahmedabad.

Susman, P. and Schnlts, E. (1983) : 'Monopoly and Competition from Relations and Regional Developments in Global Capitalism', *Economic Geography*, Vol.59(20) pp 161–177.

Swamy, D. (1986) : *Multinational Corporations and the Third World Economy*, ALPS International Publishers, New Delhi.

Swamy, H. (1993) : 'New Industrial Policy : Environmentalists Worried', *The Times of India*, June 21, Bombay.

Sweezy, P. et. al (1992) : 'Globalization to What End?', *Monthly Review*, Vol.43(10), pp 1–19, New York.

Taylor, M.J. (1975) : 'Organisational Growth, Spatial Interaction and Location Decision Making', *Regional Studies*, Vol. 5.

Taylor, M.J. and Thrift, N.J. (1980) : 'Large Corporations and Concentrations of Capital in Australia: A Geographical Analysis', *Economic Geography*, Vol. 56(4), pp 261–277.

——(1981) : 'Introduction', in M. J. Taylor and N.J. Thrift (eds), *The Geography of Multinational Corporations*, Croom Helm, London.

——(1982) : 'Models of Corporate Development', in M.J. Taylor and N.J. Thrift, (eds), *The Geography of Multinational Corporations*, Croom Helm, London, pp 14–32.

Tharakan, M. (1980) : *The New International Division of Labour and Multinational Corporations*, Saxon House, Farnborough.

Thomas, M.D. (1980) : 'Explanatory Frameworks for Growth and Change in Uninational and Multinational Firm', *Economic Geography*, Vol. 56.

Thompson, J.D. (1967): *Organizations in Action*, McGraw Hill, New York.

Thrift, N. (1986) : 'Geography of International Economic Disorder' in R.J. Johnston and P.J. Taylor (eds.), *A World in Crisis*, Basil and Blackwell, U.K pp 12–67.

Thrift, N. J. (1980) : 'Frobel and the New International Division of Labour', R. Peet (ed), *Marxist Theories of Underdevelopment*, Department of Human Geography, Human Geography 14, Australian National University Press, Canberra, pp 181–9.

Times of India (1989) : Advertisement of Nippon Electric Corporation, Japan, September 11, 1991, Bombay.

Tolchin, M. and Tolchin, S. (1988) : *Buying into America*, Times Books, New York.

Tornqvist, G. (1970) : Contact Systems and Regional Development, *Lund Studies in Geography*, Series B, 38, Gleerup, Lund.

Toulings, A. (1984) : 'The International Squeeze : Double Capital Movement and Job Transfer within Philips Worldwide', *Environment and Planning*, 16, pp 597–614.

Trajtenberg, R. (1985) : *Concentration Global Υ Transnationalization*, Buenos Aires, Centros de Economia Transnational.

Ullman, E.I. (1958) : 'Regional Development and the Geography of Concentration', *Papers of the Regional Science Association*, No. 4, pp 179–198.

UNCTC (United Nations Centre on Transnational Corporations) (1978): *Transnational Corporations in World Development : A Re-examination*, New York, United Nations, E/C, 10/38.

——(1988); *Transnational Corporations in World Development*, United Nations, New York.

——(1989) : The Process of Transnationalization and Transnational Mergers, *UNCTC Current Studies*, Series A, No.8.

——(1992) : 'Transnational Corporations as Engines of Growth', *World Investment Report*, United Nations, pp 197–221, New York.

United Nations Centre on Trade and Development (1993) : *World Investment Report*, New York.

United News of India (1981) : *Backgrounders*, Vol.VI(11), UNI, New Delhi.

Vaitsos, C. (1976) : *Employment Problems and Transnational Enterprises in Developing Countries : Distortions and Inequality*, I.L.O., Geneva.

——(1976) : 'Power, Knowledge and Development Policy : Relations between Transnational Enterprises and Developing Countries', in G. K. Helleiner (ed), *A World Divided*, Cambridge University Press, 1976, pp 113–146.

Vernon, R. (1966) : 'International Investment and International Trade in the Product Cycle', *Quarterly Journal of Economics*, Vol. 80, pp 190–207.

——(1971) : *Sovereignty at Bay : The Multinational Spread of U.S. Enterprises*, Basic Books, New York.

——(1977) : *Storm Over the Multinationals : The Real Issues*, Macmillan, London.

——(1979) : 'The Product Cycle Hypothesis in a New International Environment', *Oxford Bulletin of Economics and Statistics*, 41, pp 255–68.

Vickery, G. (1984) : 'Some Aggregate Measures of New Form of Investment', in C. Oman, *Forms of International Investment in Developing Countries*, OECD, Paris.

Walker, R (1978) : 'The Geographical Organization of Production Systems', *Environment and Planning, D, Society and Space* 6, pp 377–408.

Walker, R. and Storper, M, (1981) : 'Capital and Industrial Location,' *Progress in Human Geography*, Vol. 5(4), pp 473–509.

Wallerstein, I. (1974) : *The Modern World System*, Academic Press, New York.

——(1979) : *The Capitalist World Economy*, Cambridge University Press, Cambridge.

Wall Street Journal (1972) : *Multinational Corporations*, January 13, 1972.

Warrent, F. (1991) : Le deploiement Mondial de la R & D Industrielle, Commission of the European Communities, 4, *Perspective Dossier 2*, pp 77–78.

Watts, H.D. (1974) : 'Large Firms, Multinationals and Regional Development', *Environment and Planning*, A-11, pp 71–81.

——(1980) : *The Large Industrial Enterprise: Some Spatial Perspectives*, Croom Helm, London.

——(1982) : 'The Location of European Direct Investment in the United Kingdom'. *Tijdschrift Voor Economische en Sociale Geografic*, Vol. 71, pp. 3-14.

Weber, A. (1929) : *A Theory of the Location of Industries*, University of Chicago Press, Chicago.

Westway, E.J. (1974) : 'Contact Potential and the Occupational Structure of the British *Urban System*', *Regional Studies*, Vol. 8, pp 57–73.

——(1974) : 'The Spatial Hierarchy of Business Organisations and its Implications, for the British Urban System', *Regional Studies*, Vol. 8, pp 145–55.

Wheat, L. (1973) : *Regional Growth and Industrial Location*, Lexington Books, Lexington, Massachusetts.

Wilkins, M. (1974) : 'Multinational Enterprise', in H. Daems and H. Van der Wee (eds), *The Rise of Managerial Capitalism*, Wijhoff, The Hague.

Wolf, B.M. (1977) : 'Industrial Diversification and Internalisation', *Journal of Industrial Economics*, Vol. 26(2), pp 177–181.

Wood, P.A. (1980) : 'Industrial Geography', *Progress in Human Geography*, Vol. 4, pp 406–16.

Yip, G.S. and C.A. Coundouriotis, (1991) : 'The World Chocolate Confectionary Industry,' *Planning Review*, Vol. 19(1), pp 4–14.

Index